TEACHER EDUCATION RESEARCH
IN A NEW CONTEXT

British Educational Research Association

New BERA Dialogues

The BERA Dialogues series was created by the British Educational Research Association in order to facilitate the publication of collections of high quality educational research papers on particular themes. Paul Chapman Publishers took over publication of the series – New BERA Dialogues – for BERA in 1995. To be included in the series, collections should normally meet the criteria of

(a) being internally coherent, with all the papers addressing a clearly identified theme;

(b) consisting of scholarly papers, with at least most of those in any collection being of a standard that would make them acceptable to leading journals such as the *British Educational Research Journal;*

(c) being of interest to the international educational research community.

Among appropriate starting points for editions of Dialogues can be collections of papers delivered at a BERA Day Conference or in a symposium at the BERA Annual Conference. While most collections in the series have been of papers reporting research, not all editions need be of that kind. For example, collections of papers debating methodological, political or ethical issues in educational research could be highly appropriate for the series.

Paul Chapman Publishers meet annually with the series editor, currently Donald McIntyre, to agree on a set of new editions which will meet the above criteria and which will be commercially viable. Donald McIntyre (School of Education, University of Cambridge) or Marianne Lagrange of PCP welcome suggestions for additions to the series from potential editors.

TEACHER EDUCATION RESEARCH IN A NEW CONTEXT

THE OXFORD INTERNSHIP SCHEME

edited by

Donald McIntyre

New BERA *Dialogues*

P·C·P

Paul Chapman
Publishing Ltd

Paul Chapman Publishing Ltd
144 Liverpool Road
London
B1 1LA

British Library Cataloguing in Publication Data
Teacher education research in a new context: the Oxford
Internship Scheme - (New BERA dialogues)
1. Teachers - Training of - Great Britain
I. MacIntyre, D. (Donald), 1937–
370.7'11'41

ISBN 1 85396 364 X

Typeset by Anneset, Weston super Mare, North Somerset
Printed and bound in Great Britain.

A B C D E F G H 9 8 7

Dedication

This collection of research papers is dedicated by her fellow authors to the memory of Nicola Jubeh, *née* Lindsay. Nicky died shortly after completing the M.Sc. thesis on which her chapter in this book is based and after giving birth to her second child, Sophie Claire. Nicky took her work as a teacher and as a school-based teacher educator very seriously. She wanted to know how she and the rest of us could do that work better, and she pursued that goal with insight and energy. She also made thinking together on these matters a lot of fun. It was a pleasure to know her and we shall remember her with gratitude.

CONTENTS

EDITORIAL PREFACE

In my several years as Series Editor for BERA Dialogues, this is the first book that I have edited myself. It has been a special pleasure, however, to edit this collection of research papers on initial teacher education written by some of the previous colleagues with whom I worked in the context of the Oxford Internship Scheme. In planning that scheme, we had a rare opportunity to try out in practice some of the ideas to which earlier research on initial teacher education had led us. It was a great privilege to work with a group of people who not only were ready to work very hard to take full advantage of that opportunity but also were eager to go on asking questions about the appropriateness, the implications and the consequences of the initiatives that we had taken. For me, this collection of papers is a memorial to ten much enjoyed and very intellectually rewarding years. For others, I hope and believe that it will be a stimulus both for the development of practice in initial teacher education partnerships and for further research.

Donald McIntyre

A RESEARCH AGENDA FOR INITIAL TEACHER EDUCATION

Donald McIntyre

INTRODUCTION

The Oxford Internship Scheme (Benton, 1990) was planned during 1985–87 in an attempt to tackle some of the major problems which research and experience had revealed to be endemic in the pattern of teacher education dominant in most English-speaking countries for most of this century (Judge, 1980; McIntyre, 1980, 1988). From research on teaching, it was clear that the understandings about teaching expertise which underlay that system were misguided: theory had been wrongly privileged over practice, and the necessary tensions between theory and practice ignored; teachers' practical expertise had not only been neglected, but had also wrongly been assumed to be transparently accessible; and, especially, there had been an over-confidence about the possibilities for generalised prescription of good practice. From research on teacher education itself, it was apparent that there had been inadequate attention to the processes of learning to practise as a teacher, and to the construction of a system likely to facilitate such learning: student teachers had, for example, tended to survive school placements rather than learn from the analysis of their experience, having frequently been left to cope unaided with the most difficult aspects of their learning; school practice arrangements seemed as if they had been calculated in most cases not to engage schools seriously in the task of teacher education; and college-based teacher educators were on a very large scale obliged to attempt to play key roles which they were very badly placed to play.

Given the scale of the problems, radical solutions were necessary; and the Oxford Scheme, both in its practical arrangements and in its conception of what was to be done, was indeed quite radical. But that of course meant that we were moving into new territory. If we thought that we understood the problems (and the strengths) of the old system, and the strategies and skills that could be used most effectively in it, we certainly did not know how best to do things in our new system. Even if our diagnosis of the problems of the old system was correct, that did not mean at all necessarily that we had identified effective solutions for these problems. Even if our solutions were in principle appropriate, we had yet to learn how difficult and complex the implementation of these solutions might be. It was probable, furthermore, that our organisational innovations would themselves create new problems. Finally, even if we were successful in resolving some important problems in teacher education, that would almost certainly mean that other important problems would now become more apparent.

The new scheme was not seen, therefore, as offering a solution to all the problems of initial teacher education, but much more as a framework within which tentative solutions to some problems might be tested and other unresolved problems could be identified and elucidated. Having learned from research conducted within the previous framework, we now had to start again to ask and to investigate the new research questions relevant to the new situation that we had created. In other words, we had to generate and pursue a new agenda for research in initial teacher education.

Confident as we were in 1987 that our new scheme was a move in the right direction, it was at that time quite distinctive, and so too therefore was the research agenda which we had to generate and pursue. Since then, however, the rest of the world has changed and, in particular, university or college postgraduate programmes of initial professional education for secondary school teachers in England have all, in their broad structure if not in their rationale, been required to become similar to the new programme which we developed in Oxford. All such programmes are two-thirds based in schools. In all cases, schools are paid so that some of their staff can participate in the programmes as professional school-based teacher educators. In all cases, it is necessary therefore for there to be much more serious and more equal partnerships than were previously common between the teacher educators based in higher education institutions and those based in schools. In 1996, therefore, we would not wish to make any clear distinctions between the research agenda that we have been pursuing at Oxford and that which we believe to be appropriate for initial secondary teacher education in general.

The new agenda, one would of course hope, shows important continuities with earlier research agendas. There are, for example, questions about student teachers' learning which were rightly being investigated in earlier contexts and which may still require investigation in very similar terms, but in new contexts. Other questions have to be about the adequacy of the understandings achieved on the basis of earlier research, understandings which on the one hand led to innovative aspects of the Oxford scheme and which, on the other hand, can usefully be questioned by examining those aspects of the scheme in practice. Newer kinds of research questions arise, however, when one begins to consider the kinds of understanding necessary for the effective implementation of newly conceived tasks for and within initial teacher education. This applies both to the whole range of new opportunities which are opened up for school-based initial teacher education strategies and also to the new kinds of joint university and school enterprises which should become possible. And completely new questions have to be asked in the search for understanding of new phenomena and experiences which appear as unexpected or unintended, although in some cases welcome, consequences of the innovations introduced.

Each of the research studies reported in this book is included primarily because it is in itself interesting and valuable research. Nonetheless the collection as a whole exemplifies a new research agenda which, I would suggest, can properly guide our efforts for some years to come. It is the task of this chapter to discuss that more general agenda, and to exemplify it by reference to the following chapters.

RESEARCH ON TEACHING

As noted above, the nature of the Oxford Internship Scheme was greatly influenced by research on teaching. The most fundamental premise of the scheme – that there is not, nor could be, any systematic corpus of theoretical knowledge from which generally valid prescriptive principles about teaching could be generated – is derived from reflection on the findings of research on teaching. This led to the key practical principle, that all suggestions about good practice, whatever their source, should be critically examined and questioned by interns; and that the course should be structured and implemented with an emphasis on helping them to do that. However, as I have argued elsewhere (McIntyre, 1993), such a principle does not absolve teacher educators from a responsibility to offer student teachers the best guidance they can, not only for understanding teaching but also for engaging in it; and the Internship rationale for university involvement in teacher education is tied to the capacity of university staff to bring research perspectives and research-based knowledge about teaching and teacher education to their work as teacher educators.

A research agenda for initial teacher education should accordingly include, as an area of major significance, research on teaching: research-based understandings of teaching should be of central importance in determining the rationale, the structure and the content of teacher education programmes. Although this book is about research on teacher education, not research on teaching, it is nonetheless useful to take a little space to elaborate on some of the kinds of research on teaching which are needed to inform initial teacher education.

First, it is important that programmes of initial teacher education should be planned in the light of good research-based understandings of the nature of teaching. At a basic level, it is important that programmes should make well-informed assumptions about what teachers in the early years of their careers will be asked to do and will be able to do, and for what they there-fore need to be prepared. For example, the needs of beginning teachers for preparation for the role of form tutors, and for the varying responsibilities that that may entail, should be readily apparent from research. A more complex lesson from research on teacher socialisation is about the need to prepare beginning teachers, not to be reformers in their early years, but to sustain analytical, critical and reforming perspectives during these years, while they are learning about the complex practical realities of schools. More fundamental, however, is the need for initial teacher education to be rooted in a good research-based understanding of the nature of classroom teachers' expertise, and of how it develops over the years. We are still much too inclined to base our advice to beginning teachers on naive models of what we think teachers' expertise should be like rather than on well-informed understandings of what it is like. For example, I reluctantly have to recog-nise that most secondary school teachers still depend on (generally miscon-ceived) notions of 'academic ability' in making sense of differences among their pupils; and until research allows me both to understand better why they need to depend on such ideas and also what more justifiable alternatives would meet the same need, I have to be extremely cautious in suggesting to beginning teachers that this is inappropriate.

Teacher educators are in addition especially dependent on research for well-founded ideas about effective teaching. Complaints in recent years that teacher educators' advice to their students about styles and strategies of teaching has often been ideologically based are not totally without founda-tion (although those making such complaints have generally been much more guilty of the same offence and furthermore have failed to recognise the nec-essarily value-laden choices which teachers have to make). Guidance to student teachers about effective teaching needs to be hedged about with qual-ifications about the value judgements and assumptions involved as well as about the dangers of over-generalised claims. But generalised guidance is nec-essary and should surely be informed most of all by the results of research.

There is currently, however, an absence of research on effective teaching. Partly that is because the old simplistic approach of experimental compar-isons between different 'methods' of teaching has rightly been seen as unhelpful. It is also because, perhaps prematurely, quantitative correlational studies of classroom processes and outcomes have become unfashionable. The contrast between, on one hand, the current neglect of the quite subtle cor-relational studies which are possible relating teachers' thinking, classroom processes and the experiences and learning of students and, on the other hand, the popularity of the necessarily much grosser quantitative study of 'school effectiveness' is quite striking. Whether or not correlational approaches offer the most appropriate way forward, there is an urgent need for more study of effective teaching, which must give a central place to the thinking and experiences of teachers and students (cf. Brown and McIntyre, 1993; Cooper and McIntyre, 1996), but also to the quality and extent of students' learning.

CURRICULA FOR ITE PARTNERSHIPS

One of the endemic problems of old patterns of initial teacher education (ITE), based largely in higher education contexts, was that of establishing coherent and viable conceptions of how students' work in these contexts should be related to their work in schools, on 'teaching practice' and when they began work as professional teachers. It may be argued, indeed, that it was primarily because of the lack of a satisfactory solution to that problem that the shift to a largely school-based pattern of ITE came about. However, that shift is not in itself any solution. Unless one abandons completely any higher education element in ITE, as some ideologues would of course like to do, then the problem remains of how work in the two contexts can be effectively inter-related.

'Partnership' is now the orthodox way of describing the appropriate relationship between schools and universities in ITE. For such partnerships to be effective, it is probably necessary for there to be a clearly specified, persuasively justified and mutually agreed division of labour between the two partners and also shared understandings about how their contributions should be inter-related. The rationale for the Oxford Internship Scheme partnership has been that university and school staff should each contribute what their respective positions make them best placed to offer, broadly research and theory-based knowledge and perspectives from the former, and situated knowledge of teaching and schooling and practical perspectives from the latter. These different perspectives should be brought to bear on every element of the agreed curriculum and, while they might frequently support and reinforce each other, there was no assumption that this would be the case; instead, the intention was that each should be used to interrogate the other critically.

It is only through research and evaluation studies, however, that one can discover whether or not any particular conception of school-university partnership does in practice offer clear shared understandings, and whether or not it is both viable and effective in achieving its purposes. This has therefore been an important area for research, both in order to test and improve the quality of the Oxford programme and also more fundamentally to explore how well-founded the conception of partnership underlying the scheme is. In general that research (and also reflection on experience within the scheme), while not revealing any fallacies underlying that conception of partnership, has shown it to be a very ambitious conception, to the extent that some (although not the present writer) might even conclude that it was unrealistic.

Although any joint school-university ITE scheme must, to be credible, be conceived as a single partnership following a common coherent curriculum, this single partnership has to be realised through many different interweaving threads. It is necessary on occasion to take a broad overview of the partnership as a whole (cf. Rothwell, Nardi and McIntyre, 1994), but to gain a real understanding of its working it is usually necessary to focus on particular threads. Research in this area is most clearly exemplified in this collection by the chapters by Chris Davies and Nicola Jubeh. The thread examined by Chris is that of a particular subject curriculum, English, whereas Nicola focuses on the working of the scheme in a particular school.

Chris Davies' chapter shows very effectively the importance of research on partnerships. It exemplifies vividly the different concerns of teacher educators in school and university contexts. It demonstrates how difficult and complex effective negotiation between teacher educators in these two contexts is likely to be. His account of his PGCE students' shifting intellectual enthusiasms, as they moved out of the university context and were gradually socialised into English departments in schools, is of critical importance. It seems strikingly to exemplify how little progress we have made, even here with the most vigorous of efforts in this most radical of schemes, towards persuading learner-teachers to experience the more challenging elements of the university components of their courses as directly relevant to the tasks and experiences which confront them in schools. Although we do need to recognise this uncomfortable truth, it should not surprise us; not only have school-based and university-based teacher educators had relatively little opportunity as yet to develop sophisticated ways of working together; the more fundamental problem is that our understanding of what such working together involves is still very limited. This study is therefore important primarily because of the detailed insights it offers into the various ways in which interns and their mentors reached common understandings of what were and were not acceptable agendas to work on in schools, and how these differed from what seemed to be a highly acceptable university agenda; it is on the basis of such insights that we need to generate better theories for planning partnership curricula.

Partnership curricula depend of course on their effective planning and implementation by many people working in complementary roles. Nicola Jubeh's study followed the experiences of the interns in one school with particular reference to the quality of the support and guidance which they saw themselves to be receiving from people in these several complementary roles. Her questions and her findings point to one of the central problems of such curricula, involving as they do almost as many people in key teacher educator roles as there are student teachers: the problem of quality control. While some interns receive high quality support and guidance, others in the same school can receive much more amateurish attention or may even be simply neglected. As she points out, if weight is to be given to interns' own judgements, the problem is to some extent one of misplaced energies: staff time given to training not directly related to interns' concerns with classroom and tutorial work might be better used in developing the quality of the system. This in turn raises fundamental questions, which have not yet received adequate research attention, about the kinds of autonomy for mentors, university tutors and other staff which are and are not necessary and compatible with the need for systems offering professional education of consistently high quality; and about the problems and possibilities of developing such systems.

The development of appropriate and viable ITE partnership curricula of consistently high quality continues to be the fundamental challenge towards which all other teacher education research should ultimately be directed. The quality of whole partnership curricula needs a great deal of direct research attention in relation to the assumptions on which partnership relationships are based, the tasks being attempted at the ITE level, and the operation of the partnership systems. But improvements in partnership curricula may well be more likely through other kinds of research, such as research on student teachers' learning.

STUDENT TEACHERS' LEARNING

Since teacher education is by definition concerned to bring about learning by student teachers, research to give us an understanding of student teachers' learning must be among the most important kinds of teacher education research. What do student teachers learn, from what experiences or as a result of what influences, and through what processes? We have inherited a rich and confusing vocabulary for talking about what student teachers might be learning: 'images', 'perspectives', 'metaphors', 'strategies', 'ideologies', 'dispositions', as well as more prosaic and conventional, though not necessarily less useful, terms such as 'skills', 'beliefs', 'attitudes', 'values', 'knowledge' and 'understanding'. Our theoretical apparatus for discussing the processes of learning is, however, rather more limited, relying heavily as it does on theories of professional socialisation, especially Lacey's (1977) seminal work, and on social and cognitive psychology (e.g. Tomlinson, 1995). Our strongest beliefs seem to be about the sources of student teachers' learning, with Lortie's (1975) thesis about the apprenticeship of observation, or at least that part of it that suggests that students bring to their initial teacher education strong preconceptions which are resistant to modification, apparently confirmed by extensive research evidence. Furthermore, these preconceptions are generally seen to be unhelpful. Thus, for example, commenting on the work of the National Centre for Research on Teacher Education at Michigan State

University in the USA, which had conducted intensive studies of a wide variety of teacher education programmes, Mary Kennedy concluded that:

> despite the diversity of approaches to teacher education that we studied, many of these programmes were unable to alter substantially the ideas the teachers had when they arrived. Moreover, we found that teachers' initial ideas were often limiting, and that they constrained teachers' ability to understand new ideas about teaching – about how students learn, for instance, or about the teacher's role in connecting subject matter to diverse learners. (Kennedy, 1991)

As the above quotation nicely suggests, there is a fine line between research or evaluation studies of particular teacher education curricula, on one hand, and research on student teachers' learning on the other: to understand any curriculum in practice, one has to be concerned with student teachers' learning in the context of that curriculum; and any studies of student teachers' learning must of course take account of the curricular or experiential contexts in which their learning occurs.

Linda Haggarty's (1995) book describes her investigations of the mathematics teacher education curriculum which she planned jointly with school-based teacher educators in the context of the Oxford Internship Scheme. Her chapter in this book focuses on one particular facet of her investigation of student teachers' learning in that context. It exemplifies very well one set of research questions which should, in the light of findings such as those summarised by Kennedy above, be high on our research agenda. What common misconceptions do student teachers bring with them? How can we explain the persistence of these misconceptions even when more valid ideas are thoughtfully presented to them? What kinds of conditions, in terms perhaps of social contexts, or personal experiences, or cognitive and affective states, tend to lead student teachers to be receptive to new learning and to a questioning of their preconceptions? What circumstances are conducive to the questioning of particular common misconceptions? Linda asks these questions in relation to student teachers' preconceptions about classroom management, and the evidence she reports shows that these preconceptions were indeed important and provides some very interesting and important answers to her questions.

We should not, however, take for granted as universally applicable the general thrust of earlier findings. The practical experience of most teacher educators suggests that most student teachers learn a great deal during their ITE courses, especially in terms of their competence as classroom teachers. In so far as such impressions are supported by research evidence, what is the nature of that learning? Does it involve the acquisition of new ideas, and if so how does this happen? Does it involve the abandoning of old and limiting ideas? What relation is there between the developing knowledge-in-practice of student teachers and the explicit educational theories which they espouse? We need much more detailed careful investigation of these questions in relation to the learning of individual student teachers and the contexts in which they learn. Anna Pendry's study of five student history teachers as they developed during their Internship PGCE year provides a model for such investigations. Among the important benefits gained from the combination of her very open theoretical stance, her rich data and her very painstaking analysis were: her finding that the student teachers' initial ideas, although having considerable influence on their developing thinking, were not at all simplistic or limiting; her conclusion that previous work on 'pedagogical content knowledge' was not helpful in understanding the learning of these student teachers; and her recognition that that learning, while important in the development of these student teachers, was of a very subtle kind.

We need much more research to explore the diverse conditions, sources, substance and processes of student teachers' learning, with a recognition that because of the subtlety of much of that learning this will not be an easy task. We need too more extended qualitative longitudinal investigations, examining those elements of beginning teachers' thinking and practice which remain stable and those which change over the months and years as they learn to teach and become established as members of the teaching profession. We need to find ways of gaining insight into the sources and processes of those changes that do occur. And we need more multilevel studies, exploring the interaction and mutual influence of developing theoretical ideas, classroom practices and approaches to planning and evaluation on each other. It will be mainly through the improved understandings of beginning teachers' learning provided by such research that we shall be able with confidence to plan improved teacher education curricula.

STRATEGIES TO FACILITATE STUDENT TEACHERS' LEARNING

When we introduced the Oxford Internship Scheme, we planned it to overcome two major sets of problems which had been identified through research and experience in the established system. One of these, which has already been discussed, was the set of problems concerned with the disconnectedness of university-based studies from student teachers' work in schools, and from the work they would do as newly qualified teachers. The other set of problems were those of poor conditions for the student teachers' learning in schools: in particular, teacher education was a marginal activity in schools, and the teachers with whom student teachers worked had neither any responsibility as teacher educators nor any time given to them to undertake the task. Learning was therefore largely by trial and error, with some modelling of (possibly) good practice observed by the student teachers (but generally without the commentary or discussion which might have made it useful), and with occasional feedback either from a visiting university tutor or from a particularly helpful teacher. 'School practice' was often just that, an opportunity to learn through practice, with the apparent assumption that one already knew enough about what one was practising; often it was much worse than that, more of a trial by ordeal which one had to survive in order to become a teacher.

The new organisational arrangements for the Oxford scheme were designed to provide the opportunity for these problems to be overcome. With a large number of 'interns' in the same school for most of the year, teacher education should be less of a marginal activity; and certainly the interns themselves were from the beginning treated much less as marginal figures and much more as junior members of staff. With a professional tutor on the school staff to lead the school's professional teacher education work, a general tutor from the university closely attached to the particular school, and a mentor teacher in each subject department where two interns were placed, each mentor having protected time to work with the interns, one had the basis for 'school practice' to become 'school-based initial teacher education'.

But what was school-based teacher education to be like? In particular, how should mentors, as the key school-based teacher educators, set about their work? These remain as major questions for any teacher education which is largely school-based. The great strength of mentors as teacher educators is that they are full-time practising teachers. How can they most effectively build on this strength? Their problem – the other side of the same coin – is that (even if ITE were funded generously, not in the niggardly way it is at present) they will never have as much time as they might sensibly want for mentoring. How can they most effectively use the limited time at their disposal? We are still far from having consensual or adequately founded answers to these questions, but much of the research carried out in the context of the Oxford Internship Scheme has usefully been concerned with them and offers some models for the further research that is certainly needed.

The first phase of this research was of critical importance. The organisational arrangements for the Oxford scheme having been negotiated during 1985-86, a team of experienced teachers from Oxfordshire schools were seconded to the University for 1986–87 and, under Anna Pendry's leadership, they formed the Development Group which, in collaboration with the UDE staff, planned the curriculum and the general ways of working of the scheme. They worked as a group for much of the time, but each member also undertook an individual project. Some of these projects were concerned with planning subject or other components of the curriculum, but several focused on tasks that mentors might undertake, or strategies which mentors might use. Through these several projects, potential aspects of the mentor's role were thought through and tried out in practice. Thus Geoff Rhodes examined the mentor's role in managing interns' learning in a subject department; Mike Shorthouse examined the possibilities and problems of having a pair of interns working with a mentor; Richard Aplin investigated the possibility of developing a consensual framework for mentors' diagnostic and summative assessment of their interns' teaching; and Alan Pennington investigated conditions and procedures for supporting interns in their development of skills for evaluating their own teaching. On the basis of this practical research work, it was possible to develop initial guidelines for mentors.

One of these projects concerned with aspects of the mentor's role grew into a programme of research which continued over several years. This was Hazel Hagger's investigation of how mentors or other experienced teachers might help student teachers to gain access to the 'craft knowledge' embedded in their practice, knowledge articulated rarely if ever and only with great difficulty. Hazel's chapter in this book reports some of the research from much later in that programme, when she had, in the light of her earlier research, developed her thinking about the procedures to be used, and also about the contextual conditions necessary to support these procedures, to a stage which allowed her to test her central hypothesis about how craft knowledge could be accessed. This is the most quantitative piece of research reported in this collection. I am pleased it is here not only because it is important and high quality research, which it certainly is, but also because it attests to the need for a wide variety of research strategies to enable us to answer the diverse research questions on initial teacher education which should concern us.

Hazel also took the lead in carrying forward this developmental kind of research on a broader front. After mentors had had a few years' experience working in the context of the Internship Scheme, she led a group of us in a research and development project which set out to build on that experience and on the earlier work of members of the Development Group. The aim was to be able to give practical advice to mentors – especially new mentors – in the Oxford scheme and elsewhere about how they might undertake their roles most effectively. The research approach was to explore the thinking in practice of relatively experienced mentors with regard to what was involved in doing particular aspects of the mentor's work well. The outcome of this project was *The School Mentor Handbook* (Hagger *et al.*, 1993). The chapter by Lathlean and others in this collection outlines the processes and findings of the research and evaluation work which played a part in shaping *The Handbook*. Especially during the current early years of school-based teacher education, such very practical research is of the highest importance: on one hand, if the practice of the majority of mentors were to be guided by the advice offered in *The Handbook*, then in my view the move to a more school-based ITE would already be worthwhile; on the other, the articulation in such pragmatic terms of a view of good practice provides a necessary starting point for more searching research questions to be asked about appropriate and effective mentoring in ITE.

One element of mentoring which had been of high priority from the earliest stages in planning the Internship Scheme, but which we took some time to problematise, was **collaborative teaching**. The importance for student teachers' learning of focused modelling, practice and feedback in relation to particular skills of teaching, through appropriately designed simple teaching tasks undertaken in protected environments, has been recognised since at least the 1960s. The difficulty has been that learning from such experience in university contexts, supervised by university-based teacher educators, has not been easily transferred by student teachers to the tasks of teaching in normal classrooms. School-based teacher educators, on the other hand, are in the position where they can provide appropriate, more or less simple, focused teaching tasks for student teachers in the contexts of their own class-rooms and their own ongoing teaching; the degree of complexity of the task and the amount of protection given can be determined according to the student teacher's learning needs, while the teaching in which the student teacher is collaborating is part of the normal work of the classroom. Thus collaborative teaching epitomises the advantages of school-based ITE.

Nonetheless, the effective use of collaborative teaching is not without its problems. The chapter by Katharine Burn, who as a mentor was accustomed to using collaborative teaching, and who took the lead in developing *The Handbook's* guidance on this aspect of mentoring, reports the further in-depth investigation of its uses and problems which she went on to under-take.

We are as yet in the very early stages of exploring what school-based teacher educators can most usefully do and how they can do these things most effectively. Progress will depend on research on student teachers' learning needs and problems, creative thinking on how mentors might most effectively facilitate such learning, and investigation both of the validity of claims about effective kinds of mentoring practice and also of the thinking, skills and conditions necessary for such good practice.

TEACHER EDUCATION, UNIVERSITIES AND SCHOOLS

In order to make sense of teacher education, it is important to find out about the ways in which people are selected and shaped, by their own aspirations, experiences, thinking and strategies and by the decisions and demands of others, for particular teacher education roles, just as it is important to under-stand how student teachers are shaped and what brings them into teaching. It is also important to understand how the nature of the institutions within which teacher educators work influences the ways in which they approach and think about their work. Such research questions are always important, but they are more obviously important and also more easily articulated at a time of radical change and uncertainty. How have university-based teacher educators responded to the shift towards school-based ITE? Has the shift influenced their professional identities, their commitments, the rationales that they espouse for their roles, and the nature of, and authority for, the knowledge and expertise that they see themselves as helping student teachers to develop? How have teachers been selected, by themselves or others, as school-based teacher educators? Have these new responsibilities significantly changed their professional identities? What rationales do they espouse for their teacher education roles, and what is the nature of, and authority for, the knowledge and expertise that they see themselves as helping student teachers to develop? How are the new roles of university-based and school-based teacher educators understood by people in other positions in schools and universities, and how do these understandings facilitate and constrain the work of the teacher educators?

Another complementary set of questions, however, concerns the impact of new patterns of ITE on the institutions concerned. What has happened to university departments of education as a result of the move towards school-based ITE? Has the focus on classroom teaching diminished in such departments, and if so what has it been replaced by? Has more attention been given to the quantity and quality of educational research done in such departments? Has the social structure of such departments changed? What about the impact of school-based ITE in schools? Has it led to more concern, and more explicit talk, about what happens in classrooms? In what circumstances, if any, has it led to enhanced attention being given to issues of teachers' continuing professional development? Has it led to new thinking about provision in schools for newly qualified teachers? To understand initial teacher education, we need to understand the ways in which it interacts with other activities in the institutions in which it is carried out.

One of the gaps in our research on teacher education at Oxford is our failure to investigate at all systematically the way in which the UDE as a whole and its individual members adapted to the new Internship scheme or alternatively assimilated it to existing thinking and practices. More attention, however, has been given to the ways in which schools and the teachers in them have responded to the scheme and to the impact of the scheme upon them.

David Pell was one of the members of the Development Group which in 1986-87 planned the Internship Scheme. His particular project then was to develop guidelines for the role of Professional Tutor, a role which combined managing the scheme as a whole within a school with taking particular responsibility for a school-based programme of professional education in cross-curricular issues. Having done this, he later went on to study the appropriateness of the guidelines in practice and then to the more theoretically informed study summarised in his chapter, concerning the different ways in which individual professional tutors, working in different positions and contexts, each shaped and developed their roles in distinctive ways. It is a study which demonstrates vividly the inevitability with which a partnership scheme will take on the distinctive imprint of each school and of the people in key roles within it; but also shows how the quality of the ITE work in any school will depend on such factors as the seniority, the busyness and the commitment of those given overall responsibility for ITE in schools, and perhaps especially on their knowledge and understanding of ITE.

The final chapter in this book, by Stephen Carney and Hazel Hagger, reports one of the five studies undertaken as Oxford University's contribution to a national research project, funded by the Esmee Fairbairn Charitable Trust, on mentoring in schools. As the authors note, the approach adopted in Oxford was to invite teachers in partner schools to identify the issues about school-based teacher education which concerned them and to plan investigations in relation to these issues. It is perhaps significant that in all five cases the issues identified were concerned with the impact of Internship on members of the schools other than the student teachers: newly qualified teachers; mentors' subject department colleagues; mentors themselves and other teachers, in relation to the opportunities Internship offered for their professional development; and, in the case of the study reported here, the school's pupils. In involving themselves in school-based ITE, schools are rightly very much concerned with the potential advantages and disadvantages for themselves as well as those for the student teachers.

There are perhaps generalisable lessons to be learned from the results of this small study. Comparison of the two subject departments that were studied shows that it was in the one which invested more and which approached ITE in a more corporate way that not only the interns but also the pupils and their teachers felt they gained most. As schools learn that they will benefit from involvement in ITE only in so far as they take it really seriously, so the interaction between ITE and other aspects of school life will grow in complexity, as will the choices to be made about where and how to invest. We are only just beginning on the extensive research that will be necessary to explore these matters.

CONCLUSION

The research reported in this book is only a sample, although I think a rather impressive sample, of the research into ITE conducted at Oxford in the context of the Internship Scheme initiated there ten years ago. There are of course many valuable kinds of research into ITE not exemplified in this book. Nonetheless, as I have tried to show, the research agenda pursued at Oxford during the last ten years is one which needs to be followed there and elsewhere for many years to come if we are to take full advantage of the opportunities which a principled shift towards more school-based initial teacher education can offer.

Since the authors of subsequent chapters sometimes take for granted a knowledge of the basic structure and terminology of the Oxford Internship Scheme, a brief Glossary is provided on page 202.

REFERENCES

Benton, P. (ed.) (1990) *The Oxford Internship Scheme.* Calouste Gulbenkian Foundation, London.

Brown, S. and McIntyre, D. (1993) *Making Sense of Teaching.* Open University Press, Buckingham.

Cooper, P. and McIntyre, D. (1996) *Effective Teaching: Teachers' and Pupils' Perspectives.* Open University Press, Buckingham.

Haggarty, L. (1995) *New Ideas for Teacher Education: A Framework for Mathematics.* Cassell, London.

Hagger, H., Burn, K. and McIntyre, D. (1993) *The School Mentor Handbook.* Kogan Page, London.

Judge, H. (1980) Teaching and professionalization: an essay in ambiguity, in Eric Hoyle and Jacquetta Megarry (eds.) *World Yearbook of Education 1980: Professional Development of Teachers.* Kogan Page, London.

Kennedy, M. (1991) *An Agenda for Research on Teacher Learning.* National Centre for Research on Teacher Learning, Michigan State University.

Lacey, C. (1977) *The Socialization of Teachers.* Methuen, London.

Lortie, D. C. (1975) *Schoolteacher: A Sociological Study.* University of Chicago Press, Chicago.

McIntyre, D. (1980) The contribution of research to quality in teacher education, in Eric Hoyle and Jacquetta Megarry (eds.) *World Yearbook of Education 1980: Professional Development of Teachers.* Kogan Page, London.

McIntyre, D. (1988) Designing a teacher education curriculum from research and theory on teacher knowledge, in J. Calderhead (ed.) *Teachers' Professional Learning.* Falmer Press, London.

McIntyre, D. (1993) Theory, theorizing and reflection, in J. Calderhead and P. Gates (eds.) *Conceptualizing Reflection in Teacher Education.* Falmer Press, London.

Rothwell, S., Nardi, E. and McIntyre, D. (1994) The perceived values of the role activities of mentors and curriculum, professional and general tutors, in I. Reid, H. Constable and R. Griffiths (eds.) *Teacher Education Reform.* Paul Chapman, London.

Tomlinson, P. (1995) *Understanding Mentoring.* Open University Press, Buckingham.

2

PROBLEMS ABOUT ACHIEVEMENT OF SHARED UNDERSTANDINGS ABOUT ITE BETWEEN SCHOOLS AND UNIVERSITY

Chris Davies

INTRODUCTION

This chapter reports an action research project which was carried out on the professional training of secondary English teachers in the specific context of Internship. It investigates the collaborative planning and delivery of one particular aspect of a PGCE English programme which aimed to help interns reflect on and develop their understandings about their subject for the purposes of secondary teaching.

The initial point of interest in this study was with questions, particularly pertinent at that time, concerning sharply varying views about the nature of English studies. This issue had become the source of much debate in higher education, but appeared to be still of relatively minor concern within the field of secondary education English teaching. During this particular period, many English graduates were entering teacher training having recently encountered arguments for the radical reformulation of their discipline during the course of their own higher education. Such experiences tended to intensify the problem of a discontinuity between higher and secondary education subject concerns which any beginning teacher may, to a greater or lesser extent, need to negotiate. The research, as initially formulated, therefore sought to understand how beginning teachers could be helped to explore and reconcile differing subject beliefs – ideologies of the subject – in the course of learning to teach.

It became apparent (during what was, in 1986/87, the major planning period for the Internship Scheme) that Oxford's new PGCE course constituted a particularly interesting context within which to explore this question.

As a key feature of the scheme was the partnership between university and schools in planning and delivering a PGCE course, it was necessary to establish shared understandings within the partnership about the kind of learning and explorations that are appropriate for beginning teachers. By grounding the investigation of the issue of differing subject ideologies in the Internship Scheme, the research focus inevitably came to encompass the key question of how practising teachers could be enabled to contribute to interns' learning about such issues – such as questions of an ideological or epistemological nature – that extended beyond the practicalities of classroom teaching, and what form that contribution should take.

The research reported in this chapter therefore concerns the two related questions of whether an explicit focus on questions of subject ideology is an appropriate and relevant part of the learning of beginning teachers, especially as they negotiate the difficult transition from higher education study to secondary education teaching, and how the distinctive opportunities offered by the university and school partnership might be most effectively deployed in order to achieve such learning.

THE SPECIFIC ISSUE OF DIFFERING BELIEFS ABOUT ENGLISH TEACHING

The crisis in English studies in higher education

In March 1981, during a period of somewhat confused debate both in universities and in the media about university English, Raymond Williams characterised 'recent events' in English studies in terms of a break-down in the established paradigm of the subject:

> such paradigms are never simply abandoned. Rather they accumulate anomalies until there is eventually a breaking point, and attempts are made to shift and replace the fundamental hypothesis, its definitions and what are by this stage the established professional standards and methods of enquiry. That evidently is a moment of crisis. (Williams 1983, p. 192)

This debate proved to have major implications for university English departments. Although there was little serious likelihood of simply abandoning the academic study of literature, in favour of some more inclusive discipline such as cultural studies, there was a rapid effort in many higher education English departments to incorporate a certain amount (varying widely from one department to another) of critical theory into their own English literature curriculums. English studies were, to a certain extent, formally problematized, and opened up to wider perspectives (particularly, during this period, Marxist and feminist theory).

By the mid-1980s, it was increasingly possible that English undergraduates could expect to encounter, at the very least, the arguments of cultural theorists alongside those of the 'liberal humanist' perspective most notably associated with the work of F. R. Leavis and, in some institutions, far more than a passing consideration was granted. Such perspectives were markedly at odds with the way English was viewed by their predecessors, now working in schools, and by many of their contemporaries, with whom they were about to enter Initial Teacher Education.

Subject paradigm variation at secondary level

Some prospects for comparable change can be detected in secondary education at this time but, despite isolated instances of radical approaches to the teaching of English in certain locations during the early 1980s – notably ILEA, with its increasingly influential English Centre producing teaching materials which were strongly influenced by the critical, cultural and linguistic theory emerging from higher education – there is very little evidence of any great shift in secondary teachers' commitment to the dominant paradigm of the subject, which had been firmly in place since the 1960s:

> As recently as 1966, Americans at the Dartmouth Conference were left with the impression of English teachers' solidarity of purpose, their loyalty to Leavis and the 'great traditions' of English literature. Their aim was to promote children's growth, and they hoped to achieve this by introducing them to literature, and by stimulating creativity. (Mathieson 1975, p. 198)

Caroline St. John-Brooks' study of a committedly Leavisite comprehensive school English department shows such thinking still exerting a firm hold throughout the 1970s:

> The English teachers held strong ideological commitments and beliefs, central to which were a number of truths which were taken to be self-evident, but which were essentially unproveable. They held that pupils could and would enter a fuller, freer life through writing, discussing their own and other people's writing, and by the act of making the kind of judgements which are made by writers of fiction, plays and poetry. These truths were the badges of the faithful . . . (Brooks 1983, p. 39)

Similar formulations still appeared to be commonplace in the way English teachers were articulating their beliefs well into the 1980s, illustrated by the following extracts from comprehensive school English department policy documents, collected from a number of schools in one particular authority:

- English helps personal growth; literature is central to that purpose
- As teachers of English, we consider it our duty:
  a) to enrich the child's experience and to broaden his horizons through literature,
  b) to stimulate his imagination,

c) to awaken his sensitivity to human emotions,

d) to help him think for himself and to be able to confront the pressure of the mass media.

The nature of and variation amongst different English teacher ideologies was investigated during the first stage of the research by means of a small-scale survey of the attitudes of the practising teachers in one LEA towards different views of English (reported in detail in Davies 1992). The findings of the study indicated that teachers did indeed tend to adhere to one or other distinctive subject ideology – favouring either a set of preferences for an English teaching based on the study of literary texts and the production of imaginative writing, emphasising neo-Leavisite values of promoting the personal emotional growth of pupils, or rejecting such an emphasis in favour of a more progressive view of the subject, which was more explicitly concerned with a socio-political view of language and culture. The majority of teachers appeared to prefer the former, although it must be emphasised also that this study revealed a high level of idiosyncracy underlying all these sets of beliefs.

The same attitude questionnaire administered to three successive groups of beginning PGCE students revealed the same range of beliefs, but consistently produced a far higher proportion of respondents with preferences for the more progressive paradigm than was apparent in the teacher responses. These findings were consistent with the experience of working with PGCE English students at this time, when there were frequent and striking instances of argument and debate about what should be the concerns of secondary English, reflecting on some occasions profound disagreement among different students, and indicating the likelihood of a number of beginning students finding themselves sharply at odds with the beliefs about English they were likely to encounter as they started working in secondary schools.

THE INITIAL TEACHER EDUCATION CONTEXT

The socialization of new teachers

Much of the research into initial teacher education programmes – both in the UK and the United States – has suggested that their impact has traditionally tended to be minimal in comparison with other socializing forces influencing the formation of new teachers:

> Several British and North American studies provide some evidence that the impact of campus-based preparation is 'washed out' beginning during student teaching and continuing on into later teaching experience ... (Tabachnick and Zeichner 1984, p. 29)

Training (and even subsequent experience) is not a dramatic watershed separating the perceptions of naive laymen from later judgements by knowing professionals. The lack of dramatic change in outlook . . . supports the allegation that education training has a low impact on students . . . (Lortie 1975, p. 66)

Although Lortie describes the socialization process in general as 'something that happens to people as they move through a series of structured experiences and internalize the subculture of the group' (Lortie 1975, p. 61), he characterizes the particular process of socialization in the world of school-teaching – which he sees as lacking 'a shared technical culture' – as being strongly influenced by earlier learning experiences, so that 'the attitudes, values, and orientations people bring with them tend to influence the conduct of the work' (ibid., p. 55). Lortie unambiguously views this particular process as being 'an ally of continuity rather than of change' in which 'earlier conservative influences . . . are not systematically offset in the course of induction' (ibid., p. 81).

Lacey similarly emphasises biography, but focuses on what is viewed as the possibly less conservative influence of previous university subject experiences, which constitute a 'latent culture' for novice teachers:

from which skills and shared meanings are selected and put to work in new situations. These new situations transmute the old latent culture strategies and a new perspective emerges. I call this emerging perspective a 'subject teacher perspective'. (Lacey 1977, p. 75)

There is a clear impression here that the socialization process experienced by beginning teachers involves a signficant interaction between the influence of previous experiences at school or university and the influence of the new social world of the school where novices 'acquire the values and attitudes, the interests, skills and knowledge – in short the culture – current in groups to which they are, or seek to become, a member' (Merton 1957, quoted in Lacey 1977, p. 13). Lacey postulates three distinct versions of how novices adjust to the socialization pressures of the school situation: **strategic compliance**, in which individuals merely appear to comply with the definition and constraints of the school world; **internalized adjustment**, in which individuals actually adjust their thinking to the norms of that world; **strategic redefinition**, in which individuals attempt to change the thinking of more powerful figures in the school situation (Lacey 1977, pp. 72–73).

The evidence of these and other studies (notably Tabachnik and Zeichner, 1984) strongly points to the long-standing failure of the university aspect of initial teacher education programmes to achieve any significant impact in the face of the twin influences of biography and school-based socialization. One possible solution to this lack of impact suggested by Grossman, in her study of beginning English teachers, is to emphasise and strengthen the theoretical base provided by the university, even within the school context:

Because the central person responsible for the interns' supervision was the university supervisor, interns may have avoided the 'two-worlds pitfall' (Feiman-Nemser & Buchmann, 1985) in which students must negotiate between the differing norms of university and the school site. (Grossman 1990, p. 133)

Grossman's argument is based on a firm conviction that one particular theory of teaching – Shulman's notion of pedagogical content knowledge – does constitute the kind of shared technical culture which Lortie sees as absent in the profession. In Grossman's account, though, the function of this theory of teaching is chiefly to counteract the influence of biography – especially undergraduate studies – upon new teachers. Its solution to the problem of reconciling the often conflicting agendas of university and school-based socialization – the 'two-worlds pitfall' – is to attempt to prioritize the influence of the university, and ignore that of the school.

The Internship context

In contrast, the Oxford Internship Scheme was founded on the belief that the kind of response to the twin influences of biography and tacit socialization processes proposed by Grossman is both unrealistic and undesirable. Rather than trying to extend and prioritize the influence of the university, the Internship Scheme was committed to achieving a detailed and rationalised form of co-operation between school and university experience, in which both sides of the partnership agreed to make the most appropriate uses of their distinctive contexts to achieve shared goals for the learning teacher.

The various papers produced within the Oxford University Department of Educational Studies (OUDES) during the Internship planning year of 1986/87 articulate principles and practices which would actively support novice teachers in the exploration of issues of subject ideology. The original description of a model for teacher education which formed the basis for the Internship design rejected the notion of teaching 'an essentially given set of propositions about practice' in favour of encouraging and systematically structuring 'a critical, questioning and reflective mode' that might assist student-teachers to focus on their own developing understandings and beliefs in the two contexts of school and university. It was the course's aim to provide a rich context for exploring and developing the interns' thinking, ensuring that they tested this 'against a range of alternative perspectives e.g. those offered by empirical research, by different models of the curriculum, by the epistemology of their discipline; and also by testing more abstract ideas against the realities of classrooms, and the accumulated wisdom of practising teachers' (OUDES, 1986a).

As well as emphasising the central role of the students' own construction of professional theory through their active critical engagement with the various perspectives offered by their reading, by tutors in the university and by teachers in schools, the goals for the scheme, as outlined in the Internship Commissioning Paper, specifically emphasise the need for students to examine questions about the nature of their subject in the process of adapting their thinking to the realities of schools, stating that they should come to:

> possess a critical understanding of the curriculum and pedagogy of their subject(s) i.e. they should have reconceptualised their subject(s) from university to school level and attained an understanding of different ways of organising the curriculum for their subject(s) . . . They should be aware of the rationales which may be offered for the adoption of such different approaches and of different pedagogical strategies. They should have critically considered a range of evidence related to those varied approaches and strategies, including that derived from their own personal experience. (OUDES, 1986b)

The following goal firmly establishes the shared obligation of those in both schools and university who are responsible for the interns' learning to plan together in order to ensure that explorations of this kind actually take place, and – most importantly – that these take place in the contexts of both school and university:

> The co-operative relationship between university tutors and school staff will mean a much greater sharing of responsibility for the interns' work, a more coherent programme for them and more planned support for all those involved . . . There will be much closer co-ordination of school and university experiences than there has been previously which should help interns make sense of the ideas generated, exemplified and evaluated in the two contexts. (OUDES, 1986b)

The concerns of the present research were therefore firmly located within the specific development of the Internship English programme. Given that I was committed to the twin tasks of developing this new curriculum, and of carrying out research into the issues involved, it appeared most appropriate to pursue this project through the medium of action research.

THE DESIGN OF THE ACTION RESEARCH PROJECT

The initial task of this project was to plan an Internship English programme that would ensure that interns explored questions of differing views about the nature of their subject, and the implications of such questions for classroom teaching, in a structured way throughout the year. This focus formed the basis for the main research question of the study:

To what extent is the Internship PGCE English programme capable of achieving the following broad aims:

a) providing a focus through which student-teachers may view, reflect upon and explore a wide range of approaches to secondary English teaching;
b) enabling student-teachers to identify and come to conclusions about that range of approaches without being restricted by their own preconceptions, by their learning in the university, or by the established practice and beliefs of the teachers with whom they work?

It was essential, given the decision to ground this research firmly in the context of Internship working practices, that plans for the achievement of these aims should ensure an engagement from the teachers involved – the mentors – equivalent to that of the university tutors. This entailed planning an English PGCE programme **in collaboration** with mentors which incorporated a sufficiently central place for the topic of subject ideology variation in some form.

As English curriculum tutor, I was responsible both for bringing together and guiding the deliberations of the newly formed group of English mentors during the planning year, and for ensuring that the necessary breadth and range of English teaching issues were covered. All those involved – myself as curriculum tutor, and the mentors – were of course new to this particular process of collaboration, given that our own PGCE had previously, like most, tended to leave all planning and delivery of course content to university tutors. The far more complex and delicate nature of the new dynamic is described here by one of the English mentors who had been involved in that process:

> One half of the partnership is paid to do the work involved in setting up and running the scheme. The university tutors consequently do a larger share of the work and bear the greater responsibility . . . A careful balance therefore has to be maintained – curriculum tutors must not appear to be imposing their views on mentors, nor to be asking too much of mentors in terms of preparation for meetings or writing the curriculum programme. (Parkes, V. & Stratton, J., in Benton 1990)

Thus I had both the opportunity to introduce to the English programme planning group my own agenda in relation to subject ideology variation, and the obligation to ensure that the mentors had every opportunity to accept or reject that particular emphasis within the programme. Clearly, given the principle of shared responsibility, mere acceptance would not be sufficient: it was necessary that the **commitment** of the mentors to this aspect of the English programme agenda should be achieved.

The actions taken to this end during the planning year involved the progressive introduction of the topic – referred to as 'Versions of English' – into the overall developing agenda for the new English PGCE programme. In line with the principle that the curriculum tutor should take a lead in the planning process, I was able to propose that a focus on different beliefs about the nature of English might be an appropriate topic for the programme at an early stage in the process. Given the initial ready approval of mentors, this strand was developed in the same way as all others, from early tentative discussion to subsequent elaboration of detailed plans for a programme unit on Versions of English which eventually took the form of a three page 'unit' description presented for final approval of mentors at the beginning of the 1987/88 academic year, as part of the overall course programme, alongside other detailed units on topics such as the teaching of writing, reading and oracy.

A number of activities were outlined in this document. Some were to take place in the form of university seminars discussing: interns' own past experiences of English studies; their current views of the subject; a range of views about the subject as expressed by experts in the field and within school policy documents; the implications of these views for classroom practice. The development of their thinking about lesson planning was also related to these issues, as were two of the interns' written assignments. Complementary activities were planned for the school context, including the study and discussion of English department policy documents, and guided interviews with teachers about their views of the subject.

These activities were all directed towards the achievement of the following goals:

As a result of the course, interns should be able to:

Goal 1: articulate the subject ideology which they have developed as a result of their own educational histories.

Goal 2: articulate the subject ideologies of the teachers with whom they work in schools, and develop an understanding of the options available to them as secondary English teachers.

Goal 3: explore and evaluate the implications for classroom teaching of different subject ideologies.

Goal 4: articulate whatever subject ideologies
   (i) they find themselves developing during the course of the PGCE year
   (ii) they adhere to at the end of the PGCE year, and discuss their reasons for this.

Goal 5: critically examine and justify their own teaching in terms of the subject ideologies that they have developed during the course of the PGCE year.

These activities were piloted and evaluated during the first cycle of the research, in 1987/88, and refinements were subsequently made in order to strengthen their impact for the second, main cycle of the research in 1988/89. One of the main adjustments made for this cycle involved the development of teacher interviews, which gave the interns a programmed opportunity to initiate a longer term dialogue about their own and the teachers' views of English. All adjustments were made with the full support and agreement of mentors in regular planning meetings at the university.

Data gathering and analysis

A wide range of qualitative data was gathered during this process, especially during the second cycle. This consisted of: all the written assignments of the interns; transcriptions of interviews with teachers, where these took place; individual interviews carried out with each intern on three occasions (twice during the PGCE year, and once at the end of their first year as teachers); questionnaire data; recordings and transcriptions of several university-based curriculum sessions; additional unplanned data gathered during the year, such as recordings of informal seminars run by interns, and two separate articles written by interns about this issue.

This data was analysed in two stages: first, to identify broad themes across all the intern data, both in relation to themes relating to the specified goals of the Versions of English strand, and also in order to identify, more inductively, fresh perspectives on the concerns of the research in a way that was more in tune with a grounded theory approach. Focusing on the themes which thus emerged, a second stage analysis was carried out on an intern-by-intern basis, in order to test the themes emerging from the first stage against the full data for each individual. Understandings emerging from this process were gradually identified and developed in line with Glaser and Strauss's 'constant comparative method'.

The following section outlines the findings, organised in line with this process of identifying and integrating the categories, or themes, which thus emerged from the data analysis.

THE FINDINGS

During the course of this second cycle, my own experience of what took place was, despite the efforts devoted to gathering sufficient data with sufficient rigour, predominantly from the viewpoint of an actor in the events under scrutiny, rather than from that of a researcher. My role as actor in these events was as a curriculum tutor, and in that respect my experience of the year was both positive and exciting. It appeared that my teaching concern with placing an exploration of differing views of English at the centre of the PGCE English programme had achieved considerable success, and that all the interns in my group had, to varying extents, engaged profitably with this topic.

This was, of course, very much the viewpoint from within the university context and, although I was already aware from interviews I had conducted during the course of the year that certain interns had encountered problems in trying to interview teachers in their schools about their views of English, I was not prepared for the rather more stark picture which gradually but increasingly emerged from the systematic analysis of data. In effect, there had been an almost complete failure to engage the active and committed involvement of mentors in the exploration of the Versions of English issues in the context of schools.

It is that latter outcome which raises the most interesting questions for this particular research, and this shall be the main focus of the remainder of this paper, having first outlined the key features of the more successful engagement with the Versions of English strand of the programme in the university in the next section.

The university context

The data relating to the interns' experience of the Versions of English strand of the course during the time they spent in the university reveal a remarkably strong engagement with the intended issues. Although the strength of that engagement cannot, in every case, be equated with the approval of interns, there is no doubt that the actions planned in order to encourage interns to explore the nature, and implications, of different beliefs about the aims and proper content of the English curriculum, proved effective. These findings show the explorations of ideological issues, and of their relationship to what goes on in school, flourishing in the university-based work during that year.

In general, the outcome in the university can be described in terms of the establishment of a 'shared discourse' in the interactions of the intern group about the issues relating to the nature of English. This shared discourse took the form of a continuing process of discussion and interaction about the Versions of English agenda which the data show having taken place during 1988/89. 'Discourse' is used to indicate the use of a specific set of terms, points of reference and habits of discussion, and 'shared' is used to indicate that this discourse constituted common ground for (but not necessarily shared beliefs about) a wide variety of discussions about teaching English and becoming English teachers in which every member of the intern group participated, to a greater or lesser extent.

There appeared to be a number of reasons for this. First, of course, is the fact of my own power over the situation. As curriculum tutor, I planned and sustained this particular agenda. Given my experience over the previous three years of how to manage the dynamics and preoccupations of PGCE students, and strongly informed by data from the pilot cycle the previous year, I was in a good position to introduce these topics for maximum effect.

Secondly, a significant number of interns were sympathetic to the particular concerns involved in this emphasis from the very start of the course, as a result of their previous higher education English studies, which had raised similar questions. For some students, the Versions of English strand provided a welcome (and unexpected) opportunity to apply existing preoccupations to the process of learning to teach:

> a sense of relief on all our parts that we can actually articulate our sort of ideologies here (Mary)

> the notion of 'versions of English' is simply a very convenient way to talk about what already were major concerns. The curriculum programme has helpfully touched on some of the issues, but I don't think it has shaped or altered my general position. (Roy)

Thirdly, a number of other interns who had not encountered much in the way of such perspectives before the PGCE course valued the opportunity to explore possibilities for the study of English other than those which they had previously encountered:

> that course influenced me a great deal about what I thought about English. I mean, I didn't know before what kind of English I wanted to teach. I learnt a lot about what I wanted to do, just from talking to other people. (Anne)

> it started here, I think, just from all that argument . . . about your own language, and how whatever you said is loaded with gender references and things like that, and that sort of awakened it. Although I thought, God – this is a bit far-fetched at the beginning, I felt – and then now, I just appreciate that much more. (Liz)

> My attitude to 'English' on arriving at the course was more a case of inarticulated notions than a coherent ideology. Indeed, that there could be different versions of English was in itself an education. (Paul)

Finally, it appeared to be generally the case, with very few exceptions, that interns valued the opportunity to sustain the kind of intellectual/ academic explorations with which they had become familiar during their undergraduate or higher degrees. This was most visibly illustrated by the fact that a significant proportion of interns initiated and sustained – during the first term, with its greatest concentration of time in the university – an additional series of seminars of their own devoted to the exploration of the relationship of some of the theoretical perspectives they had encountered during their higher degree English studies to the secondary English teaching context:

> in our groups and grassroots generated 'Versions of English' seminar, the issues are kept warm if not over-heated. The latter has illustrated the awesome slippiness of the topic 'English', with sessions on 'The Hidden History of English Studies', 'Propaganda and Literature', 'Fictionality and the Reader', and 'Film'. (From an item in the student newspaper)

As a result of the focus encouraged by the Versions of English strand, interns tended to explore progressive approaches to English alongside the less progressive approaches they were encountering in schools. For some, such exploration was entirely in line with the interests which they brought with them to the course, whilst for others it represented a perspective that was additional to their main subject commitments. The kinds of English subject matter and approaches involved are typically represented by the following description from one of the interns:

> I would like to teach an understanding of the relation between language and society, and all that which is inherent to this term. This would involve looking into all areas of language use written and spoken, including the media: television, press, films, advertising, magazines and comics. I want to empower students to recognize the deceptions and implications of language use in social, political and historical terms. (Anne)

All interns describe, to a greater or lesser extent, undertaking work of this kind, and the intention to pursue such interests, but this did not represent any kind of wholesale shift in the subject commitment and interests of most, who took the explorations of different approaches encountered during the course as an opportunity to develop a broad and well-balanced approach to classroom practice:

> what I wanted to do, what I still want to do in the classroom, is basically to get through to kids on whatever level I can in an exciting way. That is my ideology, I don't have any restrictions, literature-wise or anything like that. (Liz)

As indicated earlier, the mainly positive outcome (positive in that it had been identified as a desirable goal in the original plans for the English programme) also had a negative aspect: a number of interns experienced the exploration of issues of subject ideology in the university setting as personally uncomfortable. Because of the strong philosophical positions held by some interns about the subject, and the highly specialised subject knowledge that often went along with those positions, some interns found themselves either being characterised as adhering to outmoded ideologies, or simply unable to participate in certain kinds of discussion. The group dynamic which obtained in the university sessions lent itself very forcibly to such perceptions:

> all these different experiences and different versions ... you can feel, oh God, it was a waste of time doing my [i.e. undergraduate] course and I don't fit in, I don't understand. (Kate)

> I think there's a lot of group pressure, I think that people know before it was uttered that it wouldn't be accepted ... It's difficult to say where the pressure originates, it's there – whether it's from the people, or from the course, or from the group. (Yvonne)

Such discomfort, although problematic at times, can nonetheless be seen as a normal aspect of the kind of debates which might be viewed as both legitimate and desirable within a university setting, and there is no doubt – on the strength of this data – that the considerable diversity of views represented in groups of English graduates at that period in the subject's history would, unless a somewhat questionable consensus was imposed, inevitably lead to discomfort on the part of some students. For many, at any rate, the debates were as much stimulating as discomfiting:

> I think a lot of it has come from mixing with other interns. I think that's very beneficial in that you do hear people who've got very solid ideas, very – they've defined what they think, and to hear that is very helpful. (Rose)

The school context

The data indicated that the interns proved adept at interpreting their observations of the English taught in their internship schools in the kinds of terms generated by the Versions of English strand. They were able to come to their own conclusions about the kind of English being taught in their particular English departments, and to measure their own beliefs and aspirations as secondary English teachers against this. They were also, and without exception, given sufficient freedom to experiment with a range of approaches to the subject, including those which were at odds with the normal practice of a department.

With only a very few exceptions, though, they failed to engage in any sustained dialogue with teachers about questions of different ways of conceptualising the subject in the secondary context. Although some discussions did take place on a few occasions, the majority of interns soon chose not to persevere with the plan to engage with mentors in the planned dialogue about the nature of the subject. Neither did the mentors, or other teachers, encourage the pursuit of such dialogue.

This failure took a variety of forms. In a number of cases (six), interns preferred to restrict dialogue with mentors and other teachers to exchanges about practical issues of classroom management and curriculum delivery, and were content to avoid discussions of a philosophical or epistemological nature. These interns valued the kinds of conversation which did occur, and perceived no problem in the failure to engage in other kinds of conversation, despite the encouragement to do so that they received from their curriculum tutor. They had clear ideas about the kinds of conversation and learning that were appropriate in different contexts:

> I've learnt more about the kind of – my feelings about teaching etc. in those discussions downstairs than I have in school – but I've also learnt in school more about the realities of it. So I feel as though learning is definitely divided into two aspects. (Mary)

> people at the school have – I think – clarified organisational matters more than anything – they've exposed how much work has to be done, exposed how much organisation there is in things, just how much you've got to be able to handle. That's what's been most enlightening. (Ann)

These interns professed themselves entirely content with such an emphasis, and saw little problem in having failed to establish any other form of dialogue. In this respect, at least, they were very different from the interns who did attempt to pursue the recommended kind of dialogue with teachers about the nature of the subject as it was reflected in the practice of their particular school, and about their own developing beliefs. Out of these, two achieved some degree of success, and saw that as a valuable part of their experience, in sharp contrast to the five others who tried and failed, experiencing varying degrees of discomfort and frustration as a result.

The two successful interns both report an unproblematic habit of discussion with the teachers in their school departments which allowed them to clarify their ideas about the aims and content of secondary English teaching:

> in the first term people were definitely telling me how they saw it, and I – I was asking questions all the time. And they were very good about putting time aside to sort of talk to me about it. So when I observed lessons, at the beginning, in October, I was always asking questions afterwards and they were giving me sort of their views . . . and, I mean, there were very general questions as well as the specific ones – so I mean, I – and – those teacher interview sheets you gave them the first term, I found those really good, because I had an excuse to actually say, you know, 'can you sit down and talk to me about your philosophy of English' . . . I learnt quite a lot from that – (Kate)

> I think that it depends on the intern, and it depends on the teachers, really – you've got to really ask them if you want to learn. . . . I think they affected me quite a lot, Derek and Sian, so I do think that the school input has been useful, in terms of versions of English. (Yvonne)

Although this apparent success should be viewed with a certain degree of caution – neither Kate nor Yvonne demonstrated any substantial interest in these issues in university-based sessions, and both might to a certain extent have been feeding me what they felt were the desired answers – such examples do keep open the question of whether it is feasible for student teachers to engage with practising teachers in discussions of this kind. In the case of these two, the process of discussing subject philosophies and their implications for practice appears to be relatively uncontentious and straightforward.

That was certainly not the case with the final five, who encountered considerable obstacles in attempting to engage in these discussions, and yet whose failure – it will be argued – most strongly supports the case for trying to succeed.

Three out of this group – Paul, Nick and Roy – explicitly felt that the scope of their own learning had been limited by the failure of the teachers in their school departments to engage with them in shared discourse about issues of subject theory and philosophy:

> I don't think they were prepared to articulate it, to help you. I think they saw it very much as a Department [i.e. university]-centred practice . . . of working

out a version for the sake of working it out, whereas I don't think they saw the relevance for teaching. (Paul)

He felt that the lack of any sustained engagement with these issues in schools limited the development of his thinking about the kind of work he should undertake in the classroom:

> It was a definite fault, really, through the year. I think you were left to your own devices as far as working out objectives . . . (Paul)

Nick also felt the need for a dialogue which would help him find a way through the different possibilities that English seemed to offer, and was shocked to encounter impatience from the teachers over his efforts at philosophical speculation:

> they really did get fed up with me going on about varieties of English – and inevitably they exploded and said, which I'm sure didn't reflect their true feelings, never mind about all this crap – this is where it's really happening, it's what happens in the classroom that counts. (Nick)

In the end, Nick gave up trying to engage the teachers in discussion about their ideas, acknowledging how busy they were and opting for the less stressful approach of learning from observation:

> I think it is possible to pick things up from watching them. I mean, as regards to them becoming more conscious of it and getting to be able to talk about it in theoretical terms, they obviously are as you know incredibly busy. (Nick)

A critical element here seems to be the lack of commitment he perceived in these teachers to issues that they saw as belonging in the less 'real' context of the university, rather than in the more practical world of school. Nick felt a strong need to work his way through the dilemma of reconciling his past experiences of English with what appeared to be new and different demands. He looked to the teachers he admired to provide a convincing case for making a firm commitment away from the kind of English he loved towards a new, more appropriate but to him less attractive, version of the subject that his experience of the course (and especially what some of his fellow interns were advocating) appeared to be recommending.

Roy had been the leading figure in the group of interns committed to the exploration of ideological issues, and progressive theories of English teaching. He saw this very strong commitment as being crucially dependent on finding a way of putting these ideas into practice – 'the theory's not going to survive without its practical affirmation' – and he saw dialogue – with fellow interns, and with teachers – as the means to achieving that: 'Not launching into the deep end with some sort of, you know, wonderful radical sort of subject practice approach, which just will fall on completely deaf ears'. He was, consequently, profoundly disappointed by the apparent indifference of the teachers in his school to his efforts and concerns:

the relations between theory and practice have become a lot more evident. Whereas what I brought with me was a theoretically quite worked-out position – the struggle and the challenge was to do something with that in the class-room . . . I don't feel that [School 7] as an institution gave me the opportunity to do that.

He also felt that greater efforts needed to be made to achieve the co-operation of mentors in this process:

To be honest, I think time might be also well employed trying to talk to the mentors – to get them to have some sort of ideological awareness – because it's not really something that exists, to be honest. They are – given that we spend an awful lot of time in school and not here, especially for those thirteen weeks – it can become a living hell sometimes, trying to get people to understand what you mean by certain things – and you're – certainly my – towards the end I just gave up trying – there wasn't any point trying to make yourself understood. Because the barrier flew up just as soon as you started to talk about certain things.

These negative feelings seemed surprising at first, considering Roy's apparently successful experience of carrying out the formal teacher interviews with at least three different members of the department in his Internship school. The Head of English had spoken articulately and at length about her own and her department's view of the subject; for instance, in the following explanation for her department's lack of engagement with media study:

When I say I'm not ultra-keen on it I do feel quite strongly that what's left to English Departments is actually what we read, and no one else is doing that. No one is dealing with how stories or poems work and affect you and help you develop yourself as a person and understand other people. That's where I think our main work is, but having said that it would be a nonsense to exclude related things happening within English work. (Head of English, School 7)

Roy, though, experienced these as isolated and artificial occasions of direct engagement. He looked for a more sustained dialogue in which his own ideas were listened to and valued. Far from achieving such a dialogue, he was conscious of the pressure of underlying assumptions about the nature of the subject which seem to belong firmly within a traditional model of the socialization of new teachers:

they didn't need to articulate it, it was so obvious is I think what – it was so obvious what English was about, um, that – they didn't feel that – they felt that I should understand this. (Roy)

Roy's energetic involvement in the university-based exploration of different views of English had earlier in the year indicated his commitment to a 'strategic redefinition' role in school, but as time went on it is clear that the socializing pressures of the school eventually resulted instead in a 'strategic compliance' response:

> The easiest thing to do is – when somebody asks you for your opinion on something or other – they ask you what you think of this, the easiest thing is to just feed them what they want because – it's just for the sake of a quiet life, you've got so many other things to do. I mean, rather than – it's not a place to argue a case, or to try and convince somebody of something – (Roy)

Ultimately, his experience in this particular school, and the temporary nature of his stay there, made him hold back and wait for a more propitious working situation in his first appointment.

The fourth of these interns, Becky, also provided strong evidence of having encountered – but, in her case, of having accepted – a similar process of socialization. Becky did not, in general, regret the fact that the teachers in her school were no more inclined to engage in a shared discourse about Versions of English than the teachers described by Paul, Nick and Roy. She appeared to be generally satisfied with the fact that the teachers did not engage in such issues, opting rather to go along with the socialization process:

> I think in a way the interns being there, if they have a good relationship with the staff, it's sort of a process of osmosis in some way. (Becky)

She, like the six relatively contented interns described earlier, clearly preferred to avoid direct engagements with teachers about theoretical or philosophical issues. Unlike those others, though, she does seem to have been negatively affected by the teachers' negligible degree of co-operation with this aspect of the programme, moving in effect towards her own form of 'internalized adjustment'. Her account of the teachers' assumptions about the place of theoretical perspectives in her learning process (which are consistent with her own notion of learning through 'osmosis') suggests that they communicated an expectation to her that new teachers would automatically adopt the implicitly agreed subject values of the department:

> I think they assumed that you shared it – I don't think they really thought – until we made it clear that we were talking about versions of English, I don't think they thought there was more than one version of English to talk about, in a way. Or if they did, they didn't say anything about it. And it was just assumed that you'd get on with it, and do what was sort of orthodox, I suppose. (Becky)

It is therefore perhaps not surprising that serious problems occurred when she and her partner intern Kevin did try to engage their mentor/Head of Department in the explicit discussion of his subject theories and philosophy demanded by the English programme (which was clearly seen both by them and the teachers in her school as emanating entirely from the university department). The best explanation for the apparently disastrous outcome of the programmed discussion with the mentor is that, having already accepted the implicit values of the department, Becky and her intern partner Kevin had left it too late to raise issues which questioned those values, especially from a perspective external to the school English department:

> I think my most uncomfortable hour with Geoff was when I asked him to give
> me his version of English – which was an extremely embarrassing experience –
> because he was made so uncomfortable by it. (Kevin)

Becky's comments about this interview were evasive at first, but ultimately
consistent with Kevin's account –

> Geoff hates intellectualisation of the subject, and I think he'd resent interfer-
> ence on that sort of – on those terms quite a lot – and see it as sort of – def-
> initely as interference that is unmerited, really, or unjustified.

– and she very directly warned me off future plans of this kind in a way that
was entirely defensive of the school department's position, as she saw it:

> I think they would resent it a lot.
> CD If they felt the way they see things was being questioned, or questioned
> critically?
> Becky: If the department was trying to change the way they taught –
> CD – well we're not –
> Becky: – in sort of quite a dramatic way. (Becky)

Although Lacey points in his study towards certain occasions where student-
teachers' views might have influenced practising teachers' thinking in a manner consistent with strategic redefinition taking place, the more compelling
evidence from his study suggests that strategic compliance or internalized
adjustment are far more likely options for student-teachers during the school
placement time of their initial training:

> Often it wasn't worth bringing conflict with teacher-tutor to a head, since there
> was a definite non-communication and it was a waste of precious school time.
> It was more useful and peaceful to go away and do your own thing quietly.
> (Lacey 1977, pp. 74–5)

Certainly, this is the view of Tabachnik and Zeichner, who report three students in their own study who reacted strongly 'against the constraints posed
by their placements', but who 'because of the severe nature of the constraints
and their status as student teachers':

> generally acted in ways demanded by their situations while maintaining strong
> private reservations about doing so. (Tabachnick and Zeichner 1984, p. 33)

The implications of these studies are entirely in line with the Oxford study,
in which all the students – even if their own views (mainly those developed
as a result of their own educational histories) were strongly at odds with
what they encountered in schools – chose either to accept, or avoid argument about, the tacit views and values of the teachers who guided their learning in schools.

But the present study additionally indicates that the problem does not –

as the studies quoted above do suggest – exclusively concern ways in which beginning students have to negotiate and conceal differing beliefs about what and how to teach as English teachers: a potentially distinctive issue emerges from these findings concerning beginning teachers' need to engage confidently and freely with teachers in discussions of a theoretical nature, in addition to the more practically oriented discussions which do evidently take place during the course of their training in the school context.

Certainly, the difficulties experienced by the three students – Paul, Nick and Roy – who were most frustrated by having to adopt compliance strategies (and for whom internalized adjustment was not an option) appear to be located more in the failure to achieve a dialogue with teachers about differing views of the subject, than with the fact that actual redefinition of the teachers' views was an unrealistic goal.

Considering the importance which those three interns appeared to attach to that failure – and the value which the two successful interns attributed to the dialogue which they achieved – the findings relating to the six interns who were not concerned about the lack of such dialogue should not be taken as sufficient evidence to claim that there is no real need to pursue this possibility further. The final section of this chapter will indeed argue that the valuable conclusions emerging from this research should concern the structural obstacles which can be seen as having hindered a fruitful process of discussion between interns and teachers, rather than in the conclusion that the aim to achieve such discussion was in itself inappropriate or misguided.

CONCLUSIONS

This action research project developed and investigated an element of a PGCE programme – the Versions of English strand – which aimed to help beginning teachers to explore the nature of their subject for the purposes of secondary teaching. The research was concerned to discover whether such issues would prove to be of relevance to those student-teachers, and whether it was possible to take advantage of the opportunities offered by the Internship Scheme so that these issues could be made meaningful in and relevant to the school context of their learning.

The research findings provided some compelling evidence that the planned focus on ideologies of the subject did indeed prove to be relevant for this particular group of interns. They became intensively involved in this topic, to the extent that these concerns were sustained throughout the year, and informed wide aspects of their developing thinking about teaching secondary English. Not all interns were equally enthusiastic about their experience of the Versions of English strand, but the quality of the discussions and written work related to it suggested both a substantial need to make sense of the issues involved on the part of all interns, and an increased understanding of current issues in secondary English teaching arising out of many of the planned activities. This was especially so for those activities taking place in the university context, but similar impact can be detected in relation to some of the teaching which they undertook in school.

On the basis of these findings, it seems reasonable therefore to suggest that the learning of beginning teachers – specifically, those negotiating the transition from higher degree subject studies towards secondary school subject teaching – should include opportunities to explore broadly theoretical and epistemological questions of this kind in some depth in the course of their inital teacher training.

The findings have also shown, though, how a central element of the planned activities – the open and sustained dialogue between students and teachers about various views of English – failed to take place. This failure restricts the extent to which the actions planned for the research may ultimately be judged successful, and points to a generalisable question about whether it is realistic to expect to involve the school side of an initial teacher education partnership in the exploration of questions that extend beyond the practicalities of classroom teaching.

In attempting to make such explorations take place, this action research project aimed, in effect, to intervene in the way a group of student-teachers were socialized into the values of school subject departments. The literature on beginning teachers tends to suggest that the socialization process results in an inherently conservative form of learning, in which beginning teachers tend to absorb the established values of the school insofar as they reflect values experienced in the course of their own educational histories. Where there is less of a match between the values which the students bring with them from their own education and those of the schools which they join in their training, the socialization process generally appears to teach the novices how to conceal those values and concerns which are at odds with those of the school.

In either respect, a strong case can be made for systematically addressing the problems relating to traditional processes of socialization within an initial teacher education programme, if at least it is accepted that a predominantly conservative process of induction into the profession is undesirable, and that we wish to value and encourage habits of critical thinking and intellectual engagement with the problems of teaching on the part of new teachers. A key aspect of this research therefore concerns the evidence that change of this kind, whilst desirable, is not straightforwardly achievable under current conditions if – as seems hard to refute – a rational way of dealing with a process whose chief characteristic is the inculcation of implicit values in the school setting is to strive for explicitness about such issues **in the school**.

Whilst it might well be the case that the failure to engage mentors' sustained commitment to the kinds of activity envisaged in the Versions of

English strand resulted in some measure from inexperience and lack of skill or sensitivity on my part (as the curriculum tutor co-ordinating the partnership planning with mentors), the evidence of this research does indicate the presence of more profound structural obstacles – even in a programme that appeared to have generally achieved a fairly high level of university and school collaboration such as the Internship Scheme.

Two major structural obstacles can be detected in the findings of the research:

1) the student teachers' characteristic concern to avoid situations of potential conflict with those who have power over their success on the course,
2) in the absence of having been inducted into a more developed view of their role as teacher educators, a tendency on the part of mentors to view their role as primarily being concerned with the provision of practical guidance and support.

In the case of the first of these, it is clear from the findings that a major factor in the avoidance by practically all interns of the intended dialogue with teachers was a resistance to bringing up issues which would highlight differing beliefs or subject knowledge between themselves and mentors, and other teachers. The issues of differing subject ideologies of English had come to be seen as contentious, and interns chose to avoid the danger of getting into disagreements with mentors, or of appearing to possess more developed subject understandings than these experienced teachers. It is, in particular, possible that the interns' sense of the contentiousness of these issues was increased by their experience of the debates about the subject which I, as curriculum tutor, had actively encouraged in university sessions.

But, in terms of the second structural obstacle mentioned above, it is also likely that the mentors, given a stronger commitment to engaging in the intended kind of dialogue about these issues, could have overcome the interns' own understandable caution. The findings certainly suggest a degree of readiness – and in some cases, a positive desire – on the interns' part, but it seems that the lack of encouragement or enthusiasm for such an activity on the part of the mentors generally resulted in the interns choosing not to persevere with initial attempts at dialogue. In the light of this, it seems reasonable to assume that it is this second obstacle which most needs to be addressed if there is to be any hope of achieving such dialogue.

This research suggests a number of specific reasons why the mentors did not, in the event, encourage dialogue about differing views of the aims and content of English:

• a structural hostility or indifference on the part of practising teachers to the kinds of theorising traditionally associated with university input into teacher training,
• a suspicion on the part of schools that the university's encouragement of

questions about the nature of the English taught in schools constituted an implicit attack on the schools' practice and expertise,
- the lack of time and opportunity on the part of mentors, during busy and pressured school days, to engage in philosophical debate,
- the crisis in English studies in particular which was occurring during that period was simply too contentious for free and open debate between teachers and students,
- a failure on my part to communicate the planned actions with adequate clarity to the mentors.

Given that considerable efforts were made, in terms of meetings and written communications, to explain and support the English programme, the most likely explanation for the failure of this aspect of the plans lies not in an insufficiency of communication, but rather in the inappropriateness of what was being proposed.

The Internship Scheme explicitly did not conceive of the mentor/intern relationship as one of expert/apprentice, demanding an unquestioning respect for the wisdom of the expert on the part of the apprentice. Rather, the role of mentor was conceived of in terms of school-based teacher educator, the experienced practitioner systematically helping able beginning teachers to develop skills of critical thinking within the real-world context of the school. In order to carry out this role, though, it was necessary that the mentors should have a conscious and theorised understanding that such a role demanded more than the provision of practical support and guidance, and access to their own classroom teaching skills (however important these things undoubtedly were in themselves).

This particular project was certainly dependent upon mentors understanding the nature and value of the contribution which they were able to make to the interns' learning, but in retrospect it is evident that the project's plans failed to conceptualise and encourage the kind of distinctive contribution to the Versions of English strand that they would be best equipped to provide and sustain. The mentors' reluctance to engage in discussion with interns about the nature and implications of different versions of English can readily be understood if we recognise that this task effectively required them to:

a) explicitly discuss understandings about their subject which they usually take for granted, and to do so in an exposed way with novices probably much more accustomed to such discussion,
b) defend well-established beliefs, potentially against alternatives which were unfamiliar, hard to comprehend, or apparently irrelevant,
c) engage in discussion in academically philosophical terms – an activity in which most would have no active expertise.

This last expectation was particularly inappropriate, and most markedly at odds with Internship's aim to ensure that all those contributing to the learning of interns should do so in terms of their distinctive expertise. The other two problems outlined above point to the difficulty in trying to achieve – or, at any rate, to sustain – any dialogue which participants perceive as uncomfortable or a waste of time.

The lessons of this research point, therefore, to the need to think about strategies and aims equally. It was somewhat simplistic to expect mentors to overcome the problems associated with the tacit socialization of novices into the established values of the school simply by encouraging the explicit philosophical examination of those values: the pace and priorities of normal school-life do not provide a suitable context for the achievement of such an aim, and given the structural nature of those contextual problems it was unreasonable to strive for a sudden change in this respect.

Nonetheless, the findings of this research do indicate many ways in which a focus on the nature and implications of subject ideology variation might be considered appropriate, feasible and valuable for beginning teachers. Epistemological questions were evidently of significant concern to the interns in this study, and their exploration worked well in the university context of their PGCE course. This research showed how readily these interns explored questions about the nature of the subject, as part of a process of orienting their thinking towards the business of teaching their subject in schools, and in a way which allowed them to sustain valued undergraduate habits of reflection and argument during the early period of the transition from university student to schoolteacher.

But in order for this aspect of their learning to be made meaningful in the school context, the outcomes of this study do suggest that the emphasis needed to have been on the kind of perspective which experienced teachers are best placed and prepared to deal with: that is, helping student-teachers to understand and explore the practical implications of various approaches to the subject. Rather than asking English teachers to expound on whether it is best to teach poetry, linguistics or media study, a more realistic, appropriate and productive approach would have emphasized questions of how one balances such choices within a pressed curriculum, how one engenders pupil enthusiasm for and engagement with such different kinds of learning, how one copes with the classroom management implications, the resource implications, the assessment implications, the demands of the outside world, and so on, of different kinds of subject content and subject aims. Perhaps, too, in the course of such explorations – which could have occurred both in discussion sessions with mentors, and in the ongoing processes of lesson planning, teaching and debriefing – teachers might also have found themselves offering philosophical justifications for one choice over another.

At any rate, it is reasonable to hypothesize that the teachers would have proved not merely able to contribute, but also to be the more capable and appropriate members of the Internship partnership when it came to theorizing about issues of working with different kinds of English in the classroom.

The findings of the research suggest, on the other hand, that it would be inappropriate to ask mentors to do the job of finding ways of relating decontextualized academic perspectives to the practical context of the classroom: it seems more reasonable to suggest that this is the kind of task which should be undertaken by tutors and interns working together in the university.

It is interesting, finally, to speculate about why these kinds of understandings about how to make best use of the distinctive roles within the Internship Scheme were not more obvious at the time of planning and carrying out this study. The first and most obvious answer must be that I – both as the person responsible for co-ordinating the development of the English programme in the new Internship Scheme, and as the person planning the action research project – was naïve in both capacities, and did not have a well-developed concept of what constituted the distinctive kinds of expertise possessed by university tutors or practising teachers.

It is also the case that the teachers were no better equipped than I to articulate what was distinctive about their expertise, and unsurprisingly accepted the suggestions for their role in this particular project that were offered them at the planning stage, even if this was not something they were ever very likely to carry out. The end result of this combined naïvety was an absence of any testing process of arguing through what each of us, in our different roles, could most appropriately and effectively have provided. Instead, superficial agreement about the desirability of the aims and strategies of the project was rapidly, and too readily, established. The impression of shared understandings thus achieved consequently obscured the need for the harder work of collaboratively figuring out, perhaps with greater initial discomfort, what was really (and valuably) different between the perspectives and concerns of those working in the university, and those working in the schools.

REFERENCES

Benton, P. (ed.) (1990) *The Oxford Internship Scheme*. London: Calouste Gulbenkian Foundation.

Brooks, C. St. John (1983) English: a curriculum for personal development, in M. Hammersley and A. Hargreaves (eds.) *Curriculum Practice*. Falmer Press, Sussex.

Dark, P. and Drake, L. (1993) School-based teacher training: a conservative practice, *Journal of Education for Teaching*, Vol. 19, no. 2, pp. 175–189.

Davies, C. (1992) English teacher ideologies: an empirical study. *British Educational Research Journal* 18 (2): 193–207.

Grossman, P. L. (1990) *The Making of a Teacher: Teacher Knowledge and Teacher Education*. Teachers' College Press, Columbia University, New York.

Lacey, C. (1977) *The Socialization of Teachers*. Methuen, London.

Lortie, D. C. (1975) *Schoolteacher: A Sociological Study*. University of Chicago Press, Chicago.

Mathieson, M. (1975) *The Preachers of Culture*. George Allen & Unwin, London.

Oxford University Department of Educational Studies (1986a) PGCE Internship Programme: Discussion Paper. Oxford: OUDES Internal Paper.

Oxford University Department of Educational Studies (1986b) The Internship Model – a Commissioning Paper. Oxford: OUDES Internal Paper.

Tabachnick, B. R., and K. M. Zeichner (1984) The impact of student teaching experience on the development of teacher perspectives. *Journal of Teacher Education* (Nov–Dec).

Williams, R. (1983) *Writing in Society*. Verso Editions, London.

3

INTERN LEARNING AND PROGRESSION: A CASE STUDY OF STUDENT TEACHERS IN ONE SCHOOL

Nicola Jubeh

This chapter explores the experiences of a group of eight student teachers attached to one Internship school. The aim of the research reported was to explore the perceptions of student teachers in relation to their learning, and to discover which aspects of their school based experience they found most significant.

In 1993, after the Internship scheme had been in operation for six years, a severe reduction occurred in the resources available for it, and the Oxford University Department of Educational Studies (OUDES) took the opportunity to conduct a review of the scheme. To inform that review, it commissioned a survey of the perceptions of all the key actors in the scheme – mentors, curriculum tutors, professional tutors, general tutors and the previous year's interns – of what were more and less useful aspects of the scheme. The findings of that survey (Rothwell, Nardi and McIntyre, 1994) were of course in generalised, quantitative terms which gave no great feel for the lived experiences of those involved. The present study – conducted contemporaneously with the survey – may therefore usefully be seen as complementing that survey by asking similar questions, in relation to the perceptions of interns, about the lives and learning of a particular group of interns in one particular school context.

Among the findings of the survey were that there was a high degree of consensus about the centrality of the mentor's role and also about which mentor activities were most valuable. A complementary finding, however, was that interns and others perceived a high level of variability in the quality of mentoring. Second in value for most respondents was the curriculum tutor role, though that was the role about which there was greatest divergence of opinion. While the majority of the suggested activities for each of the four teacher educator roles were rated as of high value by each category of respondents, ex-interns were generally less positive than the teacher educators themselves; and the professional tutor and general tutor roles seemed to be widely seen as relatively marginal. It is against the background of such general findings that this chapter should be read.

It was especially with the interns' learning in the school based component of the course that this study was concerned. In particular it focused on their perceptions of:

a) the role the mentor played in the development of their knowledge and understanding
b) other ways in which they had been provided with experience in the school to help them to develop their expertise.

RESEARCH PROCEDURES

Semi-structured group interviews were chosen as the main data collection procedure for the study. Within the broad framework of the above research concerns, it was important that the interns should be able to talk at length and to reveal unanticipated concerns and information. Group interviews were chosen because of their apparent practical and organisational advantages and because, as Watt and Ebutt (1987) have suggested, they tend to be especially appropriate when a group of people have been working together with a common purpose.

The group interviews were conducted at four times during the year:

- November 9th 1993, early in the 'J' weeks when the interns were in the school for two days each week (GI:1),
- February 23rd 1994, early in the 'S' weeks phase when the interns were wholly based in the school (GI:2),
- April 21st 1994, in the middle of the 'S' weeks phase (GI:3),
- May 13th 1994, at the end of the 'S' weeks period, when the interns were about to leave the school (GI:4).

The interviews were scheduled for times immediately after the end of the teaching day and lasted approximately one hour. The interns appeared to accept the researcher's reassurances about confidentiality and similarly appeared unconcerned about the tape-recording of the interviews. However several disadvantages of the use of group interviews became apparent:

- difficulties in getting all the interns together at the same time, so that there were absentees from three of the four interviews;
- initially, domination of the discussion by one or two of the interns;
- pressure of time within the interviews, so that some topics were perhaps

not discussed as fully as would have been useful and the researcher's own agenda was not always covered;
- a tendency which seemed to be generated by the group setting to focus on negative perceptions of the course, perhaps also contributed to by a lack of other opportunities to voice concerns;
- difficulties experienced by the researcher in following up the comments of specific members of the group.

It was therefore decided to conduct additional individual semi-structured interviews with each of the interns during the last week of their school based work (II:1-8). This proved helpful not only in allowing each individual's perceptions to be more fully pursued but also in revealing inconsistencies between privately expressed views and what had in the group context appeared to be consensual views.

In interpreting the evidence from these various interviews, one needs to bear in mind that the researcher was herself a teacher in the school and that her views about the strengths and weaknesses of the Internship scheme may not have been entirely hidden.

THE FINDINGS

The mentor

One of the main themes of group and individual interviews was about the part that mentors played in creating opportunities for interns to develop their knowledge and understanding of teaching and relating this to the more theoretical approach offered by the OUDES input.

It had been anticipated that the interns' perceptions of the role of the mentor might be varied and in fact their responses broadly covered the following areas which correlate closely with activities frequently mentioned in the prescriptive literature on mentoring (e.g. Hagger *et al.*, 1993; Tomlinson, 1995). These may be defined as:

a) providing support and reassurance,
b) setting up opportunities to observe lessons being taught,
c) collaborative lesson planning and teaching,
d) debriefing and target setting,
e) setting up opportunities to work with other teachers in the same department.

The interns also commented on other areas where they felt that their mentor's understanding or expertise was less than adequate, for example, with regards to the university's stipulations or recommendations or in providing up-to-date relevant resources.

Support and reassurance

The interns frequently commented throughout the year on the importance of the mentor with regard to providing support and reassurance either in a general sense (GI:2, GI:3) or about more specific problems which the intern perceived they were experiencing, such as the use of the Profile document (GI:2, GI:3).

> My mentor's let me take more and more responsibility for lessons, she's very gently pushing me and making it clear that I should be more confident about taking more responsibility, but she hasn't actually abandoned me. (GI:3)

Clearly the mentors here have provided counselling, which helped some of the interns to remain motivated and committed. However, for some of the interns, mentors had not provided any support at all. Two of those interns felt that they had survived the year despite, rather than because of their mentor (II:1, II:4).

Opportunities to observe

In considering the mentor's role in setting up opportunities for interns to observe lessons being taught, there was general agreement that this was particularly useful as a way of familiarising the interns with the teacher's role in the class and with specific groups of pupils in the school. This was seen as particularly significant during the early part of the year as a means of vicarious learning. Observation continued to play an important role for some interns even by the third interview, who commented that

> I still think that [observation lessons] are quite useful because I observe the classes in a year I don't teach, especially things like Year 10 French, which is my weaker language, so it's really good for me to go in and see how things are done. (GI: 3)

Here observation formed the basis for experimental imitation and the intern was actively engaged in observing in a more analytical way than had been the case earlier on in the year.

However some interns felt that the observation tasks were inappropriate, whereas others felt that too many observations of lessons were inappropriate, and that they should be spending time on other tasks. This comment is typical of many:

> They are making us do an awful lot of observation which by now is getting very boring. (GI:1).

In these cases the intern may have been merely observing the teaching action passively rather than becoming involved in the planning and rationale behind the lessons they were observing. They therefore found them difficult to relate to their own developing understanding.

Collaborative lesson planning and teaching

Interns were generally aware of the benefits of collaborative planning and teaching with their mentors and could relate these activities to their own developing understanding and skills.

Initially the interns appeared to stay within their mentor's framework and undertook limited aspects of teaching with support, but later in the year, they were experimenting with trying out and taking on a wider range of the activities, as is reflected in this intern's comment:

> The mentor periods are really useful too, where me and my mentor look forward to next week's lessons, do planning, and think about different strategies or approaches we could use to overcome problems I've been having or to introduce new techniques into my teaching. For example, we've been looking at flexible learning as a possible approach and talked through ways of resourcing and organising it. (GI:3).

The interns themselves were, however, also concerned about occasions when the collaborative planning they had undertaken with their mentor had not turned out as anticipated:

> My mentor does sit down and plan, but it doesn't always work out in practice. She overran when we planned a lesson and then my time was massively cut short and I had to alter half of the lesson at the last minute, our collaborative planning went really well, but the actual lesson was a nightmare. (GI:2)

For two of the interns in particular, collaborative planning and teaching with their mentor had played an almost non-existent role in developing their knowledge and understanding, an aspect of their school based practice which caused them some concern:

> I've never really discussed the content of any lesson with my mentor beforehand, at most he'll say on the way to the lesson 'Oh, are you all sorted?' and I'll tell him roughly what I'm doing. (GI:3)

In these cases, there was an apparent lack of understanding of the role the mentor should play which undermined the interns' confidence in their mentors at quite an early stage in their school based practice.

Debriefing and target setting

The interns made frequent comments about the nature and quality of the debriefing sessions they had with their mentor, which took place after lessons which their mentor had observed. Throughout the year, interns clearly valued this experience and felt it was reassuring and helped them to identify areas upon which they should focus their attention or to encourage them to evaluate their own classroom practice.

In the early part of the year the mentors appear to have focused the debriefing sessions on specific aspects of the classroom practice:

> I've had plenty of debriefs which have been really useful. With me, they seem to have concentrated on things like lesson planning because that's what I'm having problems with. (GI:2)

By the end of the year, the emphasis appears to have shifted towards encouraging interns to engage in the independent development of ideas:

> My mentor's been doing quite a lot of debriefing of the lessons she's been in. She'll pick upon any of the bad points and she wants to see my plans so that she can relate what actually happened to what I'd planned, which is good. She's asked me questions like 'next time, what would you do differently?' which I suppose has made me try to evaluate what I'm doing. (GI:3)

Sometimes, however, the interns felt that the debriefing sessions had been too general, and did not focus on the specific detail of their classroom teaching sufficiently, particularly in the latter part of the year when interns obviously wanted to be introduced to a range of strategies. Another problem was that the intern felt that the mentor tended to concentrate on one particular issue at the expense of evaluating other aspects of her classroom teaching:

> My mentor's tended to concentrate very much on classroom management and discipline, and although that's interesting, I don't even think I've had a problem with classroom management, but it's always dominated our discussions, and up to now the comments have been very similar and not very helpful. (GI:3)

Mentors in these instances appeared to be unaware of the progress made by their interns, and had not taken account of the changes in their abilities, understanding and needs.

In general, the interns recognised the importance of debriefing in advancing their understanding and knowledge of classroom teaching, and were concerned about the lack of time and weighting given to debriefing by their mentors on some occasions:

> I've been pretty much left to myself at the minute. I feel quite happy about going ahead and running lessons on my own, but sometimes it would be good to have more ideas on ways to approach things, in a way I don't feel that I've actually learnt much. It's just a case of carrying on with what I know works. It would have been more helpful to have had more specific debriefs. I really don't feel that I've had nearly as much help as, say, the Modern Linguists, what I've had to do is just use what I know myself rather than being given any particular help from the mentor. I have been helped with the content, but not really teaching skills. (GI:4)

This comment reflects the fact that the interns in these cases were aware of the dangers of 'satisficing' or being satisfied with what minimally suffices, and were disappointed that their mentor was not concerned with promoting reflectiveness or further development of their knowledge of a range of teaching strategies.

One intern was worried about the amount of time given to debriefing:

> I think it's very difficult for the mentor to find enough time to do debriefing
> ... I've had to squeeze mentor time into five minutes here and there to make
> it up throughout the week, which obviously isn't as good as sitting down for
> half an hour or whatever. That is a real problem when the main person you're
> trying to get information from is too busy to talk to you. (GI:4)

She was rightly concerned that this lack of time was undermining the quality of the debriefing and hampering her ability to analyse the lessons she had taught.

Setting up opportunities to work with other teachers in host departments

For two of the interns, the role that the mentor played in setting up opportunities for the interns to work with other teachers from within the same department was generally recognised as being significant. In these cases the mentor had used departmental colleagues to observe the interns' lessons, concentrating on a specific aspect of the interns' classroom practice which varied from week to week. The other teachers would debrief the intern, commenting on positive aspects of the lesson they had observed and suggesting other strategies the intern could employ. This was seen as particularly important by an intern who did not teach any of her mentor's teaching groups. The intern clearly valued the time and expertise offered by the departmental teachers. For the remaining interns, the mentor had assigned them to various teachers' classes, but had not actively followed through what went on in those lessons and the quality of these experiences varied considerably from intern to intern. Some had enjoyed the benefits of thorough debriefing, whilst others had been left very much to themselves.

Other criticisms/concerns about mentoring

The interns were critical of the lack of understanding or knowledge shown by some of the mentors with regard to the stipulations or recommendations made by the university, such as those to do with encouraging the intern pair to work together or setting up opportunities for the intern to have access to a variety of teaching styles throughout the school department. These worries tended to arise later in the year when interns perhaps had a better overview of the course as a whole.

At certain critical points in the year, interns pointed to a lack of understanding or interest in certain key processes which directly related to the monitoring of their progress, for example at the profiling points or in the transition from Phase 1 to Phase 2. The interns were also concerned about the lack of assistance the mentors gave them when they had been set tasks or assignments by the university. This is again evidence of the mentors being unwilling or unable to become more involved in the assessment aspects of their interns' practice. What is evident from the analysis of the transcripts is the extent to which the quality of mentoring varied within the practice school. Some of the mentors provided their interns with a variety of support and were clearly fulfilling their expected role. The interns attached to these mentors evidently gained considerably from the organised, economical and profitable ways in which their mentors worked. However, in a number of cases the interns commented on circumstances which called into question the ability of their mentors to assist them in the acquisition of the skills and understanding, which they, the interns, deemed necessary. Those mentors appeared to be unable to support their interns in their attempts to develop and reflect upon their practice.

The professional tutor and the Professional Development Programme (PDP)

The interns had mixed opinions about the usefulness of the Professional Development Programme which took place in the school, and was led by the professional tutor. Some of the interns clearly valued the opportunity the PDP session offered to reflect on their current practice and share experiences with the rest of the intern group based at the school. In fact, throughout the year, reference was made to the usefulness of this aspect of the sessions, compared to the more formal seminar sessions which were led by various members of the school staff. This comment reflects the views expressed by most of the interns at some stage during the year:

> Maybe it would be good to spend more of the sessions actually sharing experiences rather than having someone specific coming in to talk to us. (GI:3)

In general, the interns expressed a preference for those PDP sessions which related directly to school based issues such as form tutoring, records of achievement, the personal and social development programme followed by pupils, etc. These sessions were seen as being more immediately 'useful' since they were rooted in the reality of the practice school. As one intern put it:

> The sessions are relevant because they are in the school and about the school. The people who have done some of them are teachers here so they know what they are talking about. (II:1)

Those sessions which considered wider issues such as race and gender, or the cross-curricular themes of the National Curriculum, were generally seen as being less pertinent and useful.

There were other aspects of the PDP with which the interns appeared to be genuinely concerned. These included the order in which the programme was organised where it was felt, for example, that the session on dealing with disruptive pupils came too late in the year to be of any real use. Similarly, concern had been expressed earlier in the year at the first profiling point, about the lack of specific information or advice given about the profiling document, in particular the section on professional qualities, where it appeared that little or no discussion has been centred on this area of the document. One intern was worried about the narrowness of centring the whole of the PDP on the individual school:

> I think what they could do with instead of having it all based on the [practice] school, they could actually bring in other examples, because you need another perspective. I'm sure that other methods exist for form tutoring, and other interns that I've talked to have had quite different experiences. (GI:2)

Others felt that the topics covered by the PDP sessions would have been better dealt with by the HEI, where they would have been given a wider perspective (II:2, II:7). It was also felt that a greater emphasis on supplementary reading would have added substance and structure to the sessions (II:2, II:8). Such comments are a little puzzling since during 'J' weeks the school based PDP programme was paralleled by a university-based programme aimed at offering wider, more diverse perspectives and at introducing relevant literature.

Almost without exception, the interns felt that the amount of time given to professional development sessions was too great and that it could be spent on other activities such as finding or developing resources to be used in their teaching, or marking pupils' books. This comment is typical of many:

> I think that instead of sitting around for two hours aimlessly discussing something just to fill up time, we should be allowed to have the afternoon off to go and look at other resources, or discuss useful things like different teaching styles instead of discussing stuff that is totally irrelevant. (GI:3)

Criticisms of this type only arose in the second half of the year, when interns may have felt constrained by the amount of time available to them in school. Interns also expressed disappointment with the role played by the professional tutor, who, it was felt, was not always well organised. In addition he was perceived as being very defensive when discussing issues which related to the practice school. Most interns were concerned that these factors in combination meant that they did not always fully develop their potential understanding of particular issues.

It may be worth noting that no mention was made by any of the interns of the role of the general tutor within the Professional Development Programme.

Curriculum programme and the curriculum tutor

There was considerable divergence of opinion amongst the interns in their comments about the role the curriculum programme and the curriculum tutor played in developing their knowledge and understanding. The comments which they made are understandably diverse, since there was considerable variation in the role played by the five curriculum tutors who were attached to the school. The interns were aware of the key role the curriculum tutor could play. Many appreciated the affirmation offered by their curriculum tutor of their classroom practice. They were aware of the benefits of the discussions which took place between their curriculum tutors and their mentors, and appreciated the efforts made by their curriculum tutors to observe their lessons and give thorough debriefs. This was seen as one of the most important ways in which their curriculum tutor enhanced their knowledge and understanding, particularly as they were seen to point to aspects of the interns' classroom practice which would not otherwise have been pointed out (II:3, II:8). Their curriculum tutor also played an important part in relating university department documentation to the school particularly where the Profile document was concerned.

However, not all of the interns were satisfied with the role played by their curriculum tutor, describing them as 'daunting', 'picky', or 'very, very critical'. More specifically one intern described his relationship with his curriculum tutor as follows:

> I've found working with my particular curriculum tutor has been particularly problematic. In fact she hasn't been supportive at all. She went behind my back and talked to the General Tutor without even discussing it with me. (GI:3)

It is worth noting, however, that by the last interview, this particular intern had revised his opinion to:

> I've learnt a lot from the criticism which has come from my curriculum tutor and she's pointed out things I need to do and then I've done them. (GI:4)

Another concern raised by the interns was the frequency with which their curriculum tutor visited them in the practice school – only twice during the entire 'S' weeks period was perceived as being insufficient (II:1). Others commented that the debriefing which they were given after their tutor had observed them teaching was far from thorough. This comment is typical of the interns' understandable concerns:

> His [the curriculum tutor] visits were pretty cursory. He only visited twice and the debriefing was quite brief – sort of a couple of minutes of 'Oh yeah, that was fine' and then chatting about what my holiday plans were. (II:1)

Comments regarding the relevance of the curriculum programme to the school based practice were equally at odds. Again this may be partially explained by the diversity of the university based curriculum programmes, since each intern or intern pair would have attended a different curriculum programme, relevant to their subject area. Some of the interns clearly valued the pertinence of their curriculum programme finding it a useful source of ideas and resources which they were able subsequently to use in lessons (II:6, II:8).

Some interns were aware of the benefits of the close links between the university and the practice school, which meant that issues which had been discussed in the curriculum programme were followed up within the same week in the practice school:

> My curriculum group has done a lot of work on lesson plans and here [in the practice school] I got to put the ideas I'd developed in the curriculum group into practice straight away, before it got stale, which was really excellent, rather than just talking about things in a vacuum at the university. (GI:2)

Others felt that the curriculum programme had been good preparation for the work they were expected to do in the school and that there was clearly progression built into the tasks they were asked to complete:

> All the sessions were really good. At the start we did a couple of sessions on lesson planning in quite a lot of detail, but then we went on to look at different ways of achieving differentiation and stuff like that. (GI:3)

It is perhaps worth noting that those comments which relate to the positive benefits of the close relationship between the university and the practice school were made in the early part of the year, as would be expected, during the 'J' weeks, when interns would have been more aware of the attempts made to correlate the activities of the curriculum programme and the practice school element. Once into the 'S' weeks, the university input tended to be forgotten.

For some of the interns there were clear links between the curriculum programme which was delivered at the university, and the practice school. The input from the curriculum programme was seen as up-to-date and relevant. However for other interns their curriculum programme input from the university appeared to have little bearing so that some of them were concerned with an apparent lack of cohesion between the ideas they had been introduced to in the curriculum programme and the reality they faced in the practice school:

> It seems like there's no connection between here [the practice school] and the university. We've been given all this theory in the university which is miles in advance of what we're doing here, for example, use this language to finish a lesson, and yet we haven't even been given a whole lesson to do, and that was a couple of weeks ago. (GI:1)

Other interns were worried about the weighting given in the curriculum programme to planning lessons and felt that time would have been better spent developing an awareness of new resources with which to teach. This may be related to the sense of urgency student teachers experience with regard to wanting to get into the swing of teaching practice. Others felt that their curriculum programme was too immersed in theory or too concerned with ideological perspectives to be of any practical use in the classroom context (II:1, II:4). A further criticism of some of the curriculum programmes was that the bulk of the sessions took place when the interns had little or no practical experience of classroom teaching and therefore found it difficult to envisage how some of the activities they were asked to complete might work out in a classroom context (II:2, II:3, II:6). One intern felt that she had been set tasks in the curriculum programme which had not then been followed up at the practice school. Others felt that the curriculum programme should do more to highlight the links between subject areas within the school, and possible ways in which these might be developed. Finally, one of the interns expressed a regret that there were insufficient opportunities to return to the university during the 'S' weeks phase of the year, so that ideas and resources could be shared with other interns from within the same curriculum group:

> It would be really good to get back to the HEI and swap resources and ideas, because we're all working on different topics and producing different stuff. (GI:4)

For some of the interns, the contribution of the curriculum programme they had followed at the university to the development of their work in the practice school was significant. The effort made by the curriculum tutor to work with them within the practice school also contributed to their developing self confidence and skills. For others their curriculum programme seemed irrelevant and the visits made by their curriculum tutor to the practice school were deemed infrequent and insignificant in their attempts to bring a wider perspective to bear on the intern's classroom practice.

Teachers other than the mentor

All of the interns felt that they had gained considerably in their contact with teachers other than the mentor from within their host department. The support and guidance which these teachers gave the interns took several forms, ranging from being generally friendly and encouraging to giving them a detailed debriefing after the lesson.

Interns clearly valued the efforts made by the teachers within their host department to welcome and generally encourage them, particularly at the beginning of their school based practice.

By February they were appreciative of the low key manner in which these teachers worked with them, as they were beginning to show a willingness to engage in more independent development of ideas and teaching styles:

> She keeps a balance between not hassling me and giving some help – she's been very supportive. (GI:2)

For many of the interns, the other teachers in the host department provided them with a welcome source of teaching material and suggestions about alternative approaches as to how they might be used.

It was felt that the most common way in which these other host department teachers furthered the interns' knowledge and understanding was by their observation of the interns' teaching and debriefing which they gave the interns after the lesson. This was most commonly in the 'S' weeks, when the interns had taken over these teachers' classes as part of their teaching practice. Some general points arose from the comments the interns made about these activities. Firstly, although the interns appreciated any observation these teachers did of their teaching, they clearly felt that such observations were more beneficial if there was a specific focus to the observation itself and the subsequent debriefing. Some teachers clearly put considerable effort into this by following university recommendations (II:2), or by making detailed notes (II:1, II:2, II:4). In some other instances, the teacher had selected a particular aspect of the intern's classroom practice to focus upon and this was seen as a very productive way of helping to develop skills and understanding.

Early on in the 'S' weeks phase of the year, the focus used by the other teachers in the host department was sometimes selected by the mentor after discussion with the intern, on other occasions the focus was selected by the teacher, based on previous observations of the intern's lessons. By the final group interview, one of the interns was selecting her own focus:

> They've been excellent, I've asked them to look at specific things and they've sat in the lesson, taken notes, and discussed them with me afterwards, concentrating on ways of improving on that and in that way I've been lucky and have felt I've made progress. (GI:4)

Some of the other teachers in the host department seemed prepared to take on even more aspects of what might be considered to be the mentor's role, and became involved in collaborative planning and assessment. Again, the interns obviously valued the time and expertise offered by these colleagues, particularly those interns who had previously mentioned their disappointment with the role their mentor had played in furthering their understanding:

> One of the teachers actually went through how she might plan a lesson which we found really helpful and we now follow that approach, as a guideline, that was very good. (GI:2)

Interns also valued the opportunity to observe these other teachers in their classroom teaching, finding that this provided them with a valuable alternative perspective to that of their mentor. These included approaches to sixth form teaching (II:4), encouraging the intern to be enthusiastic and experimental in the lesson (II:2), providing an alternative perspective on developing rapport with pupils (II:8), and giving an insight into different classroom management and discipline strategies (II:6).

Within the various departments in which the interns were placed there appeared to be a range of expertise available with regards to the role played by teachers other than the mentor. Given the opportunity, some of these teachers were able to reflect upon and analyse the interns' lesson, to the obvious benefit of the interns involved.

On only one occasion did an intern cite an example of where the action of a teacher other than the mentor within the host department was considered less than helpful:

> When our mentor was ill, the teacher said, 'Right, you should both take a lesson this week' and that was horrendous because we weren't prepared for it and we didn't have any proper support, and mine was, she actually told me, to teach a book, and then it was the wrong book, so I had to teach a different book, and all I'd prepared, well I didn't have any preparation, and worse still, it was being observed by a primary head. It was a complete nightmare. (GI:2)

An incident such as this highlights the need to ensure that all the members of the host department have some understanding of the principles and ideas guiding the training of interns within their department.

Other people who were considered important

A number of other people were seen as providing valuable support and assistance to the interns, ranging from staff with whom they had prolonged and formalised contact, for example, the form tutor, to the informality of conversation interns had with auxiliary staff or their own parents. The responses interns made have been grouped accordingly.

The form tutor

Many of the interns valued the opportunity to work alongside a form tutor within the practice school. The form tutor was seen as providing a welcome contrast of classroom management style to that of the teachers, including the mentor, in the host department. Many of the interns made mention of the possibility of the form teacher acting as a role model, admiring the way in which they managed to maintain discipline, whilst relating in a friendly and relaxed way to their tutees (II:2, II:5, II:7, II:8).

> My form tutor is brilliant. She's got a really relaxed and jokey relationship with the kids, but when she wants them to listen or be serious, they really do pay attention. There are lots of things that she does, that I'd like to do. (II:5)

Other positive comments related to the consistency of approach shown by form tutors which enabled them to manage their tutor group effectively (II:6, II:8). Notwithstanding the generally positive comments made by the interns about working with the form tutor, two of the interns felt that their role in relation to the form tutor was little more than a register monitor, and that the time they spent with the form tutor was not very useful (II:1, II:4). The linking of interns to a form tutor provided the individual interns with further insights into teaching strategies, particularly those related to classroom management styles. A question arises as to how best form tutors may be able to support interns, so that they may develop a more detailed understanding of the pastoral role.

The intern partner

Of the eight interns in the practice school, six had been placed in their host department with another intern, their intern partner. This is part of the agreed structure for the school based element of the Oxford Internship model. For most of the interns, the benefit of being part of a pair was most notable in the early part of the year, where it was generally felt that it was helpful to have someone with whom to share concerns, ideas or resources. Two of the interns expressed regret that, during the 'S' weeks period, there was insufficient time to swap resources and ideas in the way in which this had been possible during the 'J' weeks phase of the year (II:2, II:6). Another intern mentioned that he was sorry that he had not an intern partner, since he would have liked the opportunity collaboratively to plan and resource lessons (II:8).

A number of interns, however, found working as part of a pair difficult. One mentioned how her intern partner was not as concerned with pre-lesson planning and organisation as she was, and so this proved to be a source of tension between them, especially at the beginning of the year when they were involved in joint teaching of lessons (II:3):

> It is very difficult with my intern partner. I think we basically have two different ways of organising ourselves. I like to plan things quite a lot of time in advance, where he likes to do it all at the last minute . . . It just turned into a nightmare. (II:3)

Another regretted that her intern partner was unwilling to be observed or become involved in collaborative planning, as she felt that these activities would have aided her development (II:1). For some of the interns, working as part of a pair was perceived as beneficial to the development to their classroom teaching and a useful means of emotional support.

The intern group

The intern group was seen as another positive form of support by the interns. It was seen as helpful to be able to share experiences and realise that other people were in a similar situation, and to share anecdotal knowledge about individual pupils and groups (II:3, II:5, II:6).

Other staff in the practice school

The interns found the friendliness and general support offered to them by other members of the staff in the school valuable. For a couple of interns, individual staff had provided them with significant support, in one case a member of staff from a department other than the intern's host department provided the intern with resources, and discussed ways of using them, an experience which the intern thought was helpful (II:7). In another case, the intern was grateful for support and advice on dealing with a disruptive pupil, from that pupil's form tutor. One of the science interns (II:3) mentioned that the departmental technicians had provided invaluable advice about equipment for practical lessons, and had generally been both helpful and encouraging.

Through their contacts with these other individuals, interns were helped in different ways either informally where they received reassurance and support, and recognition as a fellow member of staff, or in more formal ways where staff shared something of their expertise and understanding.

CONCLUDING COMMENTS

One of the most striking aspects of the information derived from the analysis is the huge variation in the experiences of these interns, even in the same school in the same year. For all of the interns the mentor was the key element in the school based part of their programme, but there were enormous differences in the manner in which the mentors worked with their interns. Firstly there were mentors who were well informed and able to adapt with apparent ease to the role of facilitator, counsellor, and critic which the interns wanted. Secondly, there was the mentor who was eager to help and set time aside to discuss and to debrief the interns, but who did not seem to have the knowledge or understanding to match her interns' perceptions about the sort of role she should be playing. Thirdly, there was the 'absent' mentor who took no apparent interest in his interns' learning and progress and who seemed by the interns' account to make no effort to assist or advise them.

The interns' reports also indicated considerable variations in the quality and quantity of provision made for them in other aspects of the school based part of the programme. In particular, for some interns the curriculum tutor had played a vital role in providing reassurance, critically appraising their classroom practice and pointing to alternative teaching strategies and resources. For others, the curriculum tutor visits were too infrequent and their comments too bland to have been of any particular use. Interns' perceptions of their various university based curriculum programmes were equally diverse: for some, but certainly not for others, these programmes were seen as vital sources of new ideas and resources and as relating well to the realities of practice in the school.

Whilst it is necessary to acknowledge the very diverse needs and perspectives of different interns, the variations in the experiences of the individual interns outlined above point to a need for greater consistency within the elements of the school based practice. Ensuring a parity of provision of effective learning opportunities for individual interns must be one of the foremost concerns of both the university and the partner school.

The role of the professional tutor may be a key issue in this respect. This person should have the understanding, expertise, status and authority to ensure that the whole school understands the nature of the partnership with the university. They should review and monitor the quality of mentoring and lead the team of mentors in the school so that they have a clear and shared sense of direction and understanding of their role. Schools should acknowledge mentors' need for training and support and should set aside sufficient funding for this. Furthermore there is a need to recognise the responsibility and changed role of the whole school in ITE and to devote resources to the preparation of all staff for this changed role. Additional funding from central government will almost certainly be needed if this is to happen, and should surely be provided by a government which wishes schools to take greater responsibility for ITE.

A major responsibility remains, however, with the university. It is the university's responsibility not only to ensure that there are clear shared understandings across schools but also, and urgently in view of evidence such as that reported here, to ensure that its altered role is understood by all its own staff and that they are effective in the new parts that they are now required to play.

REFERENCES

Hagger, H., Burn, K. and McIntyre, D. (1993) *The School Mentor Handbook*, Kogan Page, London.

Rothwell, S., Nardi, E. and McIntyre, D. (1994) The perceived values of the role activities of mentors and curricular, professional and general tutors, in I. Reid, H. Constable and R. Griffiths (eds.) *Teacher Education Reform*. Paul Chapman, London.

Tomlinson, P. (1995) *Understanding Mentoring*, Open University Press, Buckingham.
Watt, M. and Ebutt, D. (1987) More than the sum of the parts: research methods in group interviewing, in *British Educational Research Journal*, Vol. 13, No. 1, pp. 25–33.

4

READINESS AMONG STUDENT
TEACHERS FOR LEARNING ABOUT
CLASSROOM MANAGEMENT ISSUES

Linda Haggarty

INTRODUCTION

This chapter is focused on the mathematics curriculum programme of the Internship Scheme. The author had the responsibility for the original planning and negotiation of this programme, and undertook this responsibility in an action research mode, with different and (it still seems) increasingly penetrating questions being asked in three successive years about what was happening and being achieved in the evolving programme (Haggarty, 1992; 1995a). This chapter is concerned with what emerged as one important facet of the third year's research, which sought to trace the developing concerns, experiences and thinking of ten of the mathematics interns over the course of the year. Classroom management issues were not highlighted in the design of this research, but emerged as important in the experience of these interns. The ten interns had volunteered to participate in the research; there is no intention to argue here either that they are representative of a wider population or that mathematics student teachers are a special case.

A BRIEF LITERATURE REVIEW

Shulman (1986), in his categorisation of different kinds of teacher knowledge, defines 'knowledge of organisation and management for teaching' as the knowledge a teacher needs to organise: for individual, group or whole class teaching; for changes of activity; for different styles of teaching; for questioning; for control aspects such as keeping order; and being able to manage the resources available (Shulman, 1986). As one aspect of this wide and integrated field of knowledge, classroom control is worthy of attention since there is evidence to suggest that this issue is of particular concern to beginning teachers and therefore may have implications for the design of courses and the sorts of experiences offered. However, whilst the research literature suggests a complex set of issues in play in relation to classroom control, Government guidelines appear to suggest relatively simplistic solutions.

In *Initial Teacher Training: approval of courses* (DES, 1989a) the authors write that:

> all courses should contain compulsory and clearly identifiable elements of practical training which will develop in students skills in the effective management of pupil behaviour. Such training should include specific, institution-based elements on the acquisition of group management techniques.

It is also argued (DES, 1989b, *The Elton Report*) that not only this should take place but also that courses

> should involve practical learning methods, and that the skills which effective group management is based on should be an explicit part both of college work and school experience

and

> that teaching practice should be systematically used to consolidate these skills.

In addition:

> schools also have an important part to play in preparing trainee teachers to manage their classes effectively.

Presumably, implementation of this kind of advice would alleviate the problem perceived most often by beginning teachers, which is concerned with classroom discipline when they face a 'reality shock' as they begin their teaching career (Veenman, 1984). Weinstein (1988) suggests that:

> the ordeal experienced by many first year teachers stems from unrealistic expectations about the difficulty of teaching in general and about their ability to deal with the demands of the classroom in particular.

In addition she argues that student teachers have a certain amount of 'unrealistic optimism' – the tendency to believe that the problems experienced by others 'won't happen to me' and that this might contribute to a later reality shock. She also argues that there is:

> a very consistent tendency for prospective teachers to expect the tasks of teaching to be less problematic for themselves than for their peers.

Similarly, Fuller (1969) and Fuller and Bown (1975) suggest that prior to actual teaching experience, education students were characterised by 'non-concern' which changed to 'survival concerns' once they began student teaching and beginning teaching. Most intense, they say, were concerns about class control.

Lanier and Little (1986) argue that for the prospective teacher on school experience, feeling overwhelmed is common:

> the press of classroom events makes it difficult for even the experienced teacher to attend to individual children . . . in such a situation, the prospective teacher is likely to concentrate on the maintenance of order and on keeping the children attentive.

They add that:

> few other professionals conduct their practice on anything other than individuals or small groups of adults. The complexities associated with teaching, where one must deliver professional expertise in a group setting of twenty or thirty youngsters simultaneously is just coming to be understood. But the research suggests that classroom experience tends to place management at the centre of teaching, possibly at the expense of student learning.

It appears, therefore, that students on teacher education courses might arrive with little concern about classroom control issues but that at some stage either during school based work over the year or later, if problems have not yet had to be faced, their concern will rapidly develop.

This might suggest that on the issue of class control, a controlled 'reality shock' experienced during the training year when support is available is preferable to student teachers reaching the end of their teacher education course without having recognised it as an important issue for themselves. Certainly, until students feel confident about their own survival, they are unlikely to be able to move on to other concerns and, although Fuller's (1969) model may appear to oversimplify the situation, there would seem to be a great deal of truth in the idea that:

> an important task for teacher education is helping teachers to implement their concerns about pupils since better teaching is probably associated with concerns about pupils rather than concerns about self. (Fuller and Bown, 1975)

There are two additional factors which have implications for any work being done and which are linked to classroom control. The first relates to the stress caused by assessment of practical teaching. As long as the student is concerned with survival, then he or she is likely to feel under greater pressure to try to conform to perceived good practice in terms of control. Denscombe (1982) suggests that there is a 'hidden pedagogy' in schools which equates success with the establishment of classroom control and 'there is considerable pressure on teachers to execute this responsibility without calling on others for assistance'. The Elton Report (DES, 1989b) also comments that:

> teachers have tended to stay out of each others' classrooms and not to talk about their own discipline problems. Too often teachers do not seek help because

it feels like an admission of incompetence, and they do not offer it because it feels like accusing a colleague of incompetence.

Linked to this is that students who are particularly concerned with survival are unlikely to want to try innovative approaches and, if they can be persuaded to try them, are in danger of premature rejection of them when their survival, in this case their classroom control, is threatened. Both Cooper (1990) in Britain, and Haymore (1987) as part of Shulman's 'Knowledge Growth in Teaching' project describe mathematics students in case studies who reflect this tendency, the latter writing of a student for whom 'classroom management became an overarching concern and influenced her classroom plans and activities'. This contrasts with the comments made by OFSTED (1993) that 'lively and stimulating teaching is almost always associated with good behaviour'.

In summary, what has been argued here is that:

i)   classroom management is an important issue to include on a teacher education programme,

ii) student teachers perceive the importance of the issue at different stages of learning to teach,

iii) once student teachers have perceived its importance, they become concerned for their own survival and this concern can often dominate their thinking and planning,

iv) pressures of assessment and hidden pressures within school may dissuade student teachers from asking for help,

v)   student teachers may want to adopt safer, more traditional approaches in the classroom than those they are encouraged to try on teacher education courses and are in danger of rejecting innovative approaches because they threaten their survival.

Learning about both innovative approaches and classroom control is important for student teachers and school based courses which offer sheltered and controlled teaching experiences which allow, at least initially, student teachers to practise each without the added complexity of the other seems a promising strategy for improved beginning teacher learning.

THE INTERNSHIP MATHEMATICS CURRICULUM PROGRAMME

Within the general principles of the Internship course, the author negotiated a programme with the school based mathematics mentors in which it was agreed that interns would learn about issues firstly in sheltered ways and then, gradually, in more complex and demanding ways. In this way, it was hoped that interns could learn sensibly and rationally about issues without unhelpful additional complexities.

The time spent in schools was spread throughout the year, with interns for the most part spending part of each week in school and part in the university. There was, however, an entirely school based period in the middle of the year and short university based elements at the beginning and end of the course.

Classroom management was one of the agreed issues to be addressed on the course. Within the agreement, interns were required to:

- observe their mentor and other teachers, who may or may not be having classroom management problems. However, mentors had agreed in advance that this should include observing lessons which teachers themselves saw as problematic in management terms,
- talk to teachers they had observed about the issue and discover what strategies they used in relation to the issue,
- take part in university based sessions discussing both their developing thinking and what the research and practical literature had to say about the issue,
- do some sheltered teaching which helped them focus on the issue in their own practice,
- take part in discussions with teachers who had observed them teaching with this issue in mind,
- discuss with teachers their own developing theories related to the issue,
- debrief with other interns and the tutor in the university.

It can therefore be seen that there had been an attempt to address the concerns identified above in relation to the literature and its implications.

DATA COLLECTION

Data were collected from:

i)   semi-structured interviews throughout the year, with each of the ten interns in the study being encouraged to articulate any concerns they had about teaching,
ii) semi-structured interviews with each of their school based mentors after the interns had left the course. This allowed the researcher to gain another perspective on each intern's concerns during the year and how they addressed those concerns,
iii) written assignments (in one of which interns were asked to write about their developing theories on classroom management). These provided another context in which to gather information, although they were written as part of the formal requirement of the course and were subsequently used for assessment purposes. It was considered useful to be able to compare what each student said in this context of written work for assessment, with what they said or how they behaved in other circumstances,

iv) lesson evaluation proformas completed by each intern at the end of each lesson taught in school based weeks to a particular class identified by that intern. Persuading interns to complete lesson evaluation forms would provide access to their thinking and subsequent learning in terms of their own teaching in the middle part of the year. They were not collected in until the course had ended so it was hoped that this would result in interns being more honest about the thoughts they were having. In addition, the forms provided a much more personal context in which interns could record their thoughts and therefore would not rely on them having to articulate them to someone else or having to please someone else.

RESULTS

Although classroom management was not a particular focus for the author in the semi-structured interviews, concern was expressed about the issue from an early stage by some interns and by all interns at some stage of the year. It was therefore possible to look at the emerging data and consider each intern's learning about the issue. Of particular interest then was whether students had early concerns about classroom management issues; whether they expected to have problems themselves; how and what they hoped to learn about the issue during the year. It was also possible to track their developing thinking during the year, and how this influenced their decision making in school. Towards the end of the year it was helpful to look at the concerns they then had; at how they thought they had learnt, exploring both school and university based experiences; at when they had become aware of classroom management problems (if at all); what they had done to help solve their problems.

Overview of the results

The ten interns arrived on the course, broadly, in two different frames of mind about classroom management. Five did not express any concern about the issue, did not talk about it in the early weeks, appeared not to learn from the tutor input in the first term and wrote in theoretical terms about it at the end of the first term. The other five were concerned from the beginning of the course and had already identified it as a key issue for their learning.

However, the intern data collected during school based weeks suggested that however they started the course, they found this issue to be of great concern to them. Indeed, most decisions they articulated which were made in relation to their own teaching used as their main criterion whether or not the intended action would result in a subsequent loss of control.

Once interns recognised for themselves the importance of the issue, they then wanted to learn about it and at this stage, those who had expressed no early concern demonstrated how little they had learnt by that stage. That is not to say that, in particular, university tutor input was considered unhelpful by all interns: those who expressed early concerns spoke highly about it. Thus it seemed that university based tutor input was only helpful to those interns who already had the issue on their agenda.

Three interns (two of whom were concerned from the beginning) never moved beyond a major concern for classroom management in that they continued to use it as their main criterion in decision making in their own teaching. However, it would appear that classroom management was the first major hurdle for all these beginning teachers and that until they had successfully negotiated this hurdle to their own satisfaction, they could not move on to learning about other issues without this influencing, and possibly dominating, their decision making.

Early concerns about classroom management

The interns who expressed early personal concerns (i.e. made unprompted comments in the first week of the course) said things such as:

> to be able to keep order in the classroom it is essential to be strict. (Frank)

> in my view, reflecting on classroom management and putting those reflections into practice are the most important things that I will be doing this year. (Nigel)

> it is important to assert . . . dominance from the start . . . [and] establish the fact that the classroom is [his] 'territory' into which pupils can come and not vice versa. (Tony)

> I aim in the long term for complete silence when I am talking . . . I expect children to talk quietly to each other about a problem and about nothing else. (Will)

In fact, all five interns who expressed early personal concerns are male, although it is not clear whether this is significant.

On the other hand, other interns said very little without prompting at this early stage (four of whom were female and one male) and even then made comments which suggested that they were not expecting the issue to be significant. For example, one of these interns said

> a teacher should manage a lesson professionally. Each transition within the lesson, moving from one activity to another, should be effected smoothly . . . at the moment it seems almost mystical how teachers are aware of each pupil's concentration or attention. (Sarah)

Later, she wrote in her assignment:

in observing my supervising teacher it appears that the most effective method for achieving a pleasant and courteous atmosphere is to treat the children with courtesy and respect . . . [one particular reprimand] was spoken softly and gracefully and it had the desired effect.

These comments were written after the tutor input on classroom management.

Developing concerns about classroom management

All interns had recognised that classroom management was a significant issue for themselves during the entirely school based weeks when they had responsibility for whole classes on their own. Indeed, one intern who had not expressed any concern at the beginning of the course wrote about the feelings she was experiencing at this stage in her lesson evaluation proformas:

very noisy, lots of pupils walking about. I want at least the lack of movement [the usual teacher] has

noisy unruly class . . . I am now able to keep them in their seats . . . but I must look for a way of quietening them down . . . I still don't want to use detention as it is an admission of defeat and that I am not 'entertaining' the pupils sufficiently . . .

awful – noisy – uncontrolled . . . a [newspaper] article says pupils want to be worked harder – not these . . . (Sue)

The 'admission of defeat' was echoed by another intern who had not expressed earlier concerns. The intern was reluctant to exclude some disruptive girls until he was observed and the suggestion was made in the post-lesson discussion with the tutor. He said he had found this hard

because I thought it was down to my failure to excite them. (Thomas)

Some, but not all, of the interns who had expressed concerns right from the beginning were equally concerned about the issue as the course progressed:

trying to control low ability sets in years 9 and 10 still worries me most of all. (Will)

I found . . . the kind of behaviour I wanted in my classes too difficult to achieve in [the school]. Consequently I dropped my standards towards the end and became much more permissive than I would have believed at the beginning of the year. (Frank)

Another factor which emerged was that even when interns had been judged to be competent in their classroom management skills by the teachers and the university tutor, there was a reluctance by some to accept this:

I've had a year of incompetence and I'm a bit worried about my ability to teach now. (Luke)

Perhaps it is significant that Luke had talked about his concern for the issue at length from the beginning of the year so that it was high on his agenda for learning. Clearly, the standards set by the course for what a beginning teacher might achieve did not match his own and were therefore dismissed.

How concerns influenced decision making in the classroom

All the interns spoke of ways in which classroom management concerns had influenced their teaching, even though some of the interns who had expressed early concerns had found that they had no significant problems once they took over classes. However, many saw themselves facing a dilemma: pupils behaved badly when they used a traditional but familiar unstimulating approach; but pupils were likely to behave even worse (although this remained largely untested) if the lesson demanded the active involvement of pupils and the interns used what for them was an unfamiliar style of teaching. Thus, the risks associated with the latter course of action seemed too great for many of them.

Interns were observed in their teaching by both the university tutor (spending approximately half a day every two weeks with each pair of interns) and their mentor or another teacher (who had agreed to observe approximately one lesson in three). In our combined judgement, Tony had relatively few management problems, yet he said:

discussion [in the classroom] . . . involves a relaxation in control . . . it is unwise to utilise it . . . until the teacher has established firm control . . .

with practical work, it is important . . . not to begin . . . until (the teacher) has established the necessary dominance over the class and can introduce it without classroom management problems. (Tony)

Similarly, another intern who was judged to be relatively successful said:

it's very difficult to do practical work when you're not sure of the control

and spoke of one lesson where

I would have preferred to get on with some practical work but for the sake of consolidating control I felt obliged to get them working on some algebra exercises. (Nigel)

Frank and Luke were partners in the same school and were both concerned with classroom management issues from the beginning. Within a few weeks of them both talking to the tutor about the importance of being able to exclude pupils from lessons for disciplinary reasons, both did just that in early lessons and were reprimanded by the school. Indeed, in Frank's case, the pupil was returned to the lesson by a senior teacher. Both interns were unhappy about this and blamed this and subsequent problems on a variety of factors such as the school ethos, particular teachers, the all ability teaching groups, and the pupils. Luke felt that there was a tension between the school expecting him to keep pupils in the lesson and his own feeling that lessons were almost bound to fail if the pupils stayed. He felt particularly inhibited in the styles of teaching he could use:

> if it's difficult to do exposition from the front so you kick that out and it's difficult to do practical work because they break things so you kick that out, then what are you left with? ... investigations ... but the pressure is on me to [do investigations] ... and as a guest in the school, I don't want to rock the boat too much ... and the kids aren't used to other styles ... so it was a bit of a struggle. (Luke)

Interns who had not anticipated problems at the beginning of the year spoke of problems during the school based weeks. For example, when considering the use of a range of styles of teaching:

> practical work does have its drawbacks, not least classroom control (Sue)

and discussion and investigative work were identified as likely to cause classroom management problems. When discussing girls' underachievement in mathematics:

> fascinating ... how we fail girls ... but the naughty ones are the boys. They have taken all my time and I've ignored the girls. (Sue)

> girls' underachievement is secondary to classroom control. Once you've got control you can start redressing the balance. (Sarah)

In addition, the concerns did not always disappear by the end of the year:

> with all the classes I've been teaching it's only when the pupils know how much work and what sort of behaviour I expect from them that I feel happy and confident enough to go on and try more 'exciting' maths ... more open ended, investigative style maths. (Margaret)

Learning from the university tutor

Interns who spoke of early concerns for classroom management spoke positively about the tutor input in the university during the school/university integrated weeks:

> you learnt about the issue in those sessions – but when you tested them into practice, then you learnt the most. Though without those sessions, you'd never have learnt anything about it in the first place so you couldn't do without them. (Tony)

However, it was interesting to notice that those interns who had **not** expressed early concerns did not appear to remember what the issues addressed had been. Thus, Sarah said at the end of the year that she had by then learnt about 'having to wait for quiet' in the classroom. She was asked if this was learnt from university sessions and she said 'it didn't sink in at all then . . . talking to [another intern] taught me'. This conversation with another intern took place during the school based weeks when Sarah was having problems. Similarly, Thomas said at the end that 'the levels of control needed for first lessons are more than I expected when I began the course'. In his case, it would seem that he had become aware of this issue from early tutor sessions but because he had met small groups from the class before he met them altogether, he felt it was inappropriate to put into practice the ideas he had heard about. Again, however, the problems that subsequently emerged for him helped to reinforce the idea that first encounters with whole classes should be treated differently.

Thus, it might be questioned just how useful those early university based sessions had proved to be for these interns, who seemed not to have been helped to learn from what was being offered to help them.

However, all interns spoke positively about the discussions the university tutor had with them after observing their teaching:

> without these there would have been no serious discussion about this aspect of my teaching. (Sue)

> I'd say they are right at the top of what I found most beneficial . . . [the tutor] always seemed to be asking the right sort of things . . . they get to the heart of your teaching. (Tony)

These comments emphasised the value interns put on what the university tutor could offer them during conversations with them in school after their own teaching when, of course, they had recognised a need for that learning to take place.

Learning from school based experiences

It had been agreed with mentors when planning the programme that interns would be helped in their learning in school by:

- observing their mentor and other teachers, who may or may not be having classroom management problems,
- talking to teachers they had observed about the issue and discovering what strategies they used in relation to the issue,
- doing some sheltered teaching which helped them focus on the issue in their own practice,
- taking part in discussions with teachers who had observed them teaching with this issue in mind,

- discussing with teachers their own developing theories related to the issue.

In fact, each of these proved significantly more problematic than might have been anticipated.

i) Teachers in the study were happy to have interns observing lessons where there weren't significant numbers of management problems. However, this seemed unhelpful for the interns, with one commenting:

> we started off observing teachers, which got very, very, very boring – just sitting down noting things – and because the teachers there are quite good, it's even more boring. (Beth)

Thus, teachers with classes where pupils were apparently already being 'managed' were recognised as 'quite good', but for this intern at least, she had apparently not been able or motivated to find out what had been done to achieve this effective management.

On the other hand, many teachers were reluctant to have interns observe classes where they or the intern perceived there were problems and Tony talked of his mentor in relation to this with a 'bottom set' and said:

> I wouldn't have known how to ask him more directly [if I could observe him] without upsetting him. (Tony)

This in turn meant that to some extent, subsequent discussion was curtailed: what had not been observed could not be discussed.

ii) Teachers did not always find it easy to explain what they did in terms of management themselves:

> he tends not to be aware of what he's actually doing in his teaching and he takes so much for granted . . . that although you're trying to pin him down, he's not conscious of the actions he's taken to achieve what he has . . . so when you try to ask him something about what's going well he'll say 'just put it down to experience'. (Tony)

Sarah described similar problems when talking about her learning about classroom management:

> she had superb control . . . though I never got to the bottom of it. (Sarah)

Her mentor was aware that Sarah was interested in learning from her and spoke about the difficulty she had in articulating her knowledge when she said that she had not been able to be more helpful because she 'didn't really know' what she did to gain control.

iii) Sheltered teaching was generally organised by choosing small groups of pupils who the interns worked with on various issues as the year progressed. However, the small groups tended to comprise pupils who were well behaved and keen to learn so that interns did not have the challenge of any management problems with them.

iv) Discussions with teachers after the interns had taught also proved problematic, and in addition, many interns saw the problems they were having as being unique to them. After all, they were not observing anyone else having classroom management problems. In terms of the discussions with teachers, these were often dismissed as being on a trivial level:

> discussion hasn't been much use . . . for one thing I don't respect the way she teaches and I don't particularly respect what she says about my teaching. (Sarah)

> The discussions were a little bit trivial. It wasn't quite on the level I wanted it to be on. (Nigel)

> Discussions didn't amount to much . . . he'd say things briefly . . . but no indepth conversation at all. (Tony)

What seems clear is that if teachers do not let interns see the reality of their practice, then there is little subsequent talk about that reality and interns judge the conversations that do take place negatively. However, those conversations are unlikely to be on the basis of a shared concern about, in this case, classroom management so it is perhaps not surprising that interns feel this way.

v) Interns had little time to talk to teachers about their own developing theories, they and/or their mentors choosing the time they had available to talk about other things. Thus, this explicit theorising rarely took place. (Haggarty, 1995b; 1995c)

DISCUSSION

Fuller and Bown (1975) argue that:

> prospective teachers are typically anxious, and are preoccupied with their own survival. As a consequence, they are not prepared to benefit from the very real help which teacher education offers them. They are not able to attend to it.

What seems clear here is that teacher education needs to find ways of offering student teachers very real help in attending to survival concerns. At the same time, it is clearly not easy to do so.

The findings in this study indicate that individual student teachers, each having their own agenda, are likely to react in different ways to the issue. When classroom management is on their agenda, the extent to which they can attend to other issues largely depends on the extent to which they feel they are meeting the demands of their own agendas. Thus, whilst all interns in this study used criteria at some stage related to classroom management in their decision making, the issue only dominated their thinking until they were able to recognise they were achieving success in their own terms.

However, helping these student teachers to learn about the issues relating to classroom management in a rational way proved far from easy, so that the DES white paper's advice (24/89) that:

> all courses should contain compulsory and clearly identifiable elements of practical training which will develop in students skills in the effective management of pupil behaviour

appears to be far too simplistic, especially since:

> such training should include specific, institution based elements on the acquisition of group management techniques. (DES, 1989a)

If the issue is not on the student teacher's agenda, this study shows very clearly that such sessions provide little help at all.

It has already been argued that the challenge appears to be twofold: providing experiences for student teachers which move them away from a state of 'unrealistic optimism' (Weinstein, 1988) to one of concern about the issue whilst still able to learn about it in a sheltered and rational way; and persuading teachers of the need for a deeper engagement in the various activities agreed on the course. However, in relation to this second element of challenge, perhaps there was a certain amount of 'unrealistic optimism' on the part of university tutors that busy practising teachers could and would transform themselves into new, highly skilled and sophisticated teacher educators just because it was suggested to them.

Here, it emerged that teachers were reluctant to allow interns to observe (and subsequently discuss) the reality of their own teaching (Haggarty, 1995b). Consequently, interns who did not have the issue on their agenda initially were not being helped to understand its relevance and importance to experienced teachers; and therefore its importance for themselves as an issue to learn about. In addition, it emerged that the sheltered settings offered by teachers in schools so that interns could learn about issues in relative isolation in a rational way tended to be with the same hand picked small group of pupils whatever the issue being explored. One might speculate that a group of pupils hand picked to allow student teachers to try out a range of teaching approaches is not necessarily the same group one might choose to allow them to test out their classroom management strategies; nor to persuade them that there might be an issue to learn about.

CONCLUSIONS

Classroom management concerns are significant concerns for all student teachers at some stage of their learning. That should provide the opportunity for teacher education courses to help them learn about it in helpful ways, so that they can move on in their thinking to take account also of other concerns. Alerting student teachers to the issue in the university; providing small group teaching experiences in school; encouraging them to observe and discuss the issue with experienced teachers, appear not to be sufficient without more careful consideration of the thinking and actions of those involved.

Student teachers arrive on courses either already concerned and expecting problems, or already concerned and not expecting problems themselves, or unconcerned.

However, it seems clear that they will all move at some stage of their learning through a state of particular concern for classroom management. There are two alternatives: teacher educators wait until concerns arise and then try to help each student teacher's learning; or an attempt could be made to try to persuade them all that the issue concerns them at an early stage of the course and help their learning from that point. The former appears attractive yet is likely to be difficult in practice since those who can help them (tutors and teachers) may not be available; student teachers may (understandably) prefer quick and practical advice to a more thoughtful discussion on the range of alternatives available to them; decision making in the rest of their teaching may be unhelpfully restricted. It therefore seems more useful to take the latter route.

In order for all student teachers to believe that the issue is of concern they appear to need to face the problem in their own teaching. Thus, at an early stage of the year, they need to face a controlled and significantly challenging 'reality shock', thus reaching a state of 'readiness for learning' from available sources as soon as possible.

It could be speculated that such a reality shock need only be given to those who do not have the issue on their agenda already; and that it needs to take account of the likely reactions of individuals. After all, what is 'sufficiently challenging' for one may prove anything from unhelpfully overwhelming to completely inadequate for another.

In addition, it is likely to be helpful if both student teacher and teacher can plan and evaluate together for such a sufficiently challenging teaching situation, since the student teacher will then have access to the teacher's thinking, will be able to discuss their own ideas with the teacher, and will be able to reflect on the lesson in a later evaluation with the teacher, none of which appeared to happen with the interns here.

In this, as in other aspects of initial teacher education work, the need is to recognise the sophisticated skills and strategies which school based teacher education makes possible but which school based teacher educators need to learn; and also the subtlety of the ITE partnership that is needed between schools and universities.

REFERENCES

Cooper, B. (1990) PGCE students and investigational approaches in secondary maths, *Research Papers in Education*, 5, 2.

Denscombe, M. (1982) The 'hidden pedagogy' and its implications for teacher training, *British Journal of Sociology of Education*, 3, 3.

DES (1989a) *Initial teacher training: approval of courses*, Circular Number 24/89, DES.

DES (1989b) *Discipline in Schools*. Report of the Committee of Enquiry chaired by Lord Elton, HMSO, London.

Fuller, F. F. (1969) Concerns of teachers: a developmental conceptualization, *American Educational Research Journal*, 6, 2.

Fuller, F. F. and Bown, O. H. (1975) Becoming a teacher, in Ryan, K (ed.) *Teacher Education. The Seventy-fourth Yearbook of the National Society for the Study of Education. Part 2*, NSSE, Chicago.

Haggarty, L. (1992) *Investigating a New Framework for Mathematics Teacher Education: an Action Research Study*, unpublished DPhil thesis, University of Oxford.

Haggarty, L. (1995a) *New Ideas for Teacher Education: A Framework for Mathematics*, Cassell, London.

Haggarty, L. (1995b) The complexities of effective mentoring in initial teacher education, *Mentoring and Tutoring* 2, 3 pp. 32–41.

Haggarty, L. (1995c) The use of content analysis to explore conversations between school teacher mentors and student teachers, *British Educational Research Journal*, 21, 2 pp. 183–197.

Haymore, J. (1987) From successful student to frustrated student teacher. *Knowledge Growth in Teaching Project*. Stanford University.

Lanier, J. E. and Little, J. W. (1986) Research on teacher education, in Wittrock, M. C. (ed.) *Handbook of Research on Teaching, (Third Edition)*. Macmillan, New York.

OFSTED (1993) *Achieving Good Behaviour in Schools*, HMSO, London.

Shulman, L. S. (1986) Those who understand: knowledge growth in teaching, *Educational Researcher*, 15, 2.

Veenman, S. (1984) Perceived problems of beginning teachers, *Review of Educational Research*, 54, 2.

Weinstein, C.S. (1988) Preservice teachers' expectations about the first year of teaching, *Teaching and Teacher Education*, 4, 1.

5

THE PEDAGOGICAL THINKING AND LEARNING OF HISTORY STUDENT TEACHERS

Anna Pendry

ORIGINS OF THE RESEARCH

The origin of the research reported in this chapter was in my experience as a history teacher educator. Three issues were of particular interest. Firstly, the ways in which the idea of 'appropriateness' seemed to be central to our understanding of what it means to teach. Conversations with student teachers involved frequent use of the word; they revealed themselves to be grappling with the concept in their desire to make 'appropriate' decisions for their lessons; the PGCE assessment criteria required them to, for example, 'effectively praise and encourage pupils as appropriate'. A second area of interest was the individual concerns and ideas of the student teachers: the ideas they brought with them to their teacher education programme. What did they do with their own 'histories' and what were the relationships between these and their emergent ideas of appropriateness? Finally, the student teachers' lesson planning processes were of interest. Beginning teachers are dependent in their teaching on conscious, deliberate decisions which take time to make and which are made in their advance planning: this is both a very important activity for them, and – potentially – valuable as a site to gain access to their thinking about teaching.

From these concerns the following research questions, about the pedagogical decision making and more general thinking of the student teachers – interns – were formulated:

1. What is the nature of the lesson plans formulated by the interns?
2. By what processes do interns arrive at their lesson plans?

3. How do the nature and process of their planning change over the course of the internship year?

4. What kinds of preconceptions, values and aspirations about history and teaching do interns have early in the year? How do these general ideas change in the course of the internship year? How do these appear to influence lesson planning at different stages of the year?

These questions were to be explored with the history interns engaged in the internship history programme, and the researcher was also the interns' curriculum tutor.

RESEARCH DESIGN AND METHODOLOGY

The approach adopted was that of case study, understood to mean an 'approach to understanding' (Stenhouse, 1978, p. 24) in which the concern is with the 'situation as a whole'. The emphasis that Stenhouse gives to understanding the totality of the situation rather than to predetermined dimensions or variables was reflected in this study, and boundaries were determined by what was seen as the 'potential for coherence and the development of interpretation' (ibid., p. 26). The totality to be explored here was, for each of five beginning history teachers, the way in which they planned their lessons and how that related to their more general ideas about history, teaching and history teaching. The intention was to gain a phenomenological understanding of the interns' planning and thinking – how **they** construed the task of planning, what was involved for **them** in that process, what **their** more general ideas were. The design of the methods for data collection and analysis was influenced by the concept of 'grounded theory' (Glaser and Strauss, 1967). Thus the research took very little for granted: it was neither designed to test the validity of established concepts nor on the assumption that these would prove useful. Two major forms of data collection were adopted in an attempt to gain as rich a picture as possible of the product and process of the interns' thinking and the way it changed and developed. The methods were also chosen to facilitate the identification of similarities and differences within and between the interns and thus contribute to a more general understanding of the processes and product of their thinking. The principal methods adopted were semi-structured interviews and planning aloud procedures, with, on two occasions, follow-up interviews based on these planning aloud traces.

The semi-structured interviews

These were conducted with individual interns at three points in the year: at the end of October, the beginning of December and at the end of June. The interviews were designed to gain access to two aspects of the interns' think-ing: their initial preconceptions, values and aspirations and how – if at all – these general ideas about history, teaching and history teaching changed dur-ing the course of the year, and their thinking about their lesson planning in a relatively abstract context.

The planning aloud data

The second principal source of data gathered was tape recordings of the interns planning a lesson aloud.

As Morine-Dershimer states 'a teacher plan is not a simple entity to iden-tify' (1978–9, p. 84). She distinguished between the written plans that teach-ers may produce and their 'mental images or expectations of the lesson' (op. cit, p. 85). Interviews with the teachers before their teaching suggested that these mental images, 'their preactive decisions' (op. cit, p. 84), included a consideration of aspects such as pupil ability, specific objectives and seating arrangements even though their written plans rarely showed evidence of these aspects. Whilst her study was of experienced teachers rather than novices, the distinction that she makes between written plans and mental expecta-tions was adopted here.

Thus the interns were asked to plan lessons aloud, using a tape recorder, on three occasions during the year: once in early January; once in late February, several weeks into their full time school experience; and once in June during their final term. They were asked to record their name, the date, the class and the lesson at the beginning of the taping and then to verbalise what they were thinking about as they planned. Apart from reassurance that they might find it difficult at first, they were given no other instructions; the intention being to distort their normal thinking as little as possible, and to pay due attention to the effects that the preparation for the task might have on the thinking articulated.

In January and June their thinking aloud was followed by an interview, before the lesson was actually taught. For these interviews, the questions asked were dependent on the think aloud data. The purpose of the interviews was initially conceived as of value in gaining access to two areas which it was thought might not be evident in the planning aloud data. It has been suggested that the plan-ning process for a novice begins when the student teacher is told that they will be teaching the lesson (Broeckmans, 1986), and thus the interview began by asking about thinking and action undertaken prior to the formal planning ses-sion that they had recorded. The second area to be explored was their rea-soning during the process of planning as it was anticipated that this might not be fully revealed by the plan aloud trace. Prior to the interview the researcher had identified decisions which had not been explicated by the verbalisation and for each the intern was asked to recall 'why they decided . . .'.

The validity of such planning aloud data has been strongly argued by Ericsson and Simon:

> Verbal reports, elicited with care and interpreted with full understanding of the circumstances under which they were obtained, are a valuable and thoroughly reliable source of information about cognitive processes. (1980, p. 247)

They refute arguments that it is not possible to gain direct access to higher order cognitive processes (Nisbett and Wilson, 1977) and that verbal reports can be criticised on the grounds of incompleteness, irrelevance (i.e. reporting an activity that occurs in parallel with but independent of the actual thought) or that they change the nature of the cognitive processes (Ericsson and Simon, 1984). They emphasise that verbalising will not affect cognitive processes provided that the verbalisation is of information directly available in propositional form. They continue:

> However, instructions that require the subjects to perform additional cognitive processes to generate or access the information to be reported may affect these processes. (Ericsson and Simon, 1984, pp. 103–4)

Thus, for example, asking for reasons for thinking during the process of verbalisation might well distort the normal cognitive processes. Such requests were therefore carefully avoided. A second qualification they discuss, relating to experience, raises the issue of using plans later in the year. They suggest that 'practice leads to a successive fading from consciousness of information about the process' (Ericsson and Simon, 1980 p. 90), and that as experience is gained the process may move from being cognitively controlled to being a fast, automatic process, 'so that what is available for verbalisation to the novice may be unavailable to the expert' (op. cit., p. 90). This was one of the reasons why the subsequent interview on the planning process was devised – experienced teachers seem to be able to articulate their reasons retrospectively, if they are asked appropriate questions, which relate to the specifics of their actions (see, for example, Brown and McIntyre, 1993).

In these interviews the interns were being asked for a retrospective report of their thinking, and although they were encouraged to say that they couldn't remember rather than generate reasons in the interview, it is recognised that they may have reported subsequent thinking. Although the procedures recommended by Ericsson and Simon for more valid retrospective reports were followed – notably concentrating on the highly specific and reporting their own words to them – it is probably impossible to distinguish between the two types of thinking and indeed retrospective thinking will itself reveal elements of the ways in which they make pedagogical decisions in their planning.

Data analysis

The forms and procedures of the data analysis were consistent with the desire to generate from case study research a phenomenological understanding of the interns' thinking. The analysis did not depend on the *a priori* selection of categories, derived from specific theoretical models, to code and thus interpret the data. Other studies, using think aloud traces and other forms of qualitative data, appear to rely on, for example, a particular conception of the nature of pedagogical expertise (Borko and Livingston, 1989); a distinctive model of how expertise is acquired (Sabers, Cushing and Berliner, 1991), or a specific interpretation of the nature of teaching (Broeckmans, 1986). In others (Swanson, O'Connor and Cooney, 1990) it is a particular model of cognitive component processes which supplies the coding categories. In contrast, the approach here was characterised by categories suggested by the data itself in accordance with the interns' revealed thinking in relation to the specific concerns of this research; categories generated through inductive procedures.

The sort of transformation aimed at through the data analysis is that described by Schutz (1990): the generation of second order or scientific constructs which would encapsulate the common sense thinking of the intern. The intention was to devise procedures to achieve what Schutz describes thus:

> The scientific observer of human inter-relation patterns, the social scientist, has to develop specific methods for the interpretation of the subjective meaning the observed acts have for the actors. (1990, p. 27)

In developing these constructs, the process sought to meet the demanding criteria that Schutz describes: the postulates of logical consistency, of subjective interpretation and of adequacy. Thus developing constructs or concepts to adequately, and with validity, represent the interns' thinking required the design of procedures that would satisfy the following requirements. The constructs or concepts generated would need to be mutually exclusive, clearly defined, grounded in the evidence available and should be comprehensive – they should not discount any part of the data about the interns' thinking. They also needed to provide a way of making sense of all that the interns had revealed about their thinking – they should be sufficient to represent their thinking, in the respects of interest in the research. Finally, they needed to be recognisable to the interns themselves – whilst deliberately abstracted from what individual interns themselves had said, they should be valid for the interns as ways of understanding their thinking. The intention was to develop procedures that could generate concepts which met these criteria, so that these concepts could, in turn, be used to construct what Schutz refers to as the 'homunculus' (1990, p. 41) – the model or puppet of the actor. In this research, what was aimed at was a story of differences, continuities, changes and developments which would represent the ways in which each intern made sense of planning, their more general ideas about their teaching and the ways in which their thinking on different occasions and in different contexts were inter-related.

Data interpretation

The initial analysis of the data led to the construction, for each of the case study interns, of a model of each – abstracted from their reality but firmly rooted in it – that would effectively and accurately characterise their actions and thinking. Thus, the thinking and learning of Jan, James, Martha, Daniel and Stephen were represented through their own stories. The stories of Jan, James, Martha and Daniel reveal patterns of consistency, stability and development which – in conjunction with the inevitable differences reflecting distinctive concerns on particular occasions – suggested coherent ways of making sense of their thinking during the course of the year. For Stephen this did not seem to be possible: the data revealed such diversity in his thinking that few links or patterns emerged.

It was not until the individuals had been understood in their own terms that any attempt was made to draw comparisons across the cases, and it is the findings of this final stage in the interpretation of the data that are presented here: what emerged as the salient themes of difference and similarity in the thinking and learning of these interns. A detailed account of the research project can be found in the thesis (Pendry, 1994).

THE INTERNS' THINKING AND LEARNING

Differences in the interns' thinking and learning

The individual stories of the interns during their internship year suggest that each has their own concerns, their own ways of thinking about their lessons, their own ways of making sense of their roles and the purposes of history lessons, their own ways of learning: they have very different sorts of ideas about history, teaching and learning. Whilst some of their concerns and ways of thinking and developing may be shared with their peers, there is extensive evidence of their distinctive individuality and idiosyncrasy – both at the level of their general ideas and in their lesson planning.

Each talks about the nature of their discipline of history but what this means to each of them, and the relationships between their discipline and its value as a school subject, varies considerably. Thus, for Jan and James, history seems to be intrinsically valuable and worth learning. For Jan this seems to be because of its conceptual structure, a structure that makes it relevant to pupils' lives today and will, inevitably, interest them. For James it is the intellectual dimension of history that makes it valuable – being able to understand and re-create the thoughts of the past. For Martha and Daniel it seems that history for them – at least initially – is essentially a useful vehicle. Whilst they each talk of the way they view the nature of the discipline – Martha emphasising ideas of historical change and understanding the perspectives of the past, Daniel referring to the role of argument and debate in history – as teachers their interest in history seems to be that it will enable the pupils to learn skills: skills which at the beginning of the year they do not identify as specifically historical in nature. It seems that it just so happens that it is history that is useful in this way, and given that this is the subject that they have personally enjoyed, then so much the better that this is the subject that they will teach. In so far as it was possible to understand Stephen, it seems that history for him is essentially construed in terms of its propositional knowledge – the statements that it makes about the past, and the value in learning about these seems to be that in some way this helps develop an understanding of the present.

They all talk about how they see their role as teachers, and their thinking here, as well as showing some signs of change and development in several instances, provides another example of the different ways in which they construe what they are doing. A concern shared by four of them – not Stephen – seems to be their role in relation to the pupils' learning, but for James the concern with their cognitive development seems to be linked to a concern for their moral development and their understanding of the ethics of issues, whilst for Daniel, their intellectual development seems to be located within a context which will also contribute to their social development. Both Daniel and James make reference to their roles in terms of the functions of schooling and education, and seem to welcome the potentially close relationship between schooling and community. For both Martha and Jan this seems to emerge as an area of concern for them – by the end of the year they seem to be worried that as teachers they will be expected to assume responsibilities that they perceive as inappropriate. In the context of the classroom Jan seems to emphasise her role in promoting the intellectual development of the pupils, whilst for Martha both influencing the pupils' attitudes and developing their self confidence appear to be important aspects of how she construes her task. In contrast Stephen talks very little about how he sees his role – in the classroom he talks of it involving both the presentation of factual knowledge but also creating the conditions for discussion amongst the pupils, but there is no evidence of how – if at all – he sees it in broader terms.

How they talk and think about the pupils with whom they will be working similarly differs. Jan's admiration for the pupils and what they can achieve is repeatedly evident, whilst Daniel's knowledge of and concern for the individual pupils with whom he works is a striking characteristic of his thinking and developing expertise. Martha consistently shows an awareness of a diverse range of pupil characteristics and the pupils are so central in her thinking that by the end of the year she does not know what a question about her role might mean unless it is her role in relation to the pupils. For James, learning about the pupils appears to present him with a real challenge, and whilst he learns the sorts of questions that he thinks he should ask about their abilities and characteristics, he finds it hard to use this information, and particularly to integrate it with his understanding of the historical ideas he wants them to be able to make sense of. Stephen sees learning about the differences amongst pupils and their distinctive needs as examples of what he has learned during the course of the year, but it is not evident if it had been possible for him to make use of that understanding in his classroom practice.

With such differences in the ways they think in general terms about history, teaching and learning it is probably not surprising that they differ in the ways in which they plan their lessons. Whilst they do all seem to make decisions about **activities** in their planning – and for all of them this is the common and dominant aspect of all their plans – their other decision areas are not amenable to common classification. This reflects the fact that as individuals they tended to make different types of decisions on each occasion, and the few patterns that exist within each case suggest that each has a different conception of what they need to attend to in their planning, and a different way of construing the task of planning which confronts them. Although it may be the case that when Martha thinks about, for example, what the lesson is to be about she is thinking of something similar to Jan's aims and objectives, they tend to consistently use different labels for their areas of decision making and these labels may reflect differences in what they understand themselves to be doing.

This seems to be similarly reflected in their processes of decision making. Whilst they do take into account quite a lot of similar factors in arriving at their decisions, exactly what some of these factors mean to them and their relative importance shows evidence of difference from individual to individual. Thus, for example, when Daniel considers time in his lessons this tends to be in broad terms of the overall amount of time in the lesson – he rarely refers to precise timings, and it seems almost as if he has some sort of mental map of how long a worksheet with a certain number of questions on it will be likely to take most of the pupils to complete. For Daniel, time seems never to be a particularly important concern. In contrast, Martha's calculations about time are very precise, rehearsed and adjusted – and getting time sorted out seems to be an important element in her planning. Jan talks in quite precise terms about time, but often with flexibility built in, a flexibility which takes account of the unpredictability – to her – of pupil response. The significance of time for Jan seems to vary from lesson to lesson. So far as their knowledge of the pupils and their characteristics is concerned it seems that Martha consistently makes reference to the most extensive range of characteristics, and increasingly talks about these in terms of either the particular class that she is teaching or the specific individuals. James, in contrast, consistently refers to a much more limited range of characteristics, and his references are often in general terms: what a class of thirteen year olds, for example, would be likely to say in response to a particular question, rather than how he anticipates that the particular pupils that he is planning for will respond. Stephen's concern with pupil characteristics seems similarly to lack specificity, and seems to draw on what he **believes** will be the case, rather than particular observations that he has made or knowledge that he has. Daniel consistently makes extensive reference to his concern for how pupils will cope with and respond to the intellectual challenges that he devises, and he appears to take most account of characteristics which relate directly to their cognitive skills and abilities. Jan seems to consider a range of characteristics as relevant in all her planning – from specifics such as their reading abilities to rather less sharply defined characteristics such as the mood that the pupils are likely to be in for a particular lesson.

Similarities in the interns' thinking and learning

Although so much of the interns' thinking and learning about history, teaching and learning can be characterised in terms of the idiosyncrasies of the individuals, there are a number of themes and patterns which emerge from the four for whom it was possible to create a coherent interpretation. In some instances there also seems to be evidence that Stephen's thinking shares some of these patterns, but this is not often the case. The consistent complexity of the interns' planning seems to be a characteristic common to all. For each lesson they were seen to be juggling with diverse concerns, making frequent references to a wide range of differing factors that they took into account in making their decisions. Their plans in January seemed to be almost as complex as those at the end of the year – whilst there might be new factors evident in June, these were often matched by factors which only emerged in January. There was some evidence of them taking into account a wider range of sorts of factors within any particular type by June, but nonetheless the overwhelming pattern to emerge was of the stability in the complexity of their thinking.

Also common to all the interns were differences in their planning on each occasion. Whilst **activities** was one common, dominant area of decision making for all of them on each planning occasion, and there was evidence that certain sorts of concerns re-emerged as salient for each of the lessons, their stories revealed the way in which on each occasion they would make different types of decisions and accord more or less emphasis to particular types of concerns. None appeared to have a model or formula for planning that was invariably applied on each occasion. Instead, it seemed that each made the decisions that they had decided were relevant to the particular lesson that they were planning, and they took account of what they deemed were the relevant concerns for that particular lesson. It seemed that they were all making decisions about what the planning task required and how they could, in their terms, appropriately meet these requirements.

Although their planning did suggest that they were varying what they were doing according to how they construed each task, on each occasion all of them did make decisions about the activities for the lesson, and for all of them this appeared to be a major aspect of their planning. Quite what thinking about activities meant for each of them did show some signs of difference. For both James and Daniel it involved a detailed consideration of historical content and ideas (such as factors related to the development of penicillin or the events leading to the outbreak of the English Civil War) as well as what they wanted the pupils to understand and the pupil and teacher activities, whilst for Martha and Jan the activities were always linked to what it was they wanted the pupils to understand but did not include the same explicit rehearsal of historical ideas. For Stephen, making decisions about activities seemed to mean something a little different on each planning occasion – sometimes solely what the pupils and he would do, sometimes linking what they would all do with the ideas that the pupils were to understand. But despite these differences the dominance of this as a common and significant element in their planning was striking – all seemed to use the planning as an opportunity to work through in very detailed ways what was going to happen during the course of the lesson, usually linking this to what it was that they wanted the pupils to understand and how that was to be brought about.

The clearest way in which they all, except Stephen, seemed to develop during the year was in terms of the fluency of their planning. A pattern emerged for the other four of a changing shape to their planning. In January, they seemed to build their lessons through a process of rehearsal and decision making that involved repeated re-visiting of decisions that they had made earlier in the planning. It seemed that they needed to check out what they had done previously at several stages in their planning: it was as if they had not yet become confident that what had previously been put into place would still be appropriate. The re-visiting rarely involved a change of decision, although sometimes timings, for example, were adjusted to accommodate subsequent plans, and occasionally an emphasis was shifted to take account of what was now known to come later. By June, the four constructed their lessons with apparently much more confidence – they tended to work through the time span of the lesson in chronological order, putting each piece or block of the lesson in place as they went, and they rarely needed to re-visit the decisions that they had made earlier in their planning. They perhaps had a clearer picture at the outset of what it was that they were striving to create, as well as how to construct the component parts of the lesson. But this growth in fluency did not necessarily mean a diminution in their attention to detail – they still thought through aspects of the lesson in great detail, such as the questions they would ask or the tasks that the pupils would engage in. An element of this fluency seemed to be the routinisation of their planning – suggested by the ways in which they tended to articulate less of their reasoning in the actual process of their planning. It seemed that by June they were taking for granted some of the factors that they had taken into account in their actual planning, although they were still conscious of the ways in which at least some of these considerations had influenced them and were able to reveal them when questioned about the thinking informing their decisions. In several cases too there was evidence of greater economy in their planning by the end of the year – they were able to complete the planning tasks in rather less time than earlier in the year.

Another characteristic shared by all is that it was in their planning that development was most evident. Although in several cases it seemed possible to identify ways in which their more general thinking may have developed during the year – for example, for Martha, Daniel, Jan and James possibly changes in the distinctive ways that they understood the role of history in their teaching – these claims were more tentative and less clearly supported by the evidence. For all except Stephen, it seems that changes in their **planning** can be more confidently interpreted as developments than can changes in their general ideas.

There are though other common patterns which seem to emerge which relate to their more general ideas. The first of these is the relationship between the ideas that they expressed in the context of interview and the concerns that emerged in the context of their planning. With the exception of Stephen, there seemed to be a high degree of resonance in what was of interest and importance to them, whatever the context. Those differences that were apparent seemed to be largely explicable in terms of different kinds of discourse about teaching. Hence differing ways of articulating their views emerged. Also apparent were some examples of different concerns expressed in different contexts and examples of ways that they used their ideas to talk more generally about schooling (rather than in relation to their own teaching and planning). But more often than not what emerged were what seemed to be very coherent versions of what they wanted to achieve, how they understood history classrooms, how they viewed themselves as teachers. No evidence was found of any contradictions in what Jan, Martha, Daniel and James said in the different contexts – what they anticipated about their planning was largely evident in their planning, much of what was generally important to them was similarly evident, and what they were concerned about in their planning seemed to be linked to their more abstract views.

The stability of several of their initial ideas seemed to be another characteristic of all except Stephen. Whilst there was also evidence of ways in which these ideas appeared to be elaborated or refined during the course of the year, it seemed to be possible to identify strong links between what was talked about in October and what were to re-emerge in June as salient concerns to them. Their views of learners and the nature of learning was one element which for all four showed evidence of stability. For James, the centrality of his discipline also seemed to remain constant.

Another similarity was that the nature of the discipline was something that emerged for all of them at the beginning of the year as an important part of their thinking – even if its principal function to them as teachers was its role as a vehicle for the development of intellectual skills and abilities not particularly associated with history. Whilst in several cases it seemed as if their views about the role of history did show evidence of change and development, for all of them – including Stephen – it seemed to be a significant concern at the outset: it was something that they all chose to talk about in their initial interview even though they were not asked directly about it.

The final similarity identified was that none chose to use the distinctive language of their teacher education course extensively. This was most apparent in the ways that they used words other than aims, objectives and goals. Both Daniel and Jan refer to their aims and objectives in their January lessons, but not thereafter, and none of the others ever makes use of these terms in their plans. Even in interview, when one might have anticipated a greater use of such language, it was not evident. It was rare for the interns to employ these terms at all – and on the very few occasions when they did appear it was in their response to a question in which the term was used by the researcher. The interns seemed to have different ways of talking about their teaching.

THE RELATIONSHIP BETWEEN THE INTERNS' THINKING AND LEARNING AND THE INTENTIONS OF THE INTERNSHIP HISTORY PROGRAMME

The research did not investigate directly the ways in which the interns' thinking and learning was influenced by their teacher education programme. However, the position of the researcher as the tutor responsible for the programme and one of the significant actors within it does make it possible to discuss how that thinking and learning may be related to the intentions and assumptions underlying the programme.

Within the common framework of the principles of the internship scheme, the history curriculum programme was designed by the history tutor in collaboration with the team of history mentors. The planned programme was organised around a number of broad themes, such as classroom management, lesson planning, taking account of differences in learners, the variety of possible teaching strategies in history, pupil understanding in history and so on, all of which were related specifically to the teaching of history and were addressed in an order which reflected what the history team understood to be the priority concerns of beginner teachers. Thus, after an initial exploration of diverse views about the nature, purpose and practice of history teaching, the first of the units focused on issues of management before then moving on to the central concern of this research – the interns' learning about lesson planning. The programme for each of these themes was designed so that the interns engaged in university seminars and workshops, and school practice, observation and discussion which were all directed to the theme in question. Thus their work in the context of school was intended to be closely integrated with what they experienced in the university context – ideas presented by the university tutor were to be examined in various ways in school, whilst what they had seen, done and encountered in school was similarly examined in the university context. The programme had been designed to try to ensure that the school and university partners in the interns' programme offered different, distinctive but complementary contributions to the interns' learning: contributions which reflected the special expertise and occupational position of each.

In relation to the lesson planning unit, this meant that the university contribution focused on offering the interns knowledge about planning drawn from research on the nature and processes of planning. What research suggests is involved in the planning process was discussed, the criteria that might be employed in making decisions about aims, objectives and strategies were considered in thinking through what it might mean to make appropriate and worthwhile decisions in planning history lessons. The nature of and reasons for differences in planning between novice and expert teachers were examined. The interns were also given the opportunity to try out planning parts of lessons – with the examples supplied by mentors – to have the opportunity of practising their skills in a protected environment, in which they could work collaboratively with their peers. In the context of the school, the intention was that they should talk with experienced teachers about the ways in which they (the teachers) had planned lessons, what they had taken account of in their planning and why. The programme encouraged them to work collaboratively both with their partner intern and with their mentor in the planning of lessons – initially having a limited responsibility both in the planning and subsequent teaching, but increasingly assuming responsibility for whole lessons and whole classes. They were expected to test out and question the ideas presented in the university context, and to return to the university department with ideas from the school context which could be similarly subjected to scrutiny.

Thus during the period of joint weeks until the end of January, when interns worked in school two days a week and the university for the other three, the intention was that they would follow a common agenda in each context – an agenda of agreed issues within which it was assumed there had also been agreement about the distinctive but different contributions that mentor and tutor would offer. From the end of January until May, the interns worked in school full time, with occasional visits from the curriculum tutor. Whilst there were some agreed areas to be addressed by all the history interns during this time, it was assumed that the nature and pace of their learning now was largely directed by their mentor. As they gained in expertise it was anticipated that the interns would increasingly direct their own learning and, once they had satisfied the requirements of others, generate their own criteria of what was important to them and engage in a process of self evaluation to develop their understanding of these criteria and the means by which they could evaluate their own practice.

The final weeks of the year reverted to the week structure of the joint weeks, and whilst there was again a common curriculum programme for all history interns it was expected that, particularly in relation to their work in school, they would – in conjunction with their mentors – decide what sorts of emphases and priorities would be appropriate for them, given their distinctive concerns and expertise.

It is thus in the context of this type of teacher education programme that the interns' learning was located. The major themes identified from the previous discussion, about the ways in which their thinking and learning appear to vary or share characteristics, will be discussed in terms of the intentions of the programme. The aim of this discussion is not to suggest possible causal connections – there is no research evidence on which to base such claims – but to explore relevant intentions and assumptions underlying the programme and to speculate about the relationship between these and the interns' thinking and learning.

The diverse ways in which the interns vary in their thinking and learning suggest the extent of the idiosyncrasy and individuality of the process of learning to teach for these individuals. Reflecting on this in relation to their programme prompts two observations. The first is that the planned curriculum programme, delivered in the context of the university, is unlikely to have contributed to helping them, as individuals, to grapple with the processes of learning to teach. At that time, the power and potential significance of their individual concerns, their own agendas for learning, the different ways in which they would make sense of what they were learning about were simply not recognised in the programme. The group of fourteen history interns were taught as a group, and whilst there was plenty of opportunity for them to contribute, and a variety of ways of working in pairs, small groups and as a whole – with the occasional individual task – very little time was spent by the tutor with them as individuals and they had relatively few planned opportunities to work through ideas on their own. They also had few opportunities, especially in the period of the joint weeks, to direct the nature of the programme – whilst a little time was deliberately left unstructured for the discussion of the unpredictable realities of school life and for them to choose the agenda, as a proportion of the taught programme it was very small. It was also a time that was constantly vulnerable if the tutor believed that some pressing issue – identified by the tutor – simply had to be added to the programme.

In contrast to their experience in the university it is possible that in school their mentors will have accorded them individual attention. Although all interns worked in pairs in school, and the intention was that they would work collaboratively both in and outside the classroom, it was also intended that they receive individual support, guidance and criticism from both their mentors and the other teachers with whom they worked. It is possible that each of the interns in this study will have had the opportunity to engage in activities made explicit in the planned programme: to discuss their ideas with their mentors, both on their own and with their partners, to work in the classroom with their mentor but without their partner, to observe and discuss their mentors' teaching both with and without their partners and to have their own teaching observed and systematically assessed by their mentor and other teachers with whom they worked on a regular basis. Given the amount of time that these interns will have spent in school, it might be the case that in this context they will have received a programme tailored to their distinctive individual needs and concerns.

A similarity identified in the planning of all the interns was its complexity. It may be possible to understand this in terms of the intentions of their programme, but it is also possible that the programme could have led to a very different outcome. The unit on lesson planning, and specifically the university contribution, undoubtedly did emphasise planning as a complex process, and the analogy of juggling with varied and competing claims was employed by the tutor. The interns were encouraged to consider why they might plan, and also to think carefully about the differences between them and experienced teachers – they were encouraged to recognise that as beginners, effective teaching in the classroom would be strongly influenced by the ways in which they had thought through the lesson in advance and that unlike experienced teachers they would not have routinised ways of achieving their desired outcomes. They were also encouraged to recognise what experienced teachers might take for granted in their own practice, and to question teachers when they appeared to be making 'simple' decisions about what they intended to do. In the context of school it was anticipated that they would have had a range of opportunities which may have helped them to understand and learn about the complexity of planning. They may have had the chance to plan with their mentors, and to see the ways in which an experienced teacher took account of a wide range of relevant concerns. Their own planning is likely to have taken place in initially protected environments which may have meant that they were neither overwhelmed by the specific task, nor felt that they were on their own if their plan was not as successful as they had hoped. They will have had opportunities to try out their initial plans in a context which they will have already known well, and which by January was relatively familiar to them. It is possible that they will have received constructive and thoughtful feedback from their mentors about the appropriateness of what they had planned and the ways in which future plans might accommodate a wider range of concerns.

Whilst all these features of their programme (both actual and intended) might help to explain – at least in part – the complexity of their planning, it might have been anticipated that precisely because they **were** working so closely with experienced teachers they might have failed to recognise the complexity of those teachers' routinised planning and might have imitated the planning practices of many experienced teachers who appear to concentrate their planning efforts on schemes of work rather than on individual lessons. That this was not the outcome – at least for these interns – suggests that the programme might have had some success in helping them to recognise the value and purpose of planning for them and the ways in which this might differ for experienced teachers. It might also suggest that the teachers with whom they worked in school were able to articulate thinking that might normally have remained tacit and implicit in their practice. Perhaps these mentors recognised that this was necessary for the interns' learning and were able to achieve it. That this might be the explanation seems reasonable in that one of the concerns of internship as a whole has been to ensure that beginning teachers are able to gain access to the craft knowledge of experienced teachers, and thus learning about ways of achieving this has been an emphasis in both the mentors' induction and the interns' curriculum programme.

The interns' extensive work with experienced teachers might also explain the dominance of activities in the decisions that they made in their planning. This was certainly not an emphasis in the planned curriculum programme. There they had been encouraged to think about the goals or aims and objectives of the lesson and the ways in which these would be achieved: what sort of strategies and resources they would employ, the ways in which the pupils would be involved in the lesson and what their own contribution would involve. They had not been encouraged to plan in a linear fashion, and indeed a Tylerian model of planning (which suggests that planning is sequential, moving from aims to objectives on to content, organisation and resources and finishing with a consideration of ways of evaluating the lesson) had been subjected to critical analysis when they considered a range of models of planning and thought about how they might characterise their own planning processes. Although the intention was to alert the interns to different ways of understanding the nature of planning, and to discuss the value of different approaches, they were encouraged to consider the purposes of what they were planning and thus there was undoubtedly an emphasis on decisions related to the goals of lessons. It was not anticipated that they would so readily adopt what seems to be the preferred focus of planning for many experienced teachers and indeed this focus in their planning was only identified through the research process. It was not, for example, evident from their written plans nor recognised from discussions with them during the year. It might be that the explanation for this emphasis is that they did their planning with experienced teachers and may have adopted at least some of the ways of working seen to be effective for them. In addition, it seems possible that in commenting on their plans and perhaps their lessons too teachers may have focused on this as a significant aspect. The discourse of school and the ways presented there of understanding classrooms and the teacher's role in planning may have been rather more influential, and perhaps more helpful for the interns, than some of the ways of thinking about planning presented in the university context. This too might explain the reluctance of the interns to use some of the language of the planned programme to talk about their own teaching – it was perhaps not the language of schools where so much of their time was spent and where they did so much of their learning.

The extent of difference for each of the interns among their plans might also be explained by their extensive engagement in the school context. If those differences among their own plans for different lessons are understood in terms of them consistently making what they see as the decisions appropriate to specific lessons, and taking account of the factors that they see as relevant to these particular lessons, then their extended involvement in a single context about which they could develop a sophisticated knowledge and understanding might explain their readiness consistently to make what they saw as contextually appropriate decisions. It is likely that they will have had the opportunity to see experienced teachers doing this, and because of their own understanding of the context, perhaps increasingly to understand what it was that the teachers were doing. The nature of the programme may have enabled them to discover for themselves the ways in which contextual factors must influence planning if the plans are to prove effective in the classroom, and they may have had feedback from teachers who would be likely to pay attention to such considerations in their comments. This was also something that was emphasised in the university context – that planning is about making appropriate decisions and that whilst certain factors will invariably need to be considered if a decision is to avoid being inappropriate, there is no single and simple formula that will guarantee the appropriateness of decisions. In the university context they were encouraged to see planning and indeed teaching as a whole as involving the making of intelligent decisions about action.

That the interns appeared to learn how to plan with such fluency might be attributable to the nature of their programme, and a combination of elements of that experience that have already been discussed. Thus it may have been that their extended involvement in school, in a single context that they had the opportunity to come to know extremely well and regular and systematic feedback on their planning may all have contributed to their development here. Understanding this characteristic is not easy as it is not something which seems to have been reported in other studies and thus it is not known if it is a characteristic that would be relatively common amongst beginning teachers. This seems unlikely – just learning how to plan would be a big enough challenge for initial teacher education – but whether or not it is something that can be explained by distinctive features of the internship programme is not known.

A striking similarity in the interns' thinking that was observed in this study, and that replicates the findings of many others, was the stability of some of their initial ideas about teaching. That they did prove to be so stable in many respects is perhaps explicable, at least in part, in terms of the ways that the programme failed to engage in these ideas. At that time, it was not fully recognised that they would have such powerful preconceptions, and that what they brought with them would continue to influence them so strongly. When this research study was designed, it was a recent acquaintance with the literature related to this field which provided one of the research questions for the study, but although the curriculum tutor was beginning to understand that the learning of novices might be significantly shaped by the histories that they brought with them, this was not incorporated into the design of the history programme, nor had it been fully discussed with the history mentors. Whilst the mentors may have explored with the interns their initial ideas, this was not done in the context of a programme which had been systematically designed to take account of such ideas. Whilst their engagement with the research process meant that the interns were asked to articulate their ideas, these were never challenged or discussed, and in attempting to maintain the integrity of the different roles of researcher and tutor, the researcher explicitly did not comment in the teaching context on ideas that had been articulated in the research context. Of course, it cannot be known if exploring their ideas or challenging them would have made any difference to the influence that they had – but it does seem likely that failing to do these things would have been likely to contribute to their stability.

The final area of similarity in the interns' thinking to be related to their programme is what seems to have been the coherence in their thinking in different contexts. It might have been expected that as beginners contradictions and inconsistencies would emerge, and that what they would anticipate about their planning might be rather different from the actuality. That there was so little evidence of this might be explicable in terms of their programme. The curriculum programme, played out in school and university contexts, seeks to constantly integrate their learning in these two contexts and provide them with ways of making sense of the diverse perspectives that they encounter. It is possible that an integrated programme of this sort will have at least contributed to the coherence of their ideas. The planned programme seeks to emphasise a version of teaching in which action is informed by thought. The tutor's expectation is that the interns will recognise teaching and learning to teach as complex processes, worthy of serious intellectual engagement and the systematic application of diverse criteria drawn from a wide range of sources of knowledge and reflecting very different priorities: all of which need to be considered in learning about teaching and education. Such an approach at least encourages the interns consistently to think about what they are doing and learning in complex ways and to think about whether what they are doing in the classroom, for example, reflects the sort of teacher that they want to be, or what they think is important about the nature of the discipline – and if not, why not.

Whilst it may be possible to construe dimensions of the interns' thinking and learning as compatible with the intentions and assumptions underlying their programme, no claims for causality can be made, and there are ways in which it seems that their ways of thinking and learning are independent of that programme.

CONCLUSIONS

This study, like others, revealed the richness of the ideas that beginning teachers bring with them to their teacher education programme. There was though little evidence to support two findings reported in other studies: that the beginning teachers' preconceptions are essentially miseducative and unhelpful in the context of a teacher education programme (McDiarmid *et. al.*,1989), and that they are inflexible (Kagan, 1992).

Whilst it does seem likely that beginning teachers will, from their experience as learners in classrooms themselves, have seen a version of teaching and learning from a specific vantage point and that they may 'because of their vantage point and empathetic capacity . . . see it simplistically' (Lortie, 1975, p. 65), this is not the only experience on which their preconceptions are based, and the evidence of this study was that the beginning teachers' preconceptions were far from simplistic, often included thinking about pupils as learners, and suggested that several were already aware of the complexities of classrooms and ways of learning, conceptions which may derive from the **range** of experiences that they bring with them to initial teacher education.

There was also evidence that whilst initial ideas often remained stable, this did not necessarily mean that they were also inflexible – there was evidence of subtle change and development in relation to the interns' preconceptions. This echoes the finding reported by Bullough, that of the student teachers he studied:

> two began the year with very complex understandings of teaching. For these teacher education students, metaphors were not added, but understandings were deepened. (Bullough with Stokes, 1994, p. 210)

An implication here is of the need to find ways of enabling beginning teachers to articulate and examine the ideas that they bring with them to initial teacher education. There is evidence of a range of ways in which this might be done – through the construction of a course consisting of the critical analysis of selected problems of teaching (Bird *et. al.*, 1993), through the generation of personal teaching metaphors (Bullough with Stokes, 1994), through the writing of personal life histories (Knowles, 1993). But what is also evident is that the use of these methods is far from straightforward. As Bird and his colleagues report:

> the attempt to teach in a way that could engage and alter their [the student teachers'] beliefs was fraught with problems. (1993, p. 265)

This study also strongly supported the contention that 'becoming a teacher is inevitably an idiosyncratic process' (Bullough, 1992, p. 251), that:

> what is more likely is development across a range of dimensions at different times for different students. Learning to teach, in this sense, is idiosyncratic and personal. (Elliott and Calderhead, 1993, p. 173)

Thus, whilst there may be common themes that can be useful to us in understanding beginning teachers' learning – for example, that their preconceptions, of whatever nature, are likely to profoundly influence them – each individual is likely to develop in different ways, even when engaged in a common programme. Two of the interns in this study (Martha and Jan) probably had as common a programme as it is possible to provide – the same university programme, the same university curriculum tutor, the same school attachment, the same mentor (and – as it happened – developed a close personal friendship) and yet they still developed in different ways. The distinctiveness and idiosyncrasy of beginning teachers seems to persist throughout their programme. It is manifest not only in the differences in the ideas they bring with them, but in what they then learn and how they learn those things throughout the programme. It would seem that a major task for teacher educators is to find ways in which those individual needs and individual concerns can be addressed not just at the outset but on a continuing basis. As Elliott and Calderhead observe:

> there is need for considerable individual support, in both emotional and cognitive spheres, for beginning teachers if they are to develop and grow as teachers. (1993, p. 173)

There was no evidence in this study of common stages of development for the interns – a finding which seems consistent with the evidence of the idiosyncrasies of their learning, and the influence of their different personal preconceptions. Within this, there was no evidence of these beginning teachers showing an initial preoccupation in their planning with management and survival concerns: they did not:

> confirm[s] the common sense observation that trainees typically go through a number of distinct stages of development, each with its own focal concerns.

These concerns could be usefully grouped under the following headings: early idealism, survival, recognising difficulties, hitting the plateau and moving on. (Maynard and Furlong, 1993, p. 71)

Instead, in this study, the concerns of the student teachers seem to be more similar to those of the elementary students in Guillaume and Rudney's study:

student teachers spontaneously expressed concerns about their teaching and their students at the same time that they were worrying about their own survival in the classroom. (1993, p. 74)

Kagan's review of the literature suggests a pattern in which:

changes in the novice's knowledge of classrooms could be described in terms of a progression in attention: beginning with classroom management and organisation, moving on to subject matter and pedagogy and finally turning to what students were learning from academic tasks. (1992, p. 144)

This conclusion is drawn from studies which have focused on student teachers' classroom teaching, and it may be that the interns too would have shown such concerns in that context, but in their planning there was no evidence of such progression in attention in the ways that they used their knowledge about classrooms.

Related to the lack of evidence of common stages in the interns' development is the suggestion that this study also offers evidence to support the contention that changes in teacher education students' thinking might be 'quite subtle, indicating changes of degree, not kind', and that broad concepts to describe change 'may mask more than they reveal about development' (Bullough with Stokes, 1994, p. 210). Similarly, Guillaume and Rudney suggest that:

student teachers in this study did not so much think about different things as they grew; they thought about things differently. (1993, p. 79)

This study certainly suggested that, so far as their lesson planning was concerned, the key development was in the increasingly fluent way that they made their decisions – it was not so much that they became aware of different considerations to take into account as that they developed their understanding of how to take these factors into account. Similarly, the developments that could be identified in their more general ideas – and these were less easily identified than in their planning – seemed to be in terms of changing emphases (in the influence of history, for example) or increasing complexity (in ideas about learners, for example).

This subtlety of development seems to be related to the final dimension of this study which, it is suggested, contributes to our understanding of student teachers' learning – the complexity of their thinking. Very often, it seems, student teachers' thinking is characterised in relation to that of expert, experienced teachers in terms such as the following: 'initially their pedagogical conceptions were vague, global and relatively undifferentiated' (Kagan, 1992, p. 153); that their 'knowledge structures were literal and surface level' (Rovegno, 1992, p. 253). Instead of this rather impoverished view of beginners, the picture that emerged from this study suggests that beginning teachers have the potential to think about teaching and to make plans for teaching which are complex and sophisticated from an early stage in their programme, and that any model of professional development, or definition of professional growth, needs to take account of this.

Christopher Clark has suggested that research on experienced teachers' thinking:

> shows that thinking plays an important part in teaching and that the image of a teacher as a reflective professional is not farfetched . . . In sum, research on teacher thinking supports the position that teachers are more active than passive, more ready to learn than resistant, more wise and knowledgeable than deficient, more diverse and unique than they are homogenous. (1992, pp. 76–77)

Perhaps beginning teachers are too.

REFERENCES

Bird, T., Anderson, L.M., Sullivan, B.A. and Swidler, S.A. (1993) Pedagogical balancing acts: attempts to influence prospective teachers' beliefs, *Teaching and Teacher Education*, 9 (3) pp. 253–267.

Borko, H. and Livingston, C. (1989) Cognition and improvisation: differences in mathematics instruction by expert and novice teachers, *American Educational Research Journal*, 26 (4), pp. 473-498.

Broeckmans, J. (1986) Short term developments in student teachers' lesson planning, *Teaching and Teacher Education*, 2 (3), pp. 215–228.

Brown, S. and McIntyre, D. (1993) *Making Sense of Teaching*, Open University Press, Buckingham.

Bullough, R.V. Jr. (1992) Beginner teacher curriculum decision making, personal teaching metaphors and teacher education, *Teaching and Teacher Education*, 8 (3), pp. 239–252.

Bullough, R.V. Jr. with Stokes, D.K. (1994) Analysing teaching metaphors in preservice teacher education as a means for encouraging professional development, *American Educational Research Journal*, 31 (1) pp. 197–224.

Clark, C.M. (1992) Teachers as designers in self-directed professional development, in A. Hargreaves and M. Fullan (eds.) *Understanding Teacher Development*, Cassell, London.

Elliott, B. and Calderhead, J. (1993) Mentoring for teacher development: possibilities and caveats, in McIntyre, D., Hagger, H. and Wilkin, M. (eds.) *Mentoring: Perspectives on School Based Teacher Education*, Kogan Page, London.

Ericsson, K.A. and Simon, H.A. (1980) Verbal reports as data, *Psychological Review*, 87 (3) pp. 215–251.

Ericsson, K.A. and Simon, H.A. (1984) *Protocol Analysis: Verbal Reports as Data*,

MIT Press, Massachusetts.

Glaser, B.G. and Strauss, A.L. (1967) *The Discovery of Grounded Theory*, Aldine Publishing, New York.

Guillame, A.M. and Rudney, G.L. (1993) Student teachers' growth towards independence: an analysis of their changing concerns, *Teaching and Teacher Education*, 9 (1) pp. 65–80.

Kagan, D.M. (1992) Professional growth among preservice and beginning teachers, *Review of Educational Research*, 62 (2) pp. 129–169.

Knowles, J. Gary (1993) Life-history accounts as mirrors: a practical avenue for the conceptualisation of reflection in teacher education, in J. Calderhead and P. Gates (eds.) *Conceptualising Reflection in Teacher Development*, Falmer Press, London.

Lortie, D.C. (1975) *Schoolteacher: A Sociological Study*, University of Chicago Press, Chicago.

Maynard, T. and Furlong, J. (1993) Learning to teach and models of mentoring, in D. McIntyre, H. Hagger and M. Wilkin (eds.) *Mentoring: Perspectives on School Based Teacher Education*, Kogan Page, London.

McDiarmid, G.W., Ball, D. and Anderson, C. (1989) Why staying one chapter ahead doesn't really work: subject specific pedagogy, in M.C. Reynolds (ed.) *Knowledge Base for the Beginning Teacher*, Pergamon, London.

Morine-Dershimer, G. (1978/9) Planning in classroom reality: an in depth look, *Educational Research Quarterly*, 3 (4) pp. 83–99.

Nisbett, R.E. and Wilson, T. (1977) Telling more than we can know: verbal reports on mental processes, *Psychological Review*, 84 (3) pp. 231–259.

Pendry. A. (1994) *The pre-lesson pedagogical decision-making of history student teachers during the internship year*. Thesis submitted for the degree of Doctor of Philosophy at the University of Oxford.

Rovegno, I. (1992) Learning a new curricular approach: mechanisms of knowledge acquisition in preservice teachers, *Teaching and Teacher Education*, 8 (3) pp. 253–264.

Sabers, D.S., Cushing, K.S. and Berliner, D.C. (1991) Differences among teachers in a task characterised by simultaneity, multidimensionality and immediacy, *American Educational Research Journal*, 28 (1) pp. 63–88.

Schutz, A. (1990) *Collected Papers (1) The Problem of Social Reality*, Kluwer Academic Publishers, Dordrecht.

Stenhouse, L. (1978) Case study and case records: towards a contemporary history of education, *British Educational Research Journal*, 4 (2) pp. 21–39.

Swanson, H.L., O'Connor, J.E. and Cooney, J.B. (1990) An information processing analysis of expert and novice teachers problem solving, *American Educational Research Journal*, 27 (3) pp. 533–556.

6

ENABLING STUDENT TEACHERS TO GAIN ACCESS TO THE PROFESSIONAL CRAFT KNOWLEDGE OF EXPERIENCED TEACHERS

Hazel Hagger

INTRODUCTION

The research reported in this chapter is part of a larger project concerned with the problems and possibilities for student teachers of gaining access to the 'professional craft knowledge' of experienced teachers. In this introductory section, the research background, the concerns, the assumptions and the nature of that larger project will be briefly explained.

In the last twenty years, research on teachers and teaching has been increasingly dominated by a concern with teachers' cognitions; and inevitably, many different suggestions have been made about distinctions and categories that are needed for such study. The research project under discussion depends on two important distinctions made for example, by Clark and Peterson (1986) in their widely-respected review of research in this area: one between teachers' theories and beliefs and teachers' cognitions while engaged in teaching work; the other between teachers' cognitions during classroom interaction, and their cognitions while planning or reflecting on their teaching before or afterwards.

Both these distinctions are not only widely accepted but are also of considerable theoretical significance. The first distinction has been strongly emphasised by Argyris and Schon (Argyris and Schon 1974; Argyris 1982; Schon 1983) in terms of the contrast between 'espoused theory', the knowledge learned and accepted by professionals as prescribing what ought to happen and used by them to justify their actions, and 'theories-in-use', the knowledge that guides their action, knowledge that has been developed through practice, and which is usually tacit and rarely needs to be articulated. Whether or not the distinction between 'espoused theory' and ' theories-in-use' is quite so sharp in relation to teachers as Schon's (1983) rhetoric in particular would suggest must be open to question. Nonetheless, it is a highly plausible and potentially important distinction which at the very least has a considerable heuristic value for researchers.

The second distinction has no doubt been made by teachers for centuries, but in the modern research literature was made most influentially by Jackson (1968) in his seminal work on life in classrooms. He and subsequent researchers have emphasised the strikingly different conditions within which teachers' thinking during lessons and their thinking at other times has to be conducted, and have shown the implications of those different conditions in, for example, the 'immediacy' of teachers' concerns while engaged in interactive teaching.

Although both distinctions are widely accepted, there is no suggestion that they are inviolate: clearly, teachers' actions reflect their beliefs, and their interactive teaching is carried out within a framework of planning and evaluation. The distinction the researcher would want to make – which combines both those made by Clark and Peterson (1986) – is between the knowledge and thinking of teachers engaged in interactive teaching and their knowledge and thinking when not engaged in practice. It is with the former category that this research is concerned.

Again, researchers in recent years have used many different concepts and asked different questions in seeking to describe teachers' cognitions during interactive teaching. Many of these, such as Schon's influential ideas about 'reflective practice', and Shulman's similarly influential ideas about 'pedagogical content knowledge' (1986, 1987) are more concerned with how teachers **ought** to work than they are grounded in evidence about how teachers **do** work. The use of the term 'professional craft knowledge' in this study is intended to carry minimal assumptions, far less prescriptions, about teachers' cognitions during interactive teaching; and while the preference for that term over such others as 'practical knowledge' (Elbaz, 1983) or 'personal knowledge' (Lampert, 1984, 1985) is intended to imply a concern with the use to which the knowledge is put by teachers in their interactive teaching, an inclusiveness of all the knowledge used by them in that context is also intended.

This choice of terminology does not, of course, provide an escape from ambiguities or from the dangers of misinterpretation. As Tom and Valli (1990) suggest, there is 'great confusion over how craft knowledge ought to be construed' (p. 378). For example, Tom's (1984) own use of the term to celebrate 'the moral craft of teaching' and Elliott's (1989) pejorative use of the term in unfavourable comparison with 'professional' knowledge carry value judgements not intended by the use of the term in this study.

As this study has grown out of an extensive exploration of experienced teachers' professional craft knowledge carried out by Brown and McIntyre (1986, 1988, 1993), their definition of such knowledge has been adopted by the researcher. They describe it as knowledge that is:

(i) embedded in, and tacitly guiding, teachers' everyday actions in the classroom,

(ii) derived from practical experience rather than formal training,

(iii) seldom made explicit,

(iv) related to the intuitive, spontaneous and routine aspects of teaching rather than to the more reflective and thoughtful activities in which teachers may engage at other times,

(v) reflected in the 'core professionalism' of teachers and their 'theories in use' rather than their 'extended professionalism' and 'espoused theories' (1986, p. 36).

Their study focused on the nature of 'good teaching' of four primary school teachers and twelve from a secondary school, 'good teaching' defined as that judged to be good on the particular occasion by the individual teacher and his or her pupils. Each teacher was observed teaching a unit of work of two to six hours' duration. Following each lesson and again at the end of the unit the teachers were asked to talk about 'those aspects of their teaching which had particularly pleased them, they felt they had done well or had given them satisfaction' (1993, p. 32). The accounts of how each teacher evaluated and talked about his or her teaching were rich and varied, but the researchers' main interest was in determining common concepts across teachers in order to formulate and test generalisations. Figure 1 shows their model of the four main generalisable and interrelated concepts.

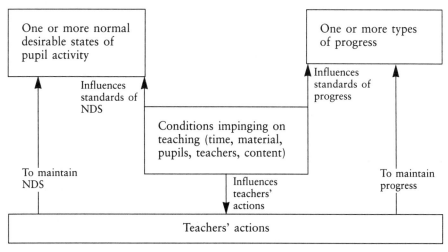

(1993, p. 70)

Figure 1: The concepts which teachers use in evaluating their own teaching

The teachers evaluated their teaching in terms of the attainment of normal desirable states of pupil activity, and types of progress. The teachers' actions and the standards they felt were appropriate for evaluating the extent to which their goals were achieved were profoundly affected by a variety of conditions, the most prominent of which were those relating to the pupils.

Brown and McIntyre's study is important in two respects. First, they appear to have come up with an answer to the question they set themselves when first thinking about the research – 'How can one discover the knowledge and thoughts which underlie the actions of a person who is engaged in a complex interaction with others?' (1993 p. 108). Their study suggests that with a suitable approach it is possible to gain access to teachers' professional craft knowledge. Secondly, while it does not add to understanding of the processes of teachers' interactive thinking, it offers an empirically grounded model of the substance and logic of teachers' professional craft knowledge.

In the Oxford Internship scheme, the relationship between university and school contributions to the learning of the student teachers is based on the assertion that there are no absolute right answers about good teaching; rather there are useful ideas from a variety of sources, all of which need to be critically evaluated by student teachers against diverse criteria of practicality and quality. Sources of knowledge seen as valuable for student teachers include research and theoretical argument, and **equally** ideas embedded in the practice of experienced teachers, the latter of which have first to be accessed and articulated. It is the accessing by student teachers of the knowledge embedded in the practice of experienced teachers that is the focus of this study.

Review of the literature on initial teacher education suggested that it was rare for student teachers to gain access to experienced teachers' craft knowledge, and indeed that little value appeared to be placed on such access. One is led to share the uncertainty expressed by Clark (1989):

> The field of research on teacher thinking is thriving and growing. But what is not so clear is how (or whether) the research can be informative and useful to teacher educators. (p. 305)

Yet if researchers can gain access to, and thence describe, the professional craft knowledge of teachers, is it not possible to learn from their approaches in order to give guidance to student teachers? It was this question that was most fundamental in shaping this study, leading as it did back to the work of Brown and McIntyre (1993). The successful research procedures employed in their study served as the foundation of the empirical study in this project: in order to access the craft knowledge of the teachers with whom they worked in schools, could student teachers use the same general approach as had been used by Brown and McIntyre?

They summarise that approach as:

- Emphasising what was good about the teaching, in the eyes of the teachers and pupils.
- Focusing on specific classroom events which occurred when both teacher and researcher were present.
- Determinedly avoiding the imposition of any researcher preconceptions about good teaching or about how to make sense of teaching.
- Helping teachers to remember what was involved in doing the things they did well, the most important element in this being to interview the teachers very soon after the observed lessons (1993, p. 48).

It is not at all self-evident that student teachers could successfully use such an approach. The above summary greatly simplifies the procedure adopted by the researchers, and gives little indication of the detailed preparation, extensive preliminary negotiations and high level of expertise which characterised the research approach. Furthermore, even if student teachers were able – and indeed willing – to replicate key features of the approach, there was no guarantee that experienced teachers would respond at all in the same way to these novices as they had done to mature and respected researchers.

The broad concern of this project was then with the possibilities and the implications of student teachers effectively gaining access to experienced teachers' craft knowledge, and more specifically with exploring the possibilities of building on the Scottish work of Brown and McIntyre for this purpose. The questions to be investigated were concerned with procedures for gaining access to experienced teachers' craft knowledge as an integral part of an initial teacher education programme, in particular the Oxford Student Internship programme.

To this end a number of studies were conducted over a three year period, mostly but not exclusively by the researcher. Since the purpose of these studies was to collect evidence and thereby acquire understandings leading to successive developments in the procedures to be used, or in the choice of contexts within which they were used, this series of studies can best be understood as following a classical action research pattern. However, this paper is concerned with the research conducted in the final third year of this three year programme. It is furthermore focused on only **one** element of that third year's work.

As a result of the first two years of the research, there had been developed:

a) a suggested set of procedures for student teachers to follow in observing and subsequently interviewing selected experienced teachers;
b) methods and materials for explaining and modelling these procedures to student teachers, and for explaining the rationale for their use;
c) arrangements whereby this aspect of the student teachers' work was firmly embedded in apparently appropriate ways within their whole programme.

The research plans for the third year were designed to answer *inter alia* the question:

> To what extent does the student teachers' use of the various suggested questions and behaviours correlate with the teachers' articulation of the craft knowledge they have used in the observed lesson?

The study was focused on student teachers following the subject programmes in English, Maths and History. As part of their school-based curriculum work in the final term of their three-term course, they were each asked to arrange to observe lessons by two teachers, selected because they were believed to have expertise of interest to the student teacher. As soon as possible after each observed lesson, the teacher was to be interviewed in order to gain access to the craft knowledge used in the lesson, and the interview was to be audio-taped. Meetings were held with each subject group to clarify the purposes, arrangements and rationale for this work.

All but eight of the fifty-six student teachers in English, Maths and History claimed to have audio-taped at least one conversation with a teacher following observation. Four of the tapes, however, were blank, three were inaudible, two were of conversations that had been carried out by student teachers operating as a pair, and on two the conversation with the teacher followed observation of the student teacher's teaching. Other tapes simply failed to materialise as the student teachers, having listened to them for the purposes of their self-evaluation assignment, became embroiled in end of course activities and mislaid the cassettes. For research purposes the final total was forty-eight taped conversations. These included, however, two conversations for each of the majority of the student teachers and since analysis of the conversations proved very time-consuming, in the end analysis was restricted to twenty-eight taped conversations, each involving a different student teacher.

This chapter concentrates on the analysis of these audio-taped conversations for the purpose of answering the above research question.

THE CONTENT ANALYSIS SYSTEM

Before turning to the development of the framework of analysis, reasons for the adoption of a quantitative method of analysis, a content analysis system, are briefly discussed. At a broad level, the choice lay between an approach that systematically analysed all the conversations with certain categories of a pre-determined nature, or an approach which took as its starting point a desire to understand the distinctive concerns, understandings and conversation of each student teacher and teacher, thus making it possible to relate the story of each pair of individuals. The correlational research question above is a closed question formulated in terms of pre-established concepts, and such a question is best addressed through applying the same categories and procedures to all the conversations. The system of analysis had to be one that made possible the operationalisation of the hypothesis on which the research was based, namely that if student teachers adopted the patterns of activity recommended to them then teachers would be more likely to reveal their craft knowledge. Interest lay in what was common to all the conversations and in the nature of variation among them; and even in relation to the nature of variation, concern was more with trying to define the variables so that they could be meaningfully applied to all of the conversations rather than with trying to highlight the uniqueness of each. This interest in issues of commonality as opposed to uniqueness can be more fully described through exemplification. One of the conversations opens with the student teacher talking about the enthusiastic manner in which the pupils in the observed lesson contributed to class discussion, and the teacher gives an account of the various strategies she uses to bring this about. The focus of interest here is not with the particular substance of those strategies, but with whether the student teacher and teacher are talking about teaching strategies, and with how far this talk resulted from the student teacher's use of the suggested questioning procedures.

As well as needing to explore the validity of the hypotheses about facilitating teachers' talk about their craft knowledge – and a content analysis system would meet such a need – the understandings as to the nature of experienced teachers' craft knowledge gleaned from the research carried out by Brown and McIntyre (1993) would provide the basis for the framework for analysis. Above all, the real test for any system of analysis is whether the claims that can be made following the analysis correspond with what the research study is designed to find out and with the concepts explicitly imported by the analyst. In this study content analysis procedures enabled one to examine the extent to which student teachers' and teachers' talk in the conversations following the observed lessons corresponds to the desired patterns, and how the characteristics of student teacher talk are correlated with the desired patterns of teacher talk; and this is what the researcher was primarily interested in finding out from these data.

In any research design using content analysis, the central problem is the establishment of appropriate units and categories: the analyst must decide on the size of the units to be coded, and select and define the categories into which content units are to be classified. For the purposes of this study, the notion of a move as the unit of analysis was adopted from the research of Bellack *et. al.* (1966) into the language of the classroom, since their interest 'in finding out which participant – teacher or student – speaks about what, how much, when, under what conditions, and with what effect' found echoes in the author's focus of concern in relation to the student teacher/teacher conversations. To Bellack's framework of four moves – structuring, soliciting, responding, reacting – was added a fifth – reacting/soliciting – to accommodate probing of the teacher's response that the student teachers had been encouraged to engage in.

To acquire as full an understanding as possible of the student teacher/teacher conversations (which preliminary listening to the audio-tapes suggested were rich and complex), it was necessary to develop a coding system comprising several different facets or dimensions on each of which several categories would be distinguished, with each move analysed in relation to each of the dimensions.

The starting point for the selection and definition of categories was the central hypothesis of the study: if student teacher does 'x', teacher is more likely to do 'y', with 'x' elaborated in the advice that had been given to the student teachers about observation of teachers with follow-up discussion, and 'y' emanating from the work of Brown and McIntyre (1993), which provides an understanding of what the major components of teachers' professional craft knowledge might be like.

Student teachers had been advised to ask open questions, to probe and to focus their attention on the specific lesson observed. In addition, they had been encouraged to ask questions about the teacher's successes or achievements in the lesson, the actions taken to bring about any such achievements, and the reasons for the actions taken. From this advice came the broad categories – or dimensions – of openness, nature of reaction, level of specificity, positiveness and nature of solicitation. From Brown and McIntyre (1993) came the three content dimensions of pedagogical actions, goals, and factors of which account is taken, as well as some of the categories within the latter two.

The central hypothesis then, was the main structuring device in the content analysis system, but the researcher was also interested in being able to describe the main patterns of what took place between student teachers and teachers in the conversations, and so be in a position to answer one of the other research questions, namely:

> Apart from articulating the craft knowledge used in the particular lesson, how else do teachers talk about their teaching, and how does that relate to the part student teachers play in the post-lesson conversation?

Since there were no prior theoretical concepts for coding those things that were not formally specified in the research questions, these additional broad categories were necessarily grounded in the data. The process of developing those categories which were not pre-determined is illustrated in relation to the concept of 'use made of past experience'.

While the central hypothesis concerned both student teachers and teachers focusing on the specific observed lesson, it became apparent that teachers were inclined to refer to other lessons when talking about the observed lesson. In the transcripts, such statements as:

> It's always important to start off this topic with practical experience. When I taught it first, I used to kick off with definitions written up on the board, but that wasn't half as effective . . .

seemed to indicate a potentially interesting and valuable way in which teachers were elaborating on the craft knowledge used in the observed lesson. The decision was made, therefore, to introduce the dimension of 'use made of past experience' to take account of statements of this kind, and further reading of transcripts led to a number of distinctions being made among different ways of using past experience.

Such commonsense distinctions carry no theoretical weight; the modest claim made for them is that they represented – albeit somewhat crudely – the use student teachers and teachers made of past experience in the conversations. The same process applied to two further dimensions, namely, 'mental activites in relation to teaching' and 'how the teacher knows and understands'. These were aspects of the conversations that were recognised as related to craft knowledge and as potentially useful to student teachers, but they had not been formally specified in the research questions, nor were the distinctions drawn based on theory; again, the categories were born of common sense logic.

The process of development through which a final system was arrived at was both lengthy and detailed. As Holsti (1968) points out:

> the analyst is often faced with the task of constructing appropriate categories by trial-and-error methods. This process usually consists of moving back and forth from theory to data, testing the usefulness of tentative categories, and then modifying them in the light of data. (p. 646)

Since the research questions went beyond the central hypothesis, as well as extensively reading the transcripts to test and elaborate the *a priori* definitions in order that they could be made sensitive to the data without violating or distorting the initial concepts, it was necessary to refine those categories developed in response to the data. The process was further complicated by the need to develop categories that would encompass the ways of thinking of both student teachers and teachers, an especially challenging task in the light of the evidence from, among others, Calderhead (1983), Housner and Griffey (1985), and Berliner (1987, 1988), that suggests that they are likely to have different ways of thinking about teaching and use different language when talking about it.

In developing the categories, then, the aim was to make distinctions that were practically viable, preserved the clarity of the concepts, and were potentially useful in relation to the general concern of getting access to professional craft knowledge. This was no easy task, and issues of operationalisation abounded.

Reliability study

In order to check on the reliability of the coding system, a second coder was trained and transcripts of three conversations, which turned out to involve about 120 moves, were coded independently by the two coders.

Using Scott's Coefficient (1955) as a measure of coder reliability, the formula for which is:

$$\Pi = \frac{po - pe}{1 - pe}$$ Where po is the actual proportion of agreement and pe is the expected proportion of agreement by chance

the coders found that they were much more successful in agreeing on what categories things belonged to than they were in noticing instances of things. Subsequent discussion of instances noticed by one coder but not the other confirmed that when attention was drawn to a particular phrase there was rarely disagreement on what it was an instance of; but noticing all such instances, embedded as they were in complex texts, proved difficult.

In the light of the lessons learned from the reliability trial, and especially the fuller and clearer operational rules that were subsequently developed, a second small scale reliability trial was carried out with the second independent coder. This trial seemed to show that the new rules had considerably improved the system's reliability. Forty moves were coded, involving 260 or more decisions or identifications. The two coders disagreed on only twelve of these decisions, nine of these disagreements being concerned with factors taken account of, a dimension that was subsequently simplified.

The content system finally arrived at is presented in the following section within tables which report descriptive information on the extent to which student teachers followed the suggested guidelines in relation to specificity, openness, positiveness and probing, and on the patterns of student teachers' and teachers' talk.

DESCRIPTIVE EVIDENCE ABOUT THE CONVERSATIONS

Specificity

In order to access the knowledge and expertise used by the teacher in the observed lesson, student teachers had been encouraged to relate their questions to the particular lesson observed, and to avoid framing questions as generalisations. Of interest, therefore, was the extent to which both the student teachers' questions and the teachers' responses were related to the observed lesson.

Table 1

Level of specificity	% within different types of move		
	intern solicitations	intern reacting/solicitations	teacher responses
(a) particular action, event, section, phase or aspect of the observed lesson, including products of the lesson and thinking about the lesson	49	37	42
(b) on another specified occasion or other specified occasions – including those in the future – focus on particular action, event, section, phase or aspect of the lesson or lessons	6	7	7
(c) a move formulated in terms of a generalisation which is nonetheless concerned with, or is closely tied to, a specific aspect of the observed lesson which is explicitly mentioned in that move or in a related prior move	26	31	23
(d) a generalisation that is not directly related to an action, event etc., as above	19	26	28

Nature of reaction

This dimension of the system applied only to REACTING and REACTING/SOLIC-ITING moves and was operated as a sign system rather than a category system. Student teachers had been encouraged to help teachers to talk about the observed teaching by probing responses and asking for elaboration. They had, on the other hand, been expressly discouraged from asking questions which led teachers to try and justify their teaching. It was important, therefore, to distinguish between a probe seeking clarification and/or elaboration, and one seeking justification.

Table 2

Nature of reaction	Average % in all interns reacting and reacting/soliciting moves
(a) assent or dissent	
1. an expressed agreement or concurrence with the views to which it is a reaction e.g. *Yes, I quite agree That's how I see it Agreed Exactly*	25
2. an expressed disagreement or lack of concurrence with the views expressed to which it is a reaction e.g. *No I disagree I can't go along with you there*	1
(b) affect – an expression of emotion in relation to what was said in the move occasioning the reaction	
1. positive – expression of emotion in relation to what was said in the move occasioning the reaction e.g. *That's great Thank you That's very interesting*	5
2. negative – expression(s) of displeasure, horror, anger, shock, alarm, desbelief e.g. *What! Your must be joking! You really believe that!*	0.5
(c) qualification – expression of a reservation about the adequacy or inadequacy of the view(s) which was being assented to or dissented from e.g. *Yes, but it's not always that simple Perhaps Not in all cases*	4
(d) elaboration – that part of the reacting or reacting/soliciting move that extends or exemplifies a theme already present in the move that occasioned the reacting or reacting/soliciting move	24
(e) probing – that part of the reacting/soliciting move which digs into what has been said in the move occasioning it to seek either:	
1. clarification and/or elaboration e.g. *Could you say a bit more about that?*	38
2. justification e.g. *Are you sure they were listening?*	2

Nature of solicitation

Since student teachers had been encouraged to seek explanations of why teachers had done things or how they had done or achieved things, these two kinds of explanation were distinguished, and everything else put in a residual category.

Table 3

Type of solicitation	% of intern solicitations	
	solicitations	reactions/solicitations
(a) solicitation seeking causal or purposive explanations	25	19
Example: When you actually started looking at them, the documents, did you decide to read them out yourself because you didn't want to allow any room for disruption, and them reading it out?		
(b) solicitation seeking procedural explanations	16	9
Example: How did you manage to get that group at the back to take the work seriously?		
(c) residual category	59	72
Example: So when you first started out teaching, did you ever follow an approach?		

Although student teachers had not been asked to concentrate exclusively on questions seeking explanations, it was nonetheless disappointing that the purely descriptive type of question (type c) tended to be dominant.

Student teacher solicitations: openness

It is clear that on a very wide scale, student teachers either were not persuaded of the merits of asking open questions (type a), or that they found it difficult to ask such questions. In most of the twenty-eight conversations, the split between open questions (including type b, partially open), and closed questions (type c) was around 50%.

Table 4

Degree of openness	% of intern solicitations	
	solicitations	reaction/solicitations
(a) open – respondent free to construct a response *I noticed that you let the pupils decide which groups to work in* and *What were your particular reasons for getting them into groups?*	42	19
(b) partially open – either a solicitation to which the respondent is left to construct a response, but the solicitation only makes sense on the basis of an assumption made by the solicitor about the respondent's concerns or reasoning: *When you asked that question why did you think it would motivate the class?*, or a solicitation in which the respondent is offered a suggestion to assent or to dissent from and is also offered an open alternative: *Did you let them pack up early because they'd finished or what?*	4	1
(c) closed – a solicitation to which either the response could be simply 'yes' or 'no': *Did you move him because he was misbehaving?*, or a solicitation which invites the respondent to choose from among suggestions given by the solicitor *Did you ask the girls at the back to lead the discussion because they're bright or because they were messing about?*	53	79

Student teacher solicitations: evaluation

Although the student teachers were not specifically asked to make positive evaluations in their questions, it was suggested that they should focus the questions on things that had gone well in the lesson, and so one might expect positive evaluation in them. It is, therefore, interesting to note that while in the great majority of questions, evaluations were neither positive nor negative, none were negative.

Table 5

Evaluation	% of intern solicitations
1. positive	10
2. negative	0
3. qualified	90

CONTENT DIMENSIONS

The content dimensions of the twenty-eight conversations are examined in relation to teacher talk – which embraces all teacher moves – and student teacher initiating moves which cover three types of student move – structuring, soliciting and reacting/soliciting. Since interest is in the ways in which the teachers talked in these conversations, all teacher moves were coded for content dimensions. The interest in the student teachers, on the other hand, is in the ways in which they initiate conversation through questions or assertions. The number of student teacher responding moves is negligible (twelve out of a total number of student teacher moves of 773), and although student teacher reacting moves are plentiful, they typically contain no substantive matter. The data for the content dimensions, therefore, are gleaned from the 746 moves which constitute teacher talk, and 585 student teacher initiating moves.

Pedagogical actions

Pedagogical actions were coded using a single category and refer only to pedagogical actions or decisions taken.

Table 6

	Proportion of moves in which pedagogical actions are mentioned
intern initiating moves	0.68
teacher talk	0.69

Outcomes – intended and otherwise

To capture the diversity and complexity of teachers' talk in relation to goals, it was necessary to establish two facets within this single dimension. One of these distinguishes desired outcomes from actual outcomes, and further differentiates among the desired outcomes in terms of the degrees of confidence expressed in their achievement – expectations, goals, hopes. The second facet is concerned with kinds of outcome, and here two further categories were added to those based on Brown and McIntyre's findings. The first focused on pupil teacher relationships and matters of 'rapport' and, as with the other categories, was couched in positive terms. The second was a residual category of 'other or unspecified outcomes' and catered mainly for unwanted outcomes as in the following extract from one of the conversations:

> *Teacher*: Yeah if, if I'd said at the beginning we've got four or five documents here I want you to get into pairs, and here are the questions, and go away and sort them through, I'd have been in the situation that five or six of them wouldn't have concentrated at all, for a number of reasons. They wouldn't have understood what it was, and they weren't prepared to concentrate or even try and understand it. They partly couldn't understand it, but even with me reading, they weren't prepared to work.

Table 7

Type of outcome	% of total no. of outcomes	
	intern initiating moves	teacher talk moves
(a) short-term progress expression of desire for change – actual or considered – in the pupils in terms of their attitude, learning acquired, skills mastered, artefacts produced, coverage of work. Such changes – actual or considered – are deemed to be short-term if related to the particular observed lessons or the particular topic, scheme of work or skill being taught within the particular lesson	17	26
(b) long-term effect(s) on pupils as (a) above, but relating to a time span that goes beyond the particular topic, scheme of work or skill being taught in the particular observed lesson	0.8	2
(c) desirable state of pupils or of pupil activity	32	28
(d) desirable kind of lesson/atmosphere/ teacher-pupil relationship/pupil-pupil relationship	9	12
(e) other or unspecified outcomes	41	33
Average no. of outcomes per move	0.44	1.16

Table 8

Nature of intentionality of outcome	% of total number of outcomes	
	intern initiating moves	teacher talk moves
1. expectations	4	6
2. goals (intended outcome)	32	42
3. hopes or aspirations	2	5
4. outcome(s)	63	47

Factors of which account is taken

Table 9

Kinds of factor of which account is taken	Percentage of total number of factors	
	intern initiating moves	teacher talk
(a) pupils		
1. individual pupil(s); 2. identified sub-group; 3. class or part of class; 4. classes; 5. year/age group; 6. pupils in general; 7. consideration of differences among pupils – 'they're all individuals'; 8. pupil state (tired, bored, noisy, finished work, way in which they're responding etc.); 9. pupils' knowledge, understandings, pre-conceptions, attitudes, aptitudes	66	69
(b) time	5	4
1. amount of time for, or within, lesson; 2. time of day, week, term, year		
(c) resources	3	3
(d) content	13	14
(e) phase	5	3
1. within lesson; 2. observed lesson within a series of lessons with the class		
(f) social acceptability – perceptions, attitudes, opinions of others such as colleagues, senior managers, governors, parents, local community	0.3	0.3
(g) teacher state – including perceived skills, ability, 'type' of teacher	7	5
(h) curriculum/examination considerations	0.3	0
(i) classroom circumstances created by the teacher (e.g. group work)	1	1
(j) awareness of being a teacher in the classroom	0	0
Average no. per conversation	10	45
Average no. per move	0.48	1.69

A striking feature of the data summarised in Table 9 is the similarity between the teachers and the student teachers in the kind of factors to which they referred in the conversations. The other significant feature concerning the different kinds of factors is the extent to which teachers referred to pupil factors. Teachers' preoccupation with pupil-associated factors when setting goals or taking pedagogical action is not surprising, echoing as it does the evidence provided by Brown and McIntyre (1993); rather it reassuringly suggests that in the conversations teachers were articulating their classroom craft knowledge.

Mental activities in relation to teaching

Within this dimension, the concern was with the kinds of processes the teacher is engaged in when making decisions rather than with what is decided.

Table 10

Mention of mental activites: average no. per conversation	Intern initiating moves	Teacher talk
	4	12
Category	Total no. of mentions	
(a) planning 1. planning or re-planning engaged in before the lesson; 2. planning or re-planning engaged in during the lesson; 3. future planning; 4. residual category – disconnected planning	24	27
(b) evaluation of teaching 1. positive; 2. negative; 3. qualified	35	120
(c) alternative – instead of another – when there is consideration or an action or intended outcome as an alternative to an action or intended outcome that has been explicitly mentioned within the move or a prior move. 1. action(s); 2. intended outcomes(s)	13	74
(d) hypothetical considerations – the option(s) available for the teacher in different circumstances 1. action(s); 2. intended outcomes(s)	21	69

Table 10: continued

Mention of mental activites: average no. per conversation	Intern initiating moves	Teacher talk
	4	12

Category	Total no. of mentions	
(e) validity of expectations or predictions	0	3
(f) use made of past experience 1. learning from experience; 2. aspect of particular observed lesson to illuminate a past problem; 3. drawing on past experience to extend the discussion about the particular case	3	24
(g) how the teacher knows and understands	14	33

Evaluation as a mental activity applies to all types of move but only when there is explicit evidence of direct or indirect evaluation of teaching including goals, expectations, aspirations and outcomes. In so far as they evaluated the teaching, the student teachers, in accordance with the guidelines, were overwhelmingly positive: of the 35 student teacher evaluations, 26 were positive, eight negative (three of which concerned their own teaching), and one qualified. The teachers talked in quite evaluative terms about their teaching, both positively and negatively: of their 120 evaluations, 54 were positive, 49 negative and 17 qualified. Teachers varied not in terms of whether they were positive or negative, but in how evaluative they were.

Actions, outcomes and factors – links

Table 11

Number of links in conversation	0	1–9	10–19	20–29	30–39	40–49	50+	average no. per conversation
student	0	18	7	2	1	0	0	9
teacher	0	2	8	9	3	2	4	28

As might reasonably be expected, the number of links in teacher talk is considerably greater than in student teacher initiating moves. This difference between the two groups is underlined by the fact that, in spite of wide variation among the teachers, in every conversation the teacher made more links than did the student teacher.

CORRELATIONS AMONG VARIABLES

Operationalising the hypothesis

As explained earlier, the whole content analysis system had been devised largely for the purpose of operationalising the hypothesis that if student teachers adopted the patterns of activity recommended to them then teachers would be more likely to reveal their craft knowledge. Nonetheless, a further step was necessary at this stage in order to define and select the precise variables which would be included in the correlational analysis. What variables that could be derived from the content analysis best reflected the ways in which the student teachers had been encouraged to act? What variables best reflected the researcher's defined conception of craft knowledge? Also, were there other variables about which the researcher wished to ask correlational questions?

The advice given to the student teachers had been largely in relation to their questioning, and therefore to the talk which had been coded as solicitation and reaction/solicitation moves. The attitudes reflected in their reacting moves were also relevant. It was therefore in relation to these three types of move – which accounted for 94% of student teacher talk – that the 'independent' variables concerning student teacher activity were formulated.

In particular, the different elements of activity in which student teachers had been advised to engage were operationalised by the characterisation of each conversation in terms of the following thirteen student teacher variables:

Openness

1. The proportion of student teacher solicitation and reaction/solicitation moves that had been categorised as open.
2. The proportion of such moves categorised as closed.

Specificity

3. The proportion of such moves that had been categorised as concerned with an aspect of the specific observed lesson (level of specificity a).
4. The proportion of such moves categorised as concerned with an aspect of a lesson or lessons on another specified occasion(s) – level of specificity b – in addition to those categorised as of level specificity a.
5. The proportion of such moves formulated in terms of a generalisation directly related to an aspect of the particular observed lesson, and of

which mention had been made – level of specificity c – in addition to those categorised as of level a and of b.

Type of question

6. The proportion of such moves categorised as type A ('why') questions.
7. The proportion of such moves categorised as type B ('how') questions.
8. The proportion of such moves categorised as type C ('what') questions.

Evaluation

9. The proportion of such moves categorised as positive evaluation.
10. The ratio of reactions expressing agreement to the total number of reacting and reacting/soliciting moves.
11. The total number of reactions categorised as positive affect.
12. The total number of reactions categorised as expressing qualification.

Probing

13. The ratio of reaction/solicitation moves to solicitation moves.

In relation to the teachers, all kinds of talk in which they had engaged were seen as relevant to the extent to which they had revealed their craft knowledge. With the exception of those variables concerned with specificity (teacher variables 10, 11 and 12), all the 'dependent' variables were therefore formulated in terms of all teacher talk in all their conversational moves.

Working from Brown and McIntyre's (1993) account of the nature of teachers' professional craft knowledge, each conversation was characterised in terms of the following sixteen teacher variables:

Factors of which account is taken

1. The total number of mentions of factors in teacher talk.
2. The average number of factors per teacher talk move.

Outcomes

3. The average number of outcomes per teacher talk move categorised as a (short-term progress), c (desirable state of pupils or of pupil activity), d (desirable kind of lesson), or e (general or residual outcomes).
4. The average number of outcomes per teacher talk move categorised as a, c, or d.

Pedagogical actions

5. The proportion of teacher talk moves in which mention was made of pedagogical action.

Links

6. The total number of links in teacher talk in the conversation.
7. The average number of links per teacher talk move.

Mental activities

8. The total number of mentions of those things categorised as mental activities in relation to teaching in teacher talk in the conversation.
9. The average number of mentions of mental activities per teacher talk move within the conversation.

Specificity
Taking account of all teacher moves for which specificity was coded, that is all moves with the exception of reacting moves, each conversation was characterised by:

10. The proportion of such moves that had been categorised as concerned with an aspect of the specific observed lesson (level of specificity a)
11. The proportion of such moves categorised as concerned with an aspect of a lesson or lessons on another specified occasion(s) – level of specificity b – in addition to those categorised as of level specificity a.
12. The proportion of such moves formulated in terms of a generalisation directly related to an aspect of the particular observed lesson, and of which mention had been made – level of specificity c – in addition to those categorised as of level a and of b.

Teacher knowledge and understanding

13. The total number of those things categorised as how the teacher knows and understands.
14. The average number of such mentions per teacher talk move.

Use of past experience

15. The total number of those things categorised as use of past experience.
16. The average number of such mentions per teacher talk move.

The correlational analysis

The variables for inclusion in this analysis having been formulated, it was necessary to determine the precise type of analysis that would be appropriate. The first step was to find simple correlation coefficients between individual variables, and therefore the question to be asked was about the measure of correlation that was most appropriate for this purpose. Ideally, the Pearson product-moment correlation would be used – if its use could be justified – since it would take account of all the information available. Of the three conditions that need to be satisfied in order to use it, the first, that the variables should be on an interval scale, was clearly met, since the variables were either simple counts or proportions derived from such counts. The second, that the distributions should not be highly skewed, was met in most though not all cases. The third condition, that there should be linear regression between the two variables, was checked visually and again appeared to be met in most cases.

As a further check on the appropriateness of the Pearson coefficient, the data were analysed using it and also using the Spearman Rank Difference coefficient. In general the results were very similar, although the Spearman analysis showed more moderately high correlations of around .30–.35. In these circumstances use of the Pearson results seemed justified and indeed safer.

The nature of any further analysis had to depend on the results of this basic analysis, and especially on the relationships among the student teacher variables and among the teacher variables. It was not clear in advance to what extent either the dependent (teacher) variables or the independent (student teacher) variables would be related to each other. The value of, for example, multiple regression analysis would depend on the strength of these inter-relations.

The findings in terms of the Pearson correlation coefficients are therefore presented and discussed in three successive sub-sections, showing correlations among student teacher variables, those among teacher variables and finally those between student teacher and teacher variables.

Student teacher variables

The correlation coefficients presented in Table 12 suggest first that those correlations between variables which are defined in related terms are consistent with those definitions. Open and closed questions, for example, are strongly negatively correlated, and, as expected, the levels of specificity (variables 3, 4 and 5) are strongly positively correlated. Similarly, the proportion of the residual type C (mostly 'what') questions is strongly negatively correlated with the proportion of type A ('why') questions, and to a lesser extent with type B ('how') questions. There is, however, no marked relationship between the incidence of type A questions and of type B questions. These correlations, which virtually follow from the definitions of variables, account for about half of all the correlations above 0.3. Nevertheless, the remaining high correlations are of considerable interest.

The findings in relation to the three types of student teacher questions are interesting, and in some cases, puzzling. Type A or 'why' questions are highly positively correlated with specificity A suggesting that questions seeking purposive explanations were predominantly focused on the particular observed lesson. There is, however, no connection between type A ('why') questions and degree of openness of the question.

Type B ('how') questions, on the other hand, are unrelated to specificity, while the 'what' or residual questions – type C – are negatively correlated with all three measures of specificity. These correlations, together with those between positive evaluation and specificity, and between positive affect and specificity, indicate that three elements of student teacher behaviour seen as desirable – specificity of questions, 'why' type questions and positiveness – are associated, which in turn might suggest that the student teachers were more or less attentive to the guidelines as a whole. However, the other two elements of the guidelines, probing and openness, far from being associated with this cluster of correlations, are negatively correlated with each other, in addition to which probing is negatively correlated with specificity.

To throw further light on the suggestion that there might be a general tendency for student teachers to be more or less attentive to the guidelines (but not in all respects), a principal components factor analysis was carried out on the student teacher variables. According to the Kaiser criterion of significance (eigenvalues >1), five factors were significant. Varimax rotation did not lead to a very different or clearer picture, so it is the unrotated factors which are shown in Table 13.

The first factor, accounting for one third of the total variance, confirms the suggestion of a general tendency to conform more or less with the guidelines, and also offers very clear confirmation that this tendency does not extend to the openness of questions and that it incorporates a tendency not to probe. Of course, the size of this factor might be seen to be 'artificially' enhanced by the inclusion of three measures of specificity, but it extends well beyond specificity in its scope.

The second factor, accounting for 20% of the variance, is overwhelmingly concerned with openness and closedness, two important variables that have minimal loadings on the first factor.

Factor 3 is interesting in its opposition of positive evaluation and positive affect to type A ('why') questions and probes, suggesting how real is the danger that was emphasised in the guidelines of 'why?' being interpreted by those asking the questions as a search for justification, not a search for explanation.

Factors 4 and 5 account for relatively little variance and it seems difficult to interpret them in any illuminating way.

Table 12: Pearson product-moment correlation coefficients between selected student-teacher variables (only those correlations >.30 or <.30 are presented)

Student variables	1. open	2. closed	3. spec A	4. spec A+B	5. spec A+B+C	6. why questions	7. how questions	8. what questions	9. eval	10. agreement	11. positive affect	12. qualification	13. probing
1. OPEN % open questions	**1**	-.91										-.42	
2. CLOSED % closed questions	-.91	**2**											.38
3. SPECIFICITY A % in student initiating moves			**3**	.95	.74	.61		-.69			.42		
4. SPECIFICITY A+B %			.95	**4**	.80	.52		-.61					-.46
5. SPECIFICITY A+B+C %			.74	.80	**5**	.43		-.48	.36				-.50
6. 'WHY' QUESTIONS % type A questions			.61	.52	.43	**6**		-.81					
7. 'HOW' QUESTIONS % type B questions							**7**	-.48					
8. 'WHAT' QUESTIONS % type C questions			-.69	-.61	-.48	-.81	-.48	**8**	.36				
9. EVALUATION % positive evaluation					.36				**9**				
10. AGREEMENT No. agreements per reacting + reacting/soliciting move										**10**			
11. POSITIVE AFFECT No. per reacting + reacting/soliciting move			.42								**11**		
12. QUALIFICATION No. per reacting + reacting/soliciting move	-.42											**12**	
13. PROBING Ratio rea/sol to solicitation		.38		-.46	-.50								**13**

The factor analysis results are thus consistent with the most obvious interpretation of the results from the raw correlations. In particular, they suggest that there is a factor concerned with more or less conformity to the general guidance offered, but that such a factor excludes openness and probing.

Table 13: Principal components analysis for student teacher variables

Student teacher variables	Factor 1	Factor 2	Factor 3	Factor 4	Factor 5
1. open	0.07	−0.93	0.08	−0.21	0.18
2. closed	−0.12	0.89	−0.24	0.28	−0.05
3. specificity a	0.92	0.12	−0.05	−0.02	0.18
4. specificity a + b	0.90	0.16	0.03	0.09	0.16
5. specificity a + b + c	0.83	0.34	0.18	0.24	−0.01
6. type a questions	0.66	0.15	−0.53	−0.41	0.10
7. type b questions	0.40	−0.43	−0.09	0.52	−0.16
8. type c questions	−0.79	0.17	0.51	0.08	0.01
9. positive evaluation	0.14	0.36	0.63	0.21	0.46
10. reactions-agreement	0.45	−0.31	0.01	0.36	−0.36
11. reactions positive affect	0.48	0.04	0.46	−0.52	0.13
12. reactions qualified	0.11	0.47	0.18	−0.42	−0.64
13. probes (rea/sols)	−0.54	0.26	−0.56	−0.01	0.39
Percentage of Variance Accounted for	31.9	20.3	11.4	9.8	8.5

Teacher variables

As with the student teacher variables, certain correlations are high almost by definition. Thus the correlations between the different but overlapping measures of the frequency of outcomes mentioned, and again between measures of specificity of talk, come into this category. For activities with relatively low frequency, this is also the case where both total frequency in conversation and frequency per move are included as variables: this is the case for mental activities, for teacher knowledge and for past experience.

For more frequently occurring phenomena such as links and factors, however, the total and average frequency variables tend not to be positively correlated. Indeed, they appear to be related to quite different sets of variables. The three variables defined in terms of total numbers – of links, factors and mental activities – are all highly correlated with one another, and negatively correlated with the proportion of moves in which pedagogical actions were mentioned. It seems that perhaps the more moves there were in a conversation, the more there would be of most things: links, factors, mental activities and moves in which there is no mention of pedagogical actions.

Of greater interest, however, are the correlations among variables defined in terms of proportions and averages. There are strong patterns of intercorrelation among measures of outcomes, of specificity, and average

Table 14 Pearson product-moment correlation coefficients among selected teacher variables

Teacher variables	1. Total factors	2. Av. factors	3. A, C, D, E	4. A, C, D	5. ped act.	6. No. links	7. av. links	8. no. m.a. links	9. av. m.a.	10. spec a	11. spec a+b	12. spec a+b+c	13. teacher know no.	14. t.k. average	15. P.E. No.	16. P.E. average
1 Total factors	**1**															
2. Average factors		**2**														
3. Outcomes A, C, D, E		.50	**3**													
4. Outcomes A, C, D		.58	.89	**4**												
5. Pedagogical actions	-.55		.44	.42	**5**											
6. Number links	.94				-.54	**6**										
7. Average links		.85	.62	.60	.56		**7**									
8. Number mental activities	.47					.53		**8**								
9. Average mental activities		.38	.62	.44			.44	.46	**9**							
10. Specificity A			.52	.51			.38			**10**						
11. Specificity A+B			.56	.52			.41			.95	**11**					
12. Specificity A+B+C			.50	.43			.39			.75	.84	**12**				
13. Teacher knowledge - number													**13**			
14. Teacher knowledge - average													.77	**14**		
15. Past experience - number					-.47										**15**	
16. Past experience - average															.83	**16**

numbers of factors, links, mental activities and pedagogical actions. Such associations seem to point to the existence of a general craft knowledge factor within teacher talk.

The four variables concerned with past experience and with how the teacher knows or understands show no close connection with any of the other twelve teacher variables.

Again it seemed appropriate to explore these interconnections among variables by conducting a principal components analysis. According to the Kaiser criterion, six significant factors were extracted, as shown in Table 15. As for the student teacher factors, Varimax rotation of the six teacher factors did not produce any significantly different patterns and therefore is not reported here. The two smallest factors again offer no apparent illumination, while the only variables with significant loading in Factors 3 and 4 are how the teacher knows and understands, and past experience respectively, variables which are confirmed as being quite distinct from the others. The discussion therefore focuses on Factors 1 and 2.

Table 15:   Principal components analysis for teacher variables

Teacher variables	Factor 1	Factor 2	Factor 3	Factor 4	Factor 5	Factor 6
1. total factors	0.14	0.87	0.11	−0.36	−0.01	0.24
2. average factors	0.71	0.0	0.06	−0.36	−0.09	0.49
3. outcomes − A,C,D,E	0.87	−0.06	−0.11	0.01	0.25	−0.03
4. outcomes − A,C,D	0.83	0.0	−0.10	0.02	0.21	0.13
5. pedagogical actions	0.47	−0.73	−0.17	0.08	−0.06	0.15
6. total links	0.13	0.90	0.14	−0.28	−0.04	0.17
7. average links	0.78	−0.27	0.06	−0.20	0.03	0.44
8. total mental activities	0.35	0.56	−0.03	−0.18	0.38	−0.54
9. average mental activities	0.57	−0.23	−0.19	−0.80	0.6	−0.32
10. specificity A	0.72	0.19	0.26	0.49	−0.17	−0.11
11. specificity A+B	0.75	0.20	0.27	0.49	−0.18	−0.12
12. specificity A+B+C	0.71	0.23	0.11	0.33	−0.43	−0.10
13. total how the teacher knows	−0.25	0.07	0.86	0.16	0.31	0.54
14. average how the teacher knows	−0.30	−0.40	0.73	0.13	0.34	0.15
15. total past experience	−0.35	0.58	−0.27	0.49	0.24	0.34
16. average past experience	−0.29	0.22	−0.43	0.66	0.35	0.30
Percentage of Variance Accounted for	32.5	20.0	11.4	10.8	7.9	7.5

Again the factor analysis would appear to confirm the findings from the simple correlations. Dominating Factor 1, which accounts for a third of the variance, are average number of factors, outcomes, average number of links, specificity, average number of mental activities and pedagogical actions; the combination of these variables suggests that Teacher Factor 1 is a general craft knowledge factor.

Factor 2, representing 20% of the variance, is concerned with total number of factors, number of links and number of mental activities, indicating that it is a length of conversation factor.

Correlations between student teacher and teacher variables

The central hypothesis is that teachers are more likely to articulate their craft knowledge in so far as student teachers question them in ways consistent with the guidelines they were offered. In so far as this hypothesis is interpreted as being about correlations, it is the correlations between the selected student teacher and teacher variables that are crucial. It is of course important to avoid over-interpreting the data and implying that any causal relationships can be demonstrated: the design of the research – at least the quantitative component of it – allows no such inferences to be made.

It is the basic correlations between student teacher and teacher variables which are of primary importance. However, in the light of the findings reported with regard to correlations among student teacher variables and among teacher variables, it is to be expected that any strong patterns of correlation in terms of specific variables are likely to be reflected in correlations between the student teacher factors and the teacher factors. Table 16 reports the correlations between specific student teacher and teacher variables, and Table 17 the correlations between the first three student teacher factors and the first two teacher factors.

Table 16 shows that among the highest correlations are those between the levels of specificity of student teacher questions and the levels of specificity of teacher talk. Although perhaps predictable, this was far from an inevitable finding and it is important in itself. In addition, given the demonstrated connections both between student teacher specificity and other student teacher variables and also between teacher specificity and other teacher variables, it suggests a wider pattern of correlations between student teacher and teacher variables. Table 16 confirms such a pattern, with student teacher specificity also being associated with teachers' talk about factors, outcomes and links, and with 'why' and 'how' questions posed by the student teachers, and positive affect on their part being variously associated with teacher specificity and talk about factors and links. The openness or closedness of student teacher questions seems to have very limited relationships with the selected teacher talk variables, while student teacher probing appears to be associated with a lack of specificity on the part of teachers.

Table 17 confirms and summarises these findings. Especially significant is the correlation of 0.73 between the student teacher Factor 1 (interpreted as general but not comprehensive conformity with the guidelines) and the teacher Factor 1 (interpreted as general articulation of craft knowledge). Because of the importance of this general relationship, the two sets of factor scores were plotted against one another, as shown in Figure 2. That figure shows very clearly a linear regression relationship between the two factor variables. In particular, there is no apparent tendency in these findings similar to that suggested by McAlpine *et. al.* (1988) for some teachers effectively

Table 16 Pearson product-moment correlation coefficients Teacher Variables between student teacher and teacher variables

Student Variables	1. Total factors	2. Average factors	3. Out. A, C, D, E	4. Out. A, C, D	5. Ped. actions	6. Total links	7. Average links	8. Total mental activities	9. Av. mental activities	10. Spec. A	11. Spec. A+B	12. Spec. A+B+C	13. T.K. Total	14. T.K. Ave.	15. P.E. Total	16. P.E. Ave.
1. Open																
2. Closed						.38										
3. Specificity A		.44					.40			.82	.80	.78				
4. Specificity A+B			.46	.38						.79	.82	.82				
5. Specificity A+B+C				.45			.51			.63	.70	.86				
6. 'Why' questions										.55	.47	.48				
7. 'How' questions							.46			.40						
8. 'What' questions										-.72	-.60	-.51				
9. Evaluation																
10. Agreement		.40					.38									
11. Positive affect		.43									.45	.41				
12. Qualification					-.51											
13. Probing										-.38	-.46	-.58			.49	

to articulate their craft knowledge despite 'inappropriate' questioning from student teachers.

Thus, the correlational evidence, summarised by this high correlation between these major student and teacher factors and the linear relationship indicated in Figure 2, is strongly supportive of the central hypothesis with which this quantitative analysis is concerned.

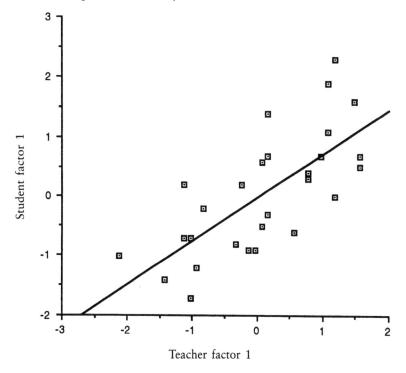

Figure 2 Factor scores for teachers and students: teacher factor 1: student factor 1

Of the other correlations reported in Table 17, three are negligible, but the other two are possibly large enough to be of interest: they indicate, albeit very tentatively, that a positive attitude on the part of the student teacher, combined with a tendency not to probe or ask 'why' questions, may be conducive in a limited way both to teachers' articulation of their craft knowledge and to longer conversations.

Table 17

	Teachers – Factor 1	Teachers – Factor 2
Students – Factor 1	0.73	0.03
Students – Factor 2	0.09	−0.08
Students – Factor 3	0.25	0.27

SUMMARY AND CONCLUSIONS

The research reported in this chapter, the quantitative part of a larger study concerned with the problems and possibilities for student teachers of gaining access to the 'professional craft knowledge' of experienced teachers, was based primarily on:

(a) the fairly well elaborated concepts in terms of which guidance was offered to student teachers about how they might engage in post-lesson conversations with experienced teachers;
(b) the understanding of teachers' professional craft knowledge derived from Brown and McIntyre's (1993) conclusions;
(c) the hypothesis that those student teachers who most fully followed the guidance given would be most likely to gain access to teachers' craft knowledge.

The detailed quantitative findings suggest many specific issues on which action might usefully be taken in any future attempts to refine the procedure used, and to clarify and elaborate on its purposes. However, many of the results can be summarised in terms of four main propositions:

1. The parts played by the student teachers in the conversations corresponded with varying degrees of closeness to the guidance they had been given. In general, they tended to

   • adopt a questioning role
   • be positive (or at least avoid being negative) about the observed teaching
   • ask follow-up questions
   • focus on the specific lessons

   On the other hand, their activities corresponded less consistently with the advice to

   • ask open questions
   • ask questions seeking explanations
   • ask follow-up questions of the kind that probed more deeply and fully the teachers' initial responses

2. In many respects, and especially in the kinds of outcomes they emphasised, the multiplicity of factors and links they discussed, and the concentration especially on pupil factors, the talk of the teachers tended to be similar to teachers' articulation of their craft knowledge as described by Brown and McIntyre (1993).

3. A strong linear relationship was revealed between the extent to which student teachers tended broadly to follow the guidance offered and the extent to which the teachers with whom they engaged in the exercise appeared to articulate their craft knowledge.

4. The readiness of student teachers to follow certain aspects of the guidance offered was **not** statistically related to teachers' apparent articulation of their craft knowledge; in particular, **openness** and **probing** were not positively correlated with such articulation. It is perhaps significant that these were two aspects of the suggested pattern of questioning which student teachers seemed least inclined to follow in the intended ways.

This study suggests that it is possible for student teachers to access experienced teachers' craft knowledge through the adoption of procedures broadly similar to those used by Brown and McIntyre (1993) when interviewing teachers following observation of their teaching. It also reveals that in two areas – those of openness and probing – the procedure needs to be reappraised.

For Brown and McIntyre (1993), openness was 'a crucial strand' of their research strategy:

> Openness on our part was seen as essential if the teachers were to be encouraged to bring to consciousness their own perceptions, concepts and decision-making processes. (p. 36)

Student teachers are, however, in a different social situation from that of researchers, with different criteria and different kinds of expertise, and it would be unreasonable to expect all of their questions to be open. Moreover, to assert that in terms of helping the teachers to reveal their craft knowledge to the student teachers, all open questions are helpful, and all closed questions problematic, is to oversimplify. From the transcripts of the conversations between the student teachers and teachers, it appears that the context of the questions is all important: the open questions that worked well tended to be when the teacher had been helped to paint a fuller picture of the lesson through responding to more closed questions. The relative frequency of open questions may not therefore in itself be a problem with the procedure; however, the lack of correlation between the openness of questions and the accessing of craft knowledge is puzzling. It is possible that the lack of correlation is associated with student teachers being in a school for a sustained period of time and getting to know the teachers very well so that they are sometimes well placed to ask well judged relatively closed questions. Of interest – and an aspect of the study that needs to be explored further – is the student teachers' capacity to convey an **openness of stance** even when asking relatively closed questions.

Probing is the second area of the procedure that calls for further work. The results show that the student teachers, while successful in avoiding follow up questions that put teachers in the position of having to justify an earlier response, tended to use probing in order to clarify or confirm their understanding of responses to earlier questions, in effect saying, 'Have I understood you properly?' Moreover, there are indications that even when probing for elaboration, student teachers are seeking wider generalisations which may encourage the teacher to talk in decontextualised terms. Clearer and more persuasive guidance about the kinds of probing that will not appear negative but can give access to richer information about teachers' craft knowledge seems to be needed.

REFERENCES

Argyris, C. (1982) *Reasoning, Learning and Action: Individual and Organizational.* Jossey-Bass, San Francisco.
Argyris, C. and Schon, D. (1974) *Theory in Practice: Increasing Professional Effectiveness.* Jossey-Bass, San Francisco.
Bellack, A.A., Kliebard, H.M., Hyman, R.T. and Smith, F.L. (1966) *The Language of the Classroom.* Teachers' College Press, New York.
Berliner, D.C. (1987) Ways of thinking about students and classrooms by more and less experienced teachers, in J. Calderhead (ed.) *Exploring Teachers' Thinking.* Cassell, London.
Berliner, D.C. (1988) *The Development of Expertise in Pedagogy.* Charles Hunt Memorial Lecture, New Orleans.
Brown, S. and McIntyre, D. (1986) How do teachers think about their craft? in M. Ben-Peretz, R. Bromme and R. Halkes (eds.) *Advances of Research on Teacher Thinking.* Lisse: Swets & Zeitlinger.
Brown, S. and McIntyre, D. (1988) The professional craft knowledge of teachers, in W.A. Gatherer (ed.) *The Quality of Teaching,* a special issue of *Scottish Educational Review,* pp. 39–47.
Brown, S. and McIntyre, D. (1993) *Making Sense of Teaching.* Open University Press, Buckingham.
Calderhead, J. (1983) *Research into Teachers' and Student Teachers' Cognitions: Exploring the Nature of Classroom Practice.* Paper presented at the annual meeting of the American Educational Research Association, Montreal, 1983.
Clark, C.M. (1989) Asking the right questions about teacher preparation: contributions of research on teacher thinking, in J. Lowyck and C.M. Clark (eds.) *Teacher Thinking and Professional Action,* Leuven University Press, Leuven.
Clark, C.M. and Peterson, P.L. (1986) Teachers' thought processes, in M.C. Wittrock (ed.) *Handbook of Research on Teaching.* Macmillan, New York.
Elbaz, F. (1983) *Teacher Thinking: A Study of Practical Knowledge.* Nichols, New York.
Elliott, J. (1989) Appraisal of performance and appraisal of persons, in H. Simons and J. Elliott (eds.) *Rethinking Appraisal and Assessment.* Open University Press, Milton Keynes.
Holsti, O.R. (1968) Content Analysis, in G. Lindzey and E. Aronson (eds.) *The Handbook of Social Psychology.* Addison-Wesley, Massachusetts.
Housner, L.D. and Griffey, D.C. (1985) Teacher cognition: differences in planning and interactive decision making between experienced and inexperienced teachers, *Research Quarterly for Exercise and Sport,* Vol. 56, no. 1, pp. 45–53.
Jackson, P.W. (1968) *Life in Classrooms.* Holt, Rinehart and Winston, New York.

Lampert, M. (1984) Teaching about thinking and thinking about teaching. *Journal of Curriculum Studies*, Vol. 16, no. 1, pp. 1–18.

Lampert, M. (1985) How do teachers manage to teach? Perspectives on Problems in Practice, *Harvard Educational Review*, Vol. 55, no. 2, pp. 178–94.

McAlpine, A., Brown, S., McIntyre, D. and Hagger, H. (1988) *Student Teachers Learning from Experienced Teachers*. Scottish Council for Research in Education, Edinburgh.

Schon, D.A. (1983) *The Reflective Practitioner: How Professionals Think in Action*. Basic Books, New York.

Scott, W.A. (1955) Reliability of content analysis: the case for nominal scale coding, *Public Opinion Quarterly*, no. 19, pp. 321–325.

Shulman, L. (1986) Those who understand: knowledge growth in teaching, *Educational Researcher*, 15(2): 4–14.

Shulman, L. (1987) Knowledge and teaching: foundations of the new reform, *Harvard Educational Review*, 57: 1–22.

Tom, A. (1984) *Teaching as a Moral Craft*. Longman, New York.

Tom, A.R. and Valli, L. (1990) Professional knowledge for teachers, in W.R. Houston (ed.) *Handbook of Research on Teacher Education*. Macmillan, New York.

7

SKILLS OF MENTORING IN INITIAL TEACHER EDUCATION

Judith Lathlean, Hazel Hagger and Donald McIntyre

INTRODUCTION

The research presented in this paper forms part of a project designed to develop materials to assist new, inexperienced mentors within a teacher preparation programme. This was known as the Development of Materials for Mentor Training (DeMMenT) Project and it led to the production of *The School Mentor Handbook* (Hagger *et. al.*, 1993). The research was in two distinct parts. First, a study of selected skills of mentoring used by mentors in the Oxford Internship Scheme was conducted over five academic terms, and second, an evaluation of the training materials which were in part derived from this research was undertaken. Whilst the purpose of this paper is not to present the whole DeMMenT project in detail but rather some of the findings of the research and the evaluation, the context and the nature of the research undertaken will briefly be described. Second, key findings from the research will be described and the implications of these for the DeMMenT project outlined. Finally, some highlights from the evaluation of the materials will be given.

THE CONTEXT AND THE PROJECT

The DeMMenT project aimed to develop materials to assist in the preparation and support of new mentors involved in the Oxford Internship Scheme. It was decided to achieve this by selecting important aspects of a mentor's role, studying what mentors actually did, and then using this understanding to inform the development of written materials. The project, therefore, went through three main stages: formulation of skill areas, the investigation with skilled and experienced mentors to see how they went about the job, and the development and evaluation of training materials. Thus, a group of teachers and university tutors identified aspects of a mentor's role and selected a number as being of critical importance for particular attention. These were: collaborative teaching; managing interns' learning; diagnostic assessment and supervision; making craft knowledge accessible; critically discussing interns' ideas; and supporting interns' self-evaluation. A consultant (i.e. an experienced mentor or professional tutor) was selected for each of the six aspects to work with the project.

Having identified the skills of mentoring that were to be the particular focus of the research, for each of the six aspects, three experienced mentors were selected from the Internship schools. A number of criteria were used for selection of the eighteen mentors. Each had to have at least one year's experience as a mentor, be recommended by one or more key persons in Internship, and importantly be judged to be especially skilful at that particular aspect of the role for which they were being recruited. Alongside these individual criteria, a mix of mentors from different schools and across all curriculum areas was sought. The final sample of eighteen mentors came from six curriculum subjects: English, history, maths, science, geography and modern languages, and from ten of the Internship schools.

The research question addressed by the study was: '**What is involved in doing a certain aspect of the mentor's job skilfully?**' This was investigated by undertaking periods of observation whilst the mentor was engaged in an aspect of their role, for example, collaborative teaching, followed by talk about the observations, that is, ethnographic interviews. The purpose of both the interviews and the observation was to gain access to the mentor's perspectives and to find out the logic of their action.

ASPECTS OF MENTORING: THE FINDINGS

The general pattern of how skilled, experienced mentors talk about specific aspects of their jobs as mentors will be described, followed by a more detailed description of some of the elements forming the pattern, with examples from the different skill areas. (All the quotes are of mentors talking.)

Mentors' talk about aspects of their job

When reflecting on a particular example of an aspect of their role that had been observed, mentors often **evaluated their performance**, comparing it with other occasions on which they had undertaken a similar activity. They talked about the **rationale** they had for engaging in the activity and the goals they hoped to achieve. They also referred, often indirectly, to how they judged the effectiveness of the enterprise or the **outcomes**. They talked a little too about the **learning processes** for interns involved in the activity.

A great deal of their discourse was about the **interns** themselves, what their needs are, what they do, and how their characteristics impinge upon or have implications for the process of collaborative teaching, diagnostic assessment etc. They also talked about the **conditions** necessary for, or that affect in some way, the activity: for example, the time available, the classes and the pupils.

When talking about these, mentors referred to both positive and negative aspects, to the challenges and the problems. They also rarely talked about them in isolation. So, for example, the goals were related to learning processes and to the characteristics of the interns. And their actions were related to many factors: the goals, the interns, the conditions and so on.

Evaluation of their own performance

When asked generally to talk about an aspect of their job that had been observed, almost invariably mentors started by evaluating their own performance, with responses ranging from 'it went quite well' to 'I could have done better if X', or 'I shouldn't have done Y'. Mentors also referred subsequently to the apparent effectiveness (or otherwise) of their performance and even though the research was not intended as evaluative, in reflecting on their actions, mentors often themselves chose to highlight the good or the less good features.

Sometimes they related this to their own characteristics (for example, 'I have a tendency to talk too much' [this was a relatively common comment]; and 'I find it difficult to stand back and to see myself as others see me'). Or they related it to the specific intern with whom they were working (for example, 'someone like Jane is very easy to talk to because she's aware of what you are doing, and she's very willing to learn'; and 'there are just some interns with whom it's very difficult to collaboratively teach'). Or they related it to the circumstances of the observed example (for example, 'we didn't really have enough time, it was very rushed, so I ended up telling him things instead of asking questions').

Rationale and goals

In talking about a particular aspect of their job, mentors articulated what they were trying to achieve, that is the rationale they had for the activity, or the goals they hoped would be attained. Most of the talk about aims for the activity was in relation to the interns; it is done to give them a 'positive experience', to 'enhance their learning', to identify problems or to ameliorate problems that they are experiencing. The aims of an activity may be couched in terms of an immediate goal, for example:

she had had a bad experience teaching a class last week, a bit of a downer, so doing [collaborative teaching] this week gave us a chance to sort out things together,

or in terms of a longer term goal, for example:

[diagnostic assessment] gives you the chance to work progressively on something over a number of lessons such as building up their confidence.

The goals may be about the development of cognitive skills such as how to plan and organise a particular type of lesson, or how to manage aspects of teaching a class; for example:

She wanted to concentrate on transitions, so I thought the best thing to do was to plan a class with lots of them, have her watch how I handle them and then talk about it together. She also noticed that I had a screwdriver handy and that gave me the opportunity to say that I always carry one, and that it's essential for all Maths teachers to have one!

Very often, though, the mentor's goal was to do with the **affective growth** of the intern, such as their confidence or assertiveness. So:

She does need to gain confidence, . . . and one way of achieving that is by planning the lesson together and just being there in the class, working with her, me having a role, rather than being seen by her as popping in and judging what she is doing.

Mentors were also concerned that the activity should maximise the learning **potential** for the intern. For example:

We plan the programme for the interns so if at all possible there is a good balance of different years, different types of class, including low and mixed ability, and different styles of teaching, as well as making sure they have some frees and aren't teaching all day.

Effectiveness and outcomes

Related to the aims and goals that mentors have for an activity were the criteria they used for **judging the effectiveness** of the actions, that is the extent to which successful **outcomes** had been gained. Again, the main focus was on the interns – on what they said and did, or on the response and behaviour of the pupils to the interns, which was viewed as an indicator of success or otherwise. So, for example:

Last week the kids looked blankly at her [i.e. the intern] when she tried to do questioning, because the questions were so vague . . . This time the kids could actually respond to them.

When asked specifically how they judged the effectiveness of say the collaborative teaching or the diagnostic assessment, mentors found it quite difficult to respond. However, spontaneously they referred to **global indicators** such as:

> You know if you have got the plan more or less right when they seem to be learning from the different experiences, and you don't get too many adverse comments back from other teachers.

Mentors **related the outcomes** back to the goals, and the extent to which goals had been achieved. On many occasions the outcome was described as positive. For example:

> In the last debriefing we had identified a problem with her not scanning the class. She said this time that she was much more conscious of doing so, and I certainly observed that for myself. I was able to confirm it to her.

But sometimes, the mentor felt that the goals had not been achieved, for example saying:

> I thought when we set the teaching [and debriefing] up that her problem was one of poor timing, and so the lesson [and subsequent discussion] was to concentrate on this. Having seen the lesson, it was more to do with poor planning. It's something we're going to have to work on next time.

In evaluating the outcomes of the skills in action, mentors sometimes used the interns' own reactions as indicators. For example:

> You can gauge a lot from listening to the interns, how they talk about the plans, how they felt about the lesson, what went well for them, what went badly.

However this was not always possible. For example:

> [Collaborative teaching] can be a threatening thing for teachers who are used to working on their own. I am not sure whether she takes the same view that I do of how valuable it can be; she didn't give any real indication that she thought it was ... perhaps you should ask her!

Mentors often related the effectiveness (or otherwise) of the outcomes to the **characteristics** of the intern. For example:

> It seemed to go quite well. That kind of discussion could be very different with another intern. Janet is very astute and she volunteers things. It could be much more difficult with someone who is less aware of their strengths and weaknesses.

Learning processes

Mentors said little about **how** they felt learning was facilitated by these aspects of mentoring, and what they did say tended to be of a generalised nature, and not related to the specific instance observed. So, for example, learning was thought to be facilitated in the examples of collaborative teaching by 'being a second person in the classroom, an extra resource', and by 'having the opportunity to plan together', in diagnostic assessment learning by 'starting with where the intern is and moving on from there', and in managing interns' learning, by 'ensuring that interns see different styles of teaching and different personalities'.

Characteristics of interns

Mentors spent a **great deal** of time talking about the characteristics of individual interns, and the effect this had on the activity, such as how they engaged in it, the approach they adopted, the timing of the activity, the benefits to the intern and even whether or not they would consider doing it at all.

In terms of **how** they conducted the activity, the personality and the needs of the intern were considered. For example:

> I think role play [in the collaborative teaching] was very appropriate. I'm not sure that I would have chosen the same strategy if [the intern] was not so extrovert.

Mentors sometimes distinguished between different **types** of activity, or different approaches to it according to the intern. So:

> I had to adopt a much more structured and directive approach to the debriefing with Ian because he doesn't yet have the insight and maturity that the other interns have.

Conditions

As well as referring to the individual needs of interns, mentors talked frequently about the conditions necessary for undertaking an activity or conditions that in some way needed to be taken into consideration. The time available was a major consideration for all mentors, and was a factor that could cause problems, or was frequently given as a reason for an example that was not as good as it could have been. Thus:

> I was in a hurry, I compromised, and told her things rather than drawing them out of her.

The classes and the pupils were almost invariably considered when setting up an activity. So, for example, whilst interns were not 'let loose' to teach a known disruptive class, followed by a debriefing designed to pick up the pieces, difficult groups of pupils were not necessarily ruled out, especially for such activities as collaborative teaching and gaining access to teachers' craft knowledge. Indeed some experience of 'difficult' and certainly mixed ability groups was considered desirable by mentors managing interns' learning. On the whole, however, if there was the possibility of choice, mentors opted for 'co-operative', 'reasonably enthusiastic' classes, and ones where it was 'appropriate' for the interns to teach a lesson or a series of lessons.

Despite the differences between mentors and the aspects of the job on which they were asked to focus, there were many commonalities and patterns in the **way** they talked. They all appeared to enjoy talking about it and thinking it through, and several said that they would like to know 'how other mentors did it'. They had a tendency to be quite self-critical or to compare, without prompting, the observed example with others in the past. Their pre-occupations were with the interns, though without exception they shared their enthusiasm for the Internship Scheme with the researcher, and both their sense of how it was contributing to their own self-development and also their quest for further learning were evident in their talk.

Mentors' conceptions of the specified skills

The mentors were chosen because they were nominated as being skilled in the aspect of mentoring that was being studied, and they were recruited on the basis of a very brief specification of the skill area. However, it was evident from the examples observed that the mentors held widely different conceptions of what that aspect of mentoring was about. For example, for one mentor collaborative teaching meant talking to an intern about a lesson before a class, and then being in the classroom with that intern whilst the intern took the lesson, whereas for another, the very detailed shared planning and shared management of the lesson, followed by an extensive period of debriefing afterwards, was critical to the whole process. In fact, for some of the skill areas, notably making craft knowledge accessible and supporting interns' self-evaluation, it was very difficult, especially from the observation alone, for the researcher, who was unfamiliar with the Internship Scheme and the world of mentoring in teacher education, to gain an understanding of what the skill was, and how it was distinctive from other aspects of the job.

An anomaly in the research design is apparent here, alongside a practically important research finding. It will be remembered that the mentoring skills to be investigated had been specified, in name and broad definition, by a steering group of tutors and teachers. These definitions were not derived from observations or accounts of practice. It now appears that the practice of even highly regarded mentors often bore little relationship to these preconceived definitions. Mentors were ready enough to talk in terms of the skill labels which had originated in the university among those teachers involved in the planning of the scheme; but the logic of the mentor's practice was often not closely connected with the meanings which the innovative planners had prescribed. The ethnographic design of the research was thus somewhat in tension with the developmental purpose which it was designed to fulfil.

CONCLUSIONS FROM THE RESEARCH PHASE

What is most striking about the ethnographic findings outlined above is the similarity between mentors' ways of talking about their practice in mentoring and teachers' ways of talking about their practice in teaching (e.g. Brown and McIntyre, 1993). Most generally, there is the dominant importance of the specific context within which they are working. More specifically, there is first and foremost the detailed attention to, and the readiness to talk about, the characteristics of students, in this case of the interns. In contrast, there is the apparent difficulty for the mentors of talking about their own actions and the relatively small part that reports of their actions play in their responses to questions about how they undertake the task.

When they do talk about their own actions, there is the dominant importance of the conditions which influence these actions, and also influence the standards they adopt in judging the success of their efforts. These conditions are concerned for example with time and timing, with their own characteristics – temporary or more permanent – and, again, with the characteristics of the interns. In relation to goals, outcomes and criteria of effectiveness, the emphasis is predominantly on the short-term, for example on what the intern does in a lesson or on how the students respond in an intern's lesson; and talk of longer-term goals tends to be somewhat vague or to reflect what looks like a shift into another mode – that of the language offered by the innovators.

A second main conclusion to be drawn is that the mentors' thinking in practice about mentoring, committed and enthusiastic about it as they are, was derived hardly at all from the explicit scheme which had been thoroughly planned, negotiated and piloted mainly by leading teachers from their own local schools, the scheme to which they had been inducted. Instead, even some of their most general working conceptions of the skills they were using were clearly derived from a commonsense which had grown out of their experience as teachers and as supervisory teachers in previous years. This is not a surprising conclusion, but it is an indication of the slow learning of some academic educators that we were surprised by it.

IMPLICATIONS OF THE RESEARCH FOR THE DEVELOPMENT OF THE TRAINING MATERIALS

It was anticipated that the understandings generated from the research and the examples gained would underpin the training materials that were to be developed in relation to each of the skill areas. In practice, while the research findings could be used to illustrate many key issues, they could not form the substantial basis of the mentor guidelines. Thus the consultants, working closely with two members of the university, were responsible for developing the materials. As a first stage, more detailed specifications of three of the skill areas were prepared, and each was sent to two mentors from each of the six curriculum subjects, involving a total of 36 mentors. In the main, their feedback agreed that the detailed specifications adequately described what those aspects of mentoring were about.

For each of the skill areas, the consultant and the two university tutors then developed guidance materials around these detailed specifications, elaborating on the contexts and purposes for which each skill was seen to be most useful, ways of using the skills most effectively, and common problems and how they might be avoided or resolved. Full use was made of the ethnographic case studies both for identifying issues and for their exemplification, although issues and examples were also imported from other sources.

By the end of the first year of the project, three sets of materials were available. These were distributed to new mentors in the Internship schools, the intention being to 'trial' them, prior to developing the other materials. An evaluation of these three sets of materials was undertaken, through interviews with mentors.

THE EVALUATION OF THE TRAINING MATERIALS

The assumption had been made in developing the materials that their availability would be useful in preparing new mentors for their roles. But little was known about the experience of being a mentor – for example, was it considered a complex job, or was it viewed simply as an extension of being a teacher – let alone what mentors perceived as being the main factors that facilitated learning about, and provided support within, the role. Especially in the light of the earlier research findings, it was felt necessary to broaden the evaluation to ascertain where the use of such materials might fit into the whole, and thus the evaluation had three aims:

- to improve our understanding of how mentors construe their roles,
- to find out how mentors perceive they learn to be mentors,
- to ascertain mentors' reactions to the draft DeMMenT materials for three of the skill areas.

Relatively structured interviews were conducted with thirty mentors, representing about one third of all mentors in the scheme. Half of the sample were new mentors, and half experienced mentors.

Being a mentor

When asked about their experience of being a mentor, almost without exception mentors described it firstly and spontaneously as 'rewarding' or 'fulfilling', 'stimulating', 'interesting' and 'enjoyable'.

The **rewards** were of four kinds: it enhanced the mentors' own teaching (e.g. it 'makes you look at your own teaching'; it 'encourages you to be reflective' and to 'question and re-evaluate your own practices'; and it 'stops you from stagnating intellectually'); it provided benefits for the department or faculty by the presence of interns who 'added a fresh dimension'; it brought the gratification of helping others to learn (e.g. 'you get a kick out of helping other people to teach'; 'it's good to see the interns change from being quite unconfident into being good teachers and knowing you've had a small hand in that process'); and the involvement with the university was deemed useful.

Various **challenges** were mentioned by about a quarter. They talked about it as being 'quite difficult', 'hard work' and 'challenging', though stressed that the rewards were worth it. Four talked abut the 'responsibility' that was vested in being a mentor. For example, one said that it was her first management experience and that it was 'quite worrying having to worry about someone else as well as [herself]'.

When asked to focus on the problems they had experienced, twenty-eight out of the thirty spontaneously mentioned time – either the lack of it or having contact time at an inappropriate point in the school week. Other problems were concerned with the logistics of the school time-table, uncooperative school colleagues and insufficient support from the university tutor.

A notable feature of their talk was once again the way in which they related their work as mentors to the interns; two-thirds of the new mentors attributed their overall enjoyment of the work of mentoring to their 'good luck in having good interns'. Conversely, new mentors who had interns they deemed weak found the job tiring and excessively time-consuming.

In summary, the main finding was that the job of mentor was not without its challenges, especially during an initial chaotic period, but was rewarding. Most saw it as a positive experience and none wanted to cease to be a mentor. The main factor that helped or alternatively hindered or constrained the job was the interns themselves.

Learning to be a mentor

Mentors were asked how they had learnt what to do as mentors, what they had found supportive and what problems in this respect they had experienced. In relation to learning to be a mentor, the six most important facets were (in order of times mentioned): contact with their university curriculum tutor; reliance on their own resources and experience – past experience, commonsense, learning by doing the job; induction; meetings with other mentors at the university; involvement in a special diploma programme; and documentation (primarily *The Mentors' Handbook*). It is interesting to note that all but one of these came from outside the school.

Reactions to the materials

Overall the materials met with the mentors' approval; they were seen as well presented, in an appropriate format, and as focusing on important aspects of a mentor's role. However, it was evident that they were not seen as part of the process of learning to be a mentor, and few had consciously worked through them in practice, for two main reasons. First, the materials had come too late or were insufficiently promoted in school, and second, the new mentors were preoccupied with the job of mentoring and there was not time to work through them.

In terms of the use made of them, many mentors felt that they confirmed the good work they were already doing, though they were comforted by reading about the dilemmas and anxieties of other mentors. And secondly, they used the materials to help colleagues in school to understand their intentions. In a positive vein, all the experienced mentors wished that they had had the materials when they started as mentors, and the new mentors said that they would use them during the next year.

In conclusion, the evaluation interviews revealed that while mentors had not internalised the materials, they approved of them. There tended to be a positive or an uncritical stance taken to materials and documentation generated by the university, though whether this indicated an overall approval of the scheme, or a relative lack of self-confidence on the part of the mentors, or perhaps both is unclear. Mentors were in general satisfied with their work as mentors, though they felt constrained by time, and they considered that their major sources of support came from outside the school. Finally, there was a pervasive feeling that mentors did not know what they needed to know until they had actually done the job – until they had experience of being a mentor. Thus in a sense their roles as mentors had to be self-made, but with the recognition that external support, such as the materials, could be of value in their development over time.

REFERENCES

Brown, S. and McIntyre, D. (1993) *Making Sense of Teaching*. Open University Press, Buckingham.

Hagger, H., Burn, K. and McIntyre, D. (1993) *The School Mentor Handbook*. Kogan Page, London.

8

LEARNING TO TEACH: THE VALUE OF COLLABORATIVE TEACHING

Katharine Burn

INTRODUCTION: THE CLAIMS FOR COLLABORATIVE TEACHING

The recent shift in initial teacher education, by which more responsibility has been passed to schools and school-based mentors have replaced teaching-practice supervisors, represents a belated recognition of the expertise possessed by practising classroom teachers. However, because this expertise is so embedded in teachers' day-to-day work and is thus highly contextualised and rarely consciously examined or articulated, it has also created an urgent need for research into the ways in which it can be made accessible to novices. Furthermore, there is a need to explore ways of taking advantage of school-based work so that student teachers can more effectively practise the skills of teaching.

The DeMMent Project, established in 1990, was one early attempt by Oxford University Department of Educational Studies to meet this need. OUDES had moved to a partnership model of initial teacher education in 1987 with the introduction of the Internship Scheme. After it had been in operation for three years the DeMMent project was set up to identify and study a number of key mentoring skills, and through the observation of good practice, to produce advice and guidelines for mentors operating both within the scheme and in other contexts. One of the skills considered worthy of investigation was that of collaborative teaching, and I was appointed as the mentor consultant for that skill.

The work of the DeMMent project has been described in the previous chapter. The training materials that were developed were published as part of *The School Mentor Handbook* (Hagger *et. al.* 1993) and a detailed description of one of the collaborative lessons was presented in *Mentoring in Schools* (Burn 1992) with suggestions as to how this process seemed to have provided the student teacher with opportunities for learning. This chapter is concerned with some further research which I did on collaborative teaching.

Definition

The process of collaborative teaching was, as an outcome of the DeMMent project, defined as:

> any lesson that is jointly planned and jointly taught by a mentor (or experienced teacher) and student teacher(s). The degree of collaboration involved in the process may vary considerably. The mentor may well plan the lesson outline and then suggest a specific slot within it for which he or she would like the student teacher(s) to take responsibility; or, at the other end of the spectrum, both mentor and student teacher(s) may together plan the whole lesson 'from scratch'. Whatever the degree of collaboration, the lesson should be planned to ensure that the student teacher(s) have a **clearly defined responsibility** within it, which is deliberately targeted to help their learning.

The benefits for student teachers' learning

It was suggested that the process made three kinds of learning possible:

1) Learning to plan lessons carefully through being involved in joint planning with an experienced teacher, finding out what the teacher takes account of, and identifying with the planning and its consequences.
2) Learning certain skills of classroom teaching through having responsibility for a specified component of the lesson, while identifying with the whole lesson and recognising the relationship of the part to the whole.
3) Gaining access to an experienced teachers' craft knowledge through observation of the teacher's actions, informed by a thorough knowledge of the planning, and probably through discussion of the lesson afterwards, with a heightened awareness because of having joint responsibility for the lesson.

The benefits for pupils

It was also suggested that the process offered a number of incidental advantages in terms of pupils' learning. Not only can two teachers working together increase the amount of individual attention and support that pupils receive; they can also present material in quite stimulating ways – using debates or role-plays, for example – and perhaps manage certain activities more smoothly, with one distributing resources while another explains the task.

Potential problems

Set against these benefits were a number of potential problems that mentors had identified in using the technique. It was thought that working collaboratively could prove threatening to both parties. Experienced teachers might find it unsettling to 'share' their class with another teacher; student teachers might feel that the teacher's contribution to the lesson undermines their own role. Shared responsibility may cause confusion, and pupils, uncertain about who is 'in charge', may further undermine the student teacher's confidence by constantly looking to their 'proper' teacher for help. The mentor's presence may even encourage the student teacher to relax and abdicate responsibility.

A further difficulty could be that of ensuring that there is adequate liaison between the student teacher and mentor during the lesson. Not every contingency can be planned for and changes may be necessary. These may be very unsettling and confusing, and the discussion necessary to plan any alteration may well appear to the pupils as 'teacher chat'.

The most problematic aspect identified by mentors, however, was the demand that collaborative teaching made on their time. Planning jointly with a student teacher took far longer than experienced teachers would normally spend preparing their own lessons, and added to this was the need to discuss the lesson together afterwards. Few mentors could find the time to engage in this process on a regular basis.

At this stage it was possible to offer some advice to mentors on how these problems could be minimised or eliminated: for example by the use of a structured pro-forma to summarise the agreed plan and clarify each responsibility, and by thoughtful consideration of when to use collaborative teaching to meet a student teacher's particular learning needs. However, it was clear that in recommending collaborative teaching as a key mentoring skill we were making considerable demands of mentors. Its inclusion rested on the claims that it could contribute to student teachers' learning in the three ways identified above (through joint planning, through the practice of certain skills, and through observation and discussion of the practice of an experienced teacher). Those involved in the initial research or who commented on the training material drafts obviously believed that these kinds of learning were taking place but it was important, if we were encouraging mentors to make use of this demanding process, to investigate these claims in more detail, seeking evidence as to whether these kinds of learning were occurring, and trying to determine whether the problems identified might not in fact outweigh the intended gains. It was therefore decided to conduct a further small-scale study of collaborative teaching in the practice of History mentors within the Internship Scheme.

CLOSER INVESTIGATION: CASE STUDIES
OF COLLABORATIVE TEACHING

Since the types of learning to be investigated apparently occurred in the three different phases of collaborative teaching – planning, classroom practice, and discussion of the practice of both intern and mentor – evidence was needed concerning all three. A tape of each planning meeting provided a complete record of the discussion without being too intrusive. For evidence of what happened in the lesson itself it was necessary to rely on a copy of the final plan and a tape of the post-lesson discussion (since neither observation by the researcher nor videotaping proved feasible). Whilst this was far from ideal, it gave access to the participants' perceptions of what had happened, and served to identify what they saw as significant within the lesson. The transcript of the discussion also allowed study of the kind of questions asked by the intern and any analysis made of the mentor's teaching. In each case both mentor and intern were asked to complete a questionnaire clarifying exactly when the lesson took place, the curriculum focus of the intern's course at the time, and what each hoped to achieve in relation to the intern's learning. The student teachers were also asked afterwards to comment on what they thought they had learned.

Initially three experienced History mentors, in addition to myself, agreed to take part in the research which took place during the first phase of the Internship year (from October to January when the interns were in their placement school for two days a week). However, the realities of school life meant that only one of them was able to collect the necessary data. To broaden the sample an experienced teacher (who was not officially designated as mentor but who had worked extensively with interns in the previous two years and shared much of the mentor's role) was also included. Each of these teachers collected data relating to one collaborative lesson, and I did the same for four others. There were thus six case studies to investigate (representing as wide a range of practice as was possible given the constraints of part-time research by a full-time teacher). Details of the participants in each, the time of the planning and lesson, and the curriculum focus at the time are presented in Table 1:

Although the concentration of the sample in weeks 8 to 13 of the course restricted the scope of the research, it was at this early stage of the interns' learning that collaborative lessons were specifically included in the History curriculum programme – essentially because it was thought to be particularly valuable at this time to offer interns a protected environment and the opportunity to focus on specific skills.

Although not consciously selected, the interns represented an interesting sample of entrants to the profession, embarking on teaching careers at very different stages and encountering various degrees of difficulty in learning to teach. Jane had spent two years in employment before starting the PGCE.

Table 1

Lesson	Taught by	Planned in week	Taught in week	Curriculum focus of interns' university programme
1	Mentor A (myself) Jane	8	9	8: lesson-planning; producing worksheets 9: lesson-plannng; aspects of language – pupil and teacher talk; review of classroom management
2	Mentor A Max	10	10	10: individual needs; behavioural problems
3	Mentor A Max	12	12	12: introduction to specific teaching strategies
4	Mentor A Ann	9	10	9: lesson planning; aspects of language; introduction to GCSE 10: individual needs
5	Mentor B Sally	13	13	13: teaching strategies – using textbooks and worksheets, questioning
6	Mentor C Adam	9	10	9: lesson planning; aspects of language; introduction to GCSE 10: individual needs

Max was a mature student, taking up teaching in his late thirties after a wide experience of other jobs. Unfortunately he decided to give up the course soon after the lessons studied, finding teaching too stressful an occupation, and recognising that he was essentially unable to come to terms with his dislike of the institutional structure of schools. Sally was also a mature student; she faced some difficulties during the year, but passed the course. Ann and Adam both began their PGCE course straight from university and completed it successfully.

The first task in the data analysis was to establish whether there were examples of the kinds of learning identified above. Did joint planning appear to offer the kind of opportunities for learning that had been suggested: were the planning processes used by the mentors made explicit, and thus more accessible to the interns? Did the mentors share with the interns specific knowledge about the class and context? Did they demonstrate clearly to the interns the necessity of careful planning?

With regard to classroom practice, which parts of lessons did the interns tend to take responsibility for, and what kind of teaching strategies did this give them the opportunity to practise? The success of the teaching or the value of the practice as a learning experience was much harder to determine, but where references were made to this in the post-lesson discussion an attempt was made to analyse these. Did the fact that they were teaching only parts of a lesson allow the interns to look critically at those particular parts?

With regard to gaining access to experienced teachers' craft knowledge, it was possible to study the interns' observations and questions about the mentors' teaching. How closely did they seem to have observed the mentors' practice, and to what extent did their understanding of the lesson plan seem to influence their questions or conclusions?

The case studies could also provide evidence of any way in which collaborative teaching was exploited for the benefit of the pupils. Did the planning suggest that they were deliberately using the opportunity presented by two teachers to vary the lesson's presentation? Was there any evidence from the discussion afterwards of ways in which the involvement of two teachers had improved the pupils' learning experience? Finally, any problems encountered in the process were identified. Did either the mentor or intern comment on the difficulty of the task, or was there any evidence from which it could be inferred that the process had created problems other than those explicitly identified by either party?

CONCLUSIONS: THE VALUE OF COLLABORATIVE TEACHING

Learning through joint planning

The nature of the planning process
The first stage in analysis of the lesson planning transcripts was to determine the kind of role played by mentor and intern respectively. How much of each lesson was actually to be planned during the joint discussion – did mentors tend to have a predetermined plan in mind, or was there scope for genuine negotiation and shared decision making? How much preparation had the interns done before the meeting and what influence did this appear to have on the contribution they made? What role did each tend to play in planning – for example, who actually identified the lesson objectives or suggested the teaching strategies to be used?

The degree of collaboration in the planning in fact varied considerably. For example, the format and activities within lesson 2 were largely predetermined since the mentor judged it necessary to include the completion of a video that pupils had begun working on the day before, and therefore already had an outline plan in mind. Lesson 3, in contrast, with the same intern two weeks later, involved him in far more creative planning: the historical content and key concepts to be taught had been identified by the mentor, but, beyond the need for a recap explaining how this work related to the previous lesson, the way in which they were to be taught was entirely open to negotiation. In fact Max suggested the teaching strategies decided upon for the first part of the lesson, and the mentor those selected for the second part. The most usual planning task, however, was somewhere between these two extremes. In every lesson the content to be covered was determined in advance by the mentor, essentially dictated by the long-term scheme of work, although occasionally there was some flexibility over timing. Mentors had also usually identified the specific resources that they wanted to use, or they offered a range from which a selection could be made. Beyond this, the way in which the particular resources were used, the particular teaching strategies, and the time spent on different tasks were open to negotiation.

There was also considerable variation in the amount of preparation done by the interns before the planning meeting. Jane and Max, for example, had done comparatively little. The former had only skimmed through the relevant parts of the pupil textbook. The latter, in preparation for lesson 2, had not looked at the textbook but happened to have seen the topic taught by another teacher the previous day. In contrast to this, his preparation for lesson 3 involved very critical study of the textbook and he had obviously spent some time developing his own ideas. Sally had taught part of the previous lesson with the class and was clearly familiar with the topic, and Ann and Adam, obviously influenced by a recent university seminar on lesson planning, had each watched the appropriate video and drawn up suggested lesson objectives, with Ann also drafting a worksheet and noting ideas for pupil discussion.

The degree of preparation clearly had some influence on the role the interns were able to play within the planning process. It is not surprising that, in planning lessons 1 and 2, interns Jane and Max did not tend to put forward their own ideas for teaching strategies or specific concepts to be developed. The latter, in particular, made very few suggestions. He asked specifically if he could conduct a session of question and answer and be responsible for explaining and setting a pupil task, but it was the mentor who suggested how these could be included in the lesson. His involvement tended to be restricted to requests for information – about the pupils, their likely understanding of certain points, exactly what he should include in his questions. The suggestions he did make were essentially selections between alternative options proposed by the mentor. It is also not surprising that where the interns were well prepared they generally made a very significant contribution to shaping the plan. All the strategies adopted for lesson 6 were suggested by Adam and merely modified or refined in the light of the mentor's suggestions. Ann determined the lesson objectives and put forward the initial proposal for all the activities and teaching strategies used in lesson 4.

It appears that it was the degree of preparation rather than constraints imposed on the plan by the previous choice of topic or resources that determined the role played by the interns in the planning process. In lesson 2 with the plan essentially predetermined by the mentor, it is true that Max made very few suggestions of his own. However, this seems more to do with his lack of preparation since the mentor was quite willing to develop an alternative approach. In lessons 4 and 6, where the content and resources were prescribed, this narrow focus seems to have helped the interns to identify for themselves the key learning objectives and to begin to develop strategies by which they could achieve these.

Making explicit the mentor's planning process

Despite the variations in the planning process all six planning sessions seem to have provided opportunities for the interns to learn from the practice and experience of the mentor. Although it cannot be concluded that the mentors demonstrated the same kinds of thinking as they would do when planning alone, they certainly made explicit the procedures they were using to determine objectives and teaching strategies for these particular lessons.

One technique which all three mentors used was that of thinking through, trying to visualise, the likely pupil response to a particular question or task as a means of assessing whether it was worthwhile or feasible. On some occasions they themselves suggested how pupils might react, on others they asked questions to try to encourage the interns to predict the likely reaction and so assess for themselves the feasibility of the proposal. When Ann suggested group-work in lesson 4, the mentor asked her to specify what she thought were the main points each group would have to contribute to the plenary – using this question to help her recognise that the suggested distribution of tasks to each group would be very unbalanced.

A similar type of process, working from the outcome back to the question or task, was also frequently displayed: focusing first on what they wanted the pupils to discover, articulating the learning objective, and then framing the questions or structuring the task clearly to encourage that particular discovery. In planning lesson 5, for example, the mentor spent a lot of time with Sally clarifying exactly what points she wanted the pupils to remember and take notes about from the previous lesson. Only when they had established this, did she suggest the task which could be presented to the pupils.

A second aspect of mentors' planning that was occasionally made explicit was the process of transforming their subject knowledge about a period or aspect of the past into a simplified form for pupils. There were few examples of this but occasionally the mentors clearly articulated this process of simplification, explaining their reasons for ignoring certain features or selecting particular terms. In the planning for lesson 3, for example, dealing with a difficult idea for a Year 9 class – Marxist theory of historical change – there was a fascinating sequence in which the mentor first narrowed the focus of what they were trying to explain and then began to simplify complex concepts into diagrams which she proposed could be made more accessible to the pupils by symbolically acting them out. Initially the simplification was done by the mentor, with Max making suggestions about historical content and the mentor translating these into specific questions to ask of pupils to lead them onto the next stage, but as the process went on, Max, whose pre-occupation continued to be the historical content, also started to suggest questions to ask of pupils and ways of demonstrating the historical changes through the role-play.

This process of transformation of the subject knowledge seemed to be made most accessible to the interns on the occasions when they had quite a detailed knowledge of the subject. The depth of their knowledge meant firstly that their own proposals tended to be quite complex and the mentors there-fore took steps to help them modify their suggestions; and secondly that the interns were much more aware of the extent to which the history had been simplified. In lessons 1 and 2 where the interns had not studied the topic in detail in advance they were probably less aware of how much was being omitted or adapted. Thus the process would have meant less to them and the mentor did not perceive a need to explain it.

A third way in which the mentors' planning process was made explicit was in their explanations of the rationale underlying their decisions. There were numerous examples of the mentors justifying their choices: the use of one strategy rather than another, for example, or the creation of certain size pupil groupings. The decisions were based on a wide range of criteria, such as the need for variety within a lesson, or the knowledge of which pupils tend to dominate discussion.

In simply observing and discussing a lesson taught by an experienced prac-titioner, interns may well ask why some of these decisions were made; by being involved in the planning process they are made aware of the alterna-tives that might have been considered, and are given an insight into the way in which their mentor establishes priorities – what factors are taken into account at any particular time, and why they are perceived as the important ones.

Demonstrating the need for careful planning

Even though the three mentors studied may not routinely produce detailed plans for their own lessons, their expectations that the interns should do so at this early stage were clearly spelt out. Even after the planning discussions the interns left with further specific preparation to do, such as making the final choice between a selection of resources, or framing the exact questions for a written exercise. During the discussions the mentors not only provided frequent reminders of routine issues to consider in planning specific activi-ties – for example that a change of room to watch a video would probably mean a late start – but they also encouraged the interns to keep sight of the lesson as a whole, alerting them to the need to consider the connections between activities, pace and variety within the lesson, and links to previous and future work.

However, the case studies also provided some evidence to suggest that collaboration may in fact obscure the issue of careful planning. There was, for example, some confusion during lesson 1 because there had been no discussion of timing; and in reviewing lesson 5 both intern and mentor commented on pupil boredom in the early part of the lesson – attributed by the mentor to the fact that she had failed to recognise the element of overlap between this lesson and the previous one. The transcript of the planning discussion gives the impression that the mentor had become so involved in detailed discussions with Sally about content and strategy that in this case she lost sight of the lesson as a whole and of the issue usually central to her own planning – that of pupil motivation.

Although there were few problems of this kind they demonstrate the demands imposed on mentors by collaborative planning. Mentors are trying to open up their thinking to the interns, while encouraging them to develop their own ideas, and endeavouring to keep sight of the pupils' needs. It is a difficult juggling act requiring intense concentration.

Sharing their knowledge of class and context

Not surprisingly the collaborative planning provided an opportunity for the mentors to give the interns very detailed information about the particular class and context. It seems likely that this knowledge not only helped to make the interns' teaching of these particular lessons more successful, but also gave them further insights into the range of issues that experienced teachers take account of. For example, mentors often made explicit judgements about what they thought the pupils were likely to understand. This was particularly evident in the two cases where the interns knew a great deal about the subject matter. The gulf between their perceptions and those of the pupils was very obvious, and their natural inclination to overload the lesson with detail or complexity meant that the mentors frequently had to give advice or sound a warning. Mentors also offered their judgements as to how the class was likely to react to certain activities, such as debating or reading aloud, illustrating another part of the planning process – the consideration and prediction of pupils' responses as a means of evaluating a particular strategy. They also shared with the interns their knowledge of the demands of external or internal examinations, reminding them of the need for pupils to have some form of written notes from which to revise and giving advice on how to frame questions to help pupils recognise and practise the techniques required for GCSE papers.

Rehearsing parts of the lesson

The case studies revealed one other way in which collaborative planning could prove useful to interns' learning – an aspect not identified in the preliminary stages of the research. In all but one of the planning discussions the mentors at some stage 'rehearsed' particular sequences of questions, explanations or instructions that could be given to the pupils. However, although the interns occasionally used these 'rehearsals' to probe the mentor's thinking – asking about specific choices of vocabulary, for example – they did not always find them helpful. As his mentor talked through the sort of questions he might ask at one point in the lesson, Max panicked and began frantically to write them down. Rather than being able to concentrate on the process of sequencing questions and the need to build from one to the next, he interpreted the 'rehearsal' as a detailed plan which he could not write fast enough, and so lost the thread. Collaborative planning, because it involves two people, creates opportunities for confusion and misinterpretation that simply do not exist when one plans alone!

Practising certain skills of classroom teaching

Removing worries about maintaining discipline

The only conclusions about discipline that can be drawn from the evidence are essentially negative: there was no reference in any post-lesson discussion to any discipline difficulties. Whilst it cannot be concluded that this was due to collaborative teaching, nor that the interns were not worried about discipline, there is evidence to suggest that both mentors and interns used the flexibility offered to allow the intern to avoid more difficult management tasks early on.

In five cases the beginning of the lesson was taught by the mentor; and on two of these occasions this was done specifically at the request of the intern who considered it too demanding at that stage. The one exception was Sally, since she had been involved in teaching the same group the previous lesson and was well placed to give a recap on that work. Even so, in the planning discussion the mentor spelt out very clearly the management issues that she would need to consider.

There were other examples of the interns opting not to teach parts of the lesson that they considered too demanding, usually in terms of pupil management. Max, confident about the initial explanation involved in the lesson on Marxism, asked for the more complex enactment to be managed by the mentor.

Practising certain skills

There is clear evidence that both mentors and interns sought to use collaborative teaching to allow the interns to concentrate on and practise certain other specific aspects of teaching. For example, before planning lesson 5 the mentor identified one aim as helping Sally to practise questioning techniques. This was one of the university topics that week; but the mentor and intern also indicated a second priority that had arisen from Sally's previous teaching – providing an opportunity for her to practise or observe methods of giving pupils notes, and in particular to concentrate on 'the reduction of material to a level appropriate to the class'. In some cases the interns suggested a particular strategy that they wanted to focus on and the lesson was planned around that, in others the lessons were planned together in outline and the interns then selected those parts which gave them the opportunity to concentrate on particular skills. In lesson 4, for example, Ann elected to design the worksheet, following a university seminar the previous week on worksheet design, and to lead the question and answer that would feed into this. She also offered to take the discussion task towards the end of lesson to gain more experience and to develop further a strategy she had used the previous week. Usually the choice of roles was made by the interns but occasionally mentors made suggestions based on their views of what their interns could usefully practise.

The particular parts of the lesson taught by the intern were sometimes but not always directly linked to the focus of the university curriculum. Mentor A, for example, consciously sought to include elements of group discussion and teacher questioning in lesson 1 when the focus was on language. On no occasion did the university focus seem to be allowed to distort the lesson in any way, but there were numerous opportunities, both planned and incidental, for the interns to practise or explore the issues they were also studying in the university context.

More difficult to assess is the value of these opportunities. There was certainly evidence that the reduced focus of the interns' attention in the planning and execution of particular tasks had allowed them to think very carefully about what they were doing. In the opinion of the mentors at least, they displayed mastery of many of the components of the skill in question or showed significant improvements over their previous performance. The following comments are typical and illustrate the sense of progress felt by interns:

Sally: I was very much more confident.

Mentor: You stuck within your time limit as you intended, so that was a real improvement in that area.

Sally: I had kept the questions simple and they were able to come back with simple responses, which was great. And I felt this business of using the questions as building blocks – they were able to – one piece of information led to the next.

The feeling of achievement was not always quite so strong, but it must be recognised that the skills involved in teaching even a small part of a lesson are so complex that an intern can have mastered a number of them and yet the activity still not work exactly as intended. The interns naturally recalled the failures and tended not to appreciate the skills that they had successfully deployed. Usually it was the mentors who encouraged them to recognise their successes. After lesson 4 Ann felt despondent about her questioning techniques. She recognised from pupils' difficulties with the worksheet that she had rushed through certain questions too quickly; but it was the mentor who pointed out how well thought out her questions had been:

> *Mentor*: But it is very hard to do. That was a perfectly logical ordering. What you said to get to Pasteur was fine, pointing out the need to go back to the beginning.

The fact she had grasped the principle about sequencing the questions and making links meant that she was able to identify the next specific problem and discuss ways of dealing with it:

> *Mentor*: It may just be the tone of voice, a sort of emphasis, because you're very softly spoken. The phrasing of the questions gave an emphasis but your tone of voice didn't really give a stress ... You went through your questions pretty quickly: as soon as somebody had their hand up you took it ... You elaborated, but you didn't tend to repeat very much. It's a kind of thing about teaching – you say it three times! There wasn't very much of that. You need to stress it a bit more.

Because Sally, who had wanted to practise the delivery of class notes, had coped so successfully with reducing the historical content to an appropriate level and presenting a clear explanation and summary notes, the mentor was able to move her thinking on to consider pupil motivation and the way in which the dramatic potential of the 'story' could have been exploited to capture more of their interest. This was to move to a higher level, beyond the intern's initial conception of the skill.

In all the examples the mentors were able to focus their observation very closely on the problems or strategies that had been identified as the interns' priorities. They provided very detailed feedback, often recording verbatim the words the interns used in certain sections, and thus giving them considerable help in analysing what had happened.

Gaining access to experienced teachers' craft knowledge

Of the three original hypotheses the third stood up least well to detailed investigation. In the post-lesson discussions there was little evidence of interns learning through observation and evaluation of the mentors' role in the collaborative lessons. If any learning was taking place through observation the interns certainly did not talk about it: there was very little mention of the mentors' contribution and no critical analysis of it. Even when changes were made by the mentors to the plans, as happened in lesson 1 where the lack of time meant that a debate was reduced to two quick-fire questions to each half of the class, who were given three minutes to research and prepare an answer to report back, there was no discussion afterwards about why the mentor had decided to make those particular changes. It is true that the mentor and intern did discuss the need for some alteration as the lesson was going on, but no comment was made afterwards as to whether the shortened activity had met their original lesson objectives, and why the mentor had opted to keep the two sides rather than, say, simplifying the task by focusing on one argument and picking the other up in the next lesson.

The mentors clearly believed that observation of their teaching within the lesson would indeed prove useful to the interns, and they specifically chose parts of lessons to teach so that the interns could watch them. In lesson 4, where Ann had expressed fears that the homework activity would be perceived as childish, the mentor deliberately offered to take responsibility for setting the task so that she could see how it could be set up in an appropriate manner. In planning lesson 5 the mentor, who had observed that Sally tended to become nervous when using question and answer techniques with a class, suggested that for the first such activity within the lesson she would pose the questions and take the feedback while Sally made notes on the board; the roles could later be reversed when she had had the chance to observe her.

Although the interns may have found the observation valuable, they made no references to it, and it would be unsafe to conclude that they had in fact benefited from it, particularly since there was evidence on one occasion that observation of the mentor within a collaborative lesson could serve simply to demoralise the intern, highlighting his own difficulties in contrast with the mentor's skilled performance.

Interns seem to be too preoccupied with their own role in the lesson to be able to derive any significant benefit from observation. When they have more skill and confidence in their own teaching they may be able to exploit the opportunity to observe teaching which they have helped to plan, but this does not seem to be feasible early on.

The benefits for pupils

None of the lesson plans made any deliberate attempt to exploit the opportunities presented by collaborative teaching to enliven the lesson. None of the teaching strategies used required more than one teacher to be effective or followed the debate/role-play model observed in the DeMMent research. Every lesson was divided into discrete sections taught either by the mentor or the intern, except where pupils were working individually or in small groups when both tended to circulate. In this respect the pupils did gain additional help and attention, but this benefit was only commented upon in one case, lesson 5, where the positive experience did make the mentor eager to include more dramatic and debating activities within her scheme of work – activities she felt would work effectively when run by two teachers.

Problems

The original research had suggested four main problems that might be encountered: one or both parties feeling threatened by the experience; confusion for the pupils over who was in charge; inadequate liaison during the lesson; and lack of time. Since all the mentors taking part in the case studies had volunteered to do so, it is not surprising that they felt no unease about sharing a lesson with the intern, but this cannot be assumed to be true of all experienced teachers. Only one of the interns suggested that teaching alongside the mentor made the experience more stressful than it might otherwise have been, although it must be recognised that even if the interns had felt undermined they were not likely to say so to their mentors. There was no suggestion in any of the post-lesson discussions that the pupils had been confused or that they had failed to regard the intern as the teacher at those points when he or she had responsibility for the teaching. There was only one occasion when a intern abdicated part of his responsibility, which seems to have been a nervous reaction reflecting his sense of relief at having finished a complex explanation drawing on pupils' contributions. No one mentioned any difficulty over liaison during the lesson. Changes were made to the plan in two cases but neither of these seems to have presented any problems, perhaps because they were made in activities for which the mentor was responsible. Only one pair commented on the time taken, and suggested that this made the exercise essentially an unrealistic way of helping interns' learning. However, the four hours that they spent planning lesson 5 (a double period) was not typical. All the other planning sessions lasted approximately an hour, which makes the task rather more feasible though still very demanding.

The case studies also revealed further difficulties. However much the mentor may emphasise the need for careful planning, there are issues – such as timing – that they may occasionally overlook. Such failings are not unique to collaborative planning, but in the context of a joint lesson they have the potential to cause considerable difficulty or unnecessary anxiety for the interns. Joint planning can be very stressful, not only for the interns. Explaining their own ideas and the rationale for their decisions, while helping the interns to articulate and evaluate their own, can make it difficult for mentors to visualise the lesson as a whole or the experience of pupils within it. The mentors sometimes blamed themselves afterwards for failing to think

critically enough about the consequences of an intern's idea or even of a proposal they themselves made.

Validity of the findings

Although this was not conceived or conducted as an action research project,
in four of the case studies reported I acted as the mentor. Does this affect
the validity or generalisability of the findings? There is no doubt that I was
acutely aware of the hypotheses I was seeking to test as I engaged in the collaborative planning, teaching and evaluation. However this awareness does
not affect the validity of the findings since the claims advanced here apply
only to those circumstances in which, as noted in the original definition of
collaborative teaching, the student teacher's involvement is deliberately tar-
geted to help their learning. It is precisely when it involves careful and explicit
planning and conscious use of the strategy to focus on specific skills that collaborative teaching seems to promote effective learning. Similar opportunities for learning (and similar problems) seemed to occur with all three
mentors. The sample was indeed a small one, but this does not negate its
value. My main conclusions are summarised below; but, as with any case
study, responsibility for generalisation rests ultimately not with the writer but
with the reader.

CONCLUSIONS

Planning with a mentor gives student teachers access to an experienced
teacher's methods and insights and impresses upon them the need for rigor-
ous planning. Taking responsibility for parts of a lesson enables student
teachers to come to terms with real teaching while remaining in a protected
environment. By narrowing the focus and removing some of the panic and
confusion, it allows student teachers to approach the task of teaching more
rationally, both while engaged in teaching and in analysing it afterwards.

However, learning through observation and discussion of the mentor's role
in a collaborative lesson is probably too demanding, especially early on when
student teachers are understandably preoccupied with their own role. Such
learning may be able to take place later, but even then it will need careful
planning to ensure that the opportunity it offers is exploited. The incidental
benefits for pupils which it offers may similarly be capable of greater
exploitation at a later stage in student teachers' learning.

None of the problems associated with collaborative teaching appears to
detract significantly from its value. Any fears of the student teacher being
undermined, or pupils being confused about who is in charge, can be largely
removed by clarity between student teachers and mentors about their respec-

tive responsibilities. Collaborative planning is very demanding but the risk of careless omissions from the plan can be removed by the use of the kind of checksheet recommended in *The Mentor Handbook* (Hagger *et. al.* 1993). The demands that it makes on mentors' time are considerable, but given the learning opportunities that the experience offers to student teachers such an investment on three or four occasions early in training seems entirely worthwhile.

REFERENCES

Burn K. (1992) Collaborative teaching, in Wilkin, M. (ed.) *Mentoring in Schools.* Kogan Page, London.

Hagger, H., Burn, K. and McIntyre, D. (1993) *The School Mentor Handbook.* Kogan Page, London.

9

THE ROLE OF THE PROFESSIONAL TUTOR WITHIN THE OXFORD INTERNSHIP SCHEME

David Pell

INTRODUCTION

The Internship professional tutor

Within recent years, the major emphasis of most published work related to school-based schemes of initial teacher training has been upon the identification, exploration and development of the complex mentoring skills required by teachers to co-ordinate student teachers' classroom related learning experiences. While this work has rightfully received ever increasing attention, less consideration has been given to the equally significant and challenging task of managing and co-ordinating school-based training within the context of the whole school.

The management issues here are diverse and intricate, and reflect the need for a school's commitment, as an institution, to its involvement in initial teacher training, and to the deployment and co-ordination of staff and resources to that end. Once the school has made that commitment, there are clear management implications to ensure, amongst other whole school concerns, that continuity in pupils' learning is maintained. These same management issues also impinge upon the nature of the partnership between higher education institutions and the schools, especially as they concern the practicalities of managing the links between school and the higher education institution.

Within schools, the role of professional tutor is increasingly at the centre of the wider management of school-based initial teacher training programmes. The research study which is reported in this chapter focuses explicitly upon the understandings and expertise required by professional tutors, specifically within the Oxford Internship scheme, to manage, support, complement and monitor the activities of school staff involved in school-based training. The study also considers the different characteristics of schools, and the ways in which those characteristics facilitate, complicate or constrain the performance of different Internship professional tutors' work in relation to the management of school-based teacher training.

It is appropriate at this point to clarify what is meant by the term 'professional tutor'. The early stages of my research demonstrated that the term 'professional tutor', while still retaining functions deriving from the James Report (DES, 1972), was often interpreted differently from one secondary school to the next. For the purposes of the research programme, the term 'professional tutor' relates to the distinctive boundaries and functions which are specific to the role within the Oxford Internship scheme, in order to differentiate this interpretation of the role from its wider, more varying connotations.

The Internship professional tutor is a member of staff within an Oxfordshire secondary school, who, as part of the school's involvement with the Internship scheme, is designated to be responsible for work with the whole group of interns attached to the school, particularly in the field of whole school approaches to cross-curricular issues. This work will mostly take place within a structured programme (the General Programme), which is school-based and is linked with the study of cross-curricular issues which takes place at Oxford University Department of Educational Studies (OUDES). The professional tutor is responsible for the overall co-ordination of the school's involvement in the Internship scheme, and works closely with a tutor from OUDES, the General Tutor, who is attached to a particular school.

An overview of the research programme

The overall research programme (Pell, 1994) developed across three distinct phases, and originally stemmed from the researcher's involvement in the planning and early implementation of the Oxford Internship scheme. The first stage featured the devising of 'guidelines' appropriate to the role of the Internship professional tutor, and these were based upon both existing 'good practice' and the needs of the new Internship scheme. The second phase concerned a detailed evaluation of the guidelines in practice, during the first year of the Internship scheme. The third phase focused upon two research questions:

(1) How have different Internship professional tutors' different personal histories and concerns, and their experiences of their institutional contexts shaped their differing practices and expectations for their part in the Internship scheme?

(2) **What are the criteria of 'good practice' within the work of Internship professional tutors, as embodied in their concerns with notions of 'quality', which were not captured in the guidelines?**

It is with this third phase of the research that this chapter is concerned.

The research questions were formulated as a result of the findings from the earlier stages of the research, the researcher's own experiences as an Internship professional tutor, and a detailed survey of literature connected with the theory of organisations. In particular, the two research questions evolved from an analysis of Silverman's 'Action Frame of Reference' which he referred to, not so much as a theory of organisations, but 'as a method of analysing social relations within organisations' (Silverman, 1970). In that sense, Silverman's 'action framework' offered the structure by which the role of the Internship professional tutor might be understood in greater depth and with a more refined dimension of methodological rigour than had been possible before.

A second major theoretical influence upon the research questions was a study of Ball's work within schools-as-organisations, and more particularly, his analysis of 'micro-politics' (Ball, 1987) which emphasised the detailed exploration of the 'folk-knowledge' of practising teachers, and the achieving of an 'understanding of the interweaving of personal lives with organisational and social structures' (p. 279).

Also embodied within the research questions were concerns about 'quality', which derived from the researcher's own practice as an Internship professional tutor, and which were also embedded in the research surrounding the evaluation of the guidelines.

The method chosen for this phase of the study consisted of six case studies of Internship professional tutors, each of whose practices was explored through a series of semi-structured, interrelated interviews, spanning a whole year of the Internship scheme. The interviews were designed to explore, in depth, issues and concerns expressed by each Internship professional tutor. There was no assumption, on the part of the researcher, that a generalising possibility across these current concerns would necessarily emerge. Neither was there any intention to test each Internship professional tutor's understandings in terms of the validity of interpretation, or to explore reliability.

The focus of the study was to be on individual Internship professional tutors, and especially on the ways they construed and took account of the complex institutional contexts within which they worked. The variety of contexts which their different schools provided was thus central to the investigation, not in order to study the schools as organisations, but rather to study Internship professional tutors' ways of responding to, and taking account of, these diverse institutional contexts.

A summary of Silverman's 'Action Framework' and its application to the research questions

According to Silverman, the 'Action Framework', when applied to a particular organisation, 'analyses both the source of action and its often complex consequences', (op. cit., p. 155). This approach examines 'the definitions of the situation held by participants, and explains what happens in organisations as the outcome of their motivated behaviour, and the choices that they make in the light of these definitions', (ibid., p. 159). In terms of sequence, the approach offers a method to establish at the outset the context within which actors both perform their actions and give a meaning to them. Once that context has been defined, then the actions which take place within that setting may be examined, and the consequences, both intended and unintended, of those actions may be reviewed.

Silverman's 'Action Framework' is structured around six key concepts which, when transposed to the role of Internship professional tutor, provided the model for the analysis of that role. The concepts are as follows:

(1) The Internship professional tutor's professional background and institutional context.
(2) The motivation of 'ideal-typical' Internship professional tutors.
(3) The Internship professional tutor's present definition of his or her situation within the organisational framework.
(4) The typical actions of different Internship professional tutors.
(5) The nature and source of the Internship professional tutor's intended and unintended consequences of action.
(6) The influence of change upon the Internship professional tutor's performance of his or her role.

The next section of the chapter takes the six individual Internship professional tutors, and attempts to create second order, theorised accounts of the distinctive features within the practice of each individual. The accounts are presented in a way which is consistent with the addressing of the first of the two research questions referred to above.

Each account attempts to present, as accurately as possible, the way a particular Internship professional tutor sees his or her role, and seeks to reflect the language that such an individual uses to express his or her attitudes towards the interactions that each one is involved in, as part of the performance of the Internship role.

ACCOUNTS OF SIX INTERNSHIP PROFESSIONAL TUTORS ABSTRACTED FROM THEIR OWN ACCOUNTS OF THEIR WORK

The distinctive features of Gordon's involvement as Internship professional tutor

Gordon, after spending fifteen years in his present school, has extensive experience of its staff, its procedures and its hierarchies. He enjoys the support of the head who, a year prior to the study, offered him the 'new challenge' of assuming a different role as Internship professional tutor. Yet as Gordon begins his second year in the role, he is very aware of his own inexperience.

The change in responsibilities has left him confident as an expert in the practices of his school, which he sees as a strength for an Internship professional tutor, whose role encompasses the induction of interns into the complexities of the school. But, as Internship professional tutor, Gordon has had to establish different working relationships with staff he has known well in a different context, and in a different hierarchy of subject based responsibilities.

His 'inexperience', in the Internship professional tutor role, has made him eager to seek advice, to glean hints and reassurance from a number of other sources. In his first year, his initial understanding of Internship and his first encounter with the school-based General Programme were derived from the General Tutor who represented an experienced authority, and a figure well established within the school. The model of the General Programme, which Gordon experienced, was 'structured', 'authoritative', and 'formal', with 'less opportunity for feedback', where the interns were concerned. Gordon accepted the style of delivery and the approach towards interns' learning which his first General Tutor adopted as appropriate and the norm.

In his second year, Gordon's new General Tutor had a very different style from the previous incumbent. He was new to the school and new to Internship, and offered Gordon different possibilities for planning and operating the General Programme. The new General Tutor promoted a 'more relaxed atmosphere' in which the interns' learning took place. The General Programme was 'more varied in structure', allowed more time for the interns 'to reflect', and the General Tutor's approach encouraged a 'more active involvement of the interns in their learning', and an opportunity for Gordon to put forward ideas of his own.

In his first year, Gordon relied upon advice given to him by his predecessor, a deputy head who had carried out the Internship professional tutor responsibilities as part of a wider job description. This reliance upon his predecessor as a source of experience lasted into the second year, when Gordon was still seeking the deputy's opinion on how to react to staff concern about interns' dress and appearance, on their first day in the school.

Gordon's sense of his own inexperience carries over to the complex relationship he has with the group of mentors, whom he characterises, in the first interview, as 'a team that would not be of my own choosing', and, containing within the group, 'several . . . who ought to be rested and put out to grass'. He does, however, see them as a source of advice: 'I have a lot to learn from mentors, too'; but he also seeks to pre-empt their concerns, by a demonstration of his own ability to co-ordinate and manage his responsibilities as Internship professional tutor. When his preparation of induction materials for the interns was queried by some of the mentors, who said, 'It'd be good if they had . . .', Gordon was able to add, 'They've got that'. In this context, he 'felt much better organised'.

Certain aspects of the Internship network of roles, and some features of the General Programme, do not appear as high priorities within Gordon's practice. He is not concerned, in any of the interviews, with Curriculum Tutors and their visits to the school, and the kind of information they might have concerning the overall progress of the interns' teaching. He leaves the discussions surrounding interns' dissertations to the General Tutor. He sees OUDES as a source of information about Internship procedures and deadlines. He does, however, apply considerable energy, and he deploys a battery of skills, to stamp his own impression upon the administration and management of Internship within his own school.

In his first year, Gordon reacted to Internship procedures very much as they arose; his management of aspects such as the involvement of interns within the tutorial system was 'haphazard'. His concern in dealing with mentors was to 'keep them up to date on information' from OUDES. His creation of a complex 'curriculum matrix' to monitor the interns' involvement in classes was largely ineffectual, he admits, in achieving the purpose behind its design, but it had 'interested the head'.

In his second year, Gordon is concerned to plan ahead, to be proactive, to forestall others' questions and concerns, and not to be taken by surprise. He selects and arranges information for the interns' induction, and issues guidelines to form tutors; he takes a pride in his own judgement in placing interns with appropriately matched form tutors. He comments: 'I've acted more or less as a marriage-broker, and I think it's worked well, with the pairings that have been organised'.

Throughout the year, Gordon seeks and sustains the support and approval of the head as a key strategy in securing control over the management of the scheme. At the beginning of the year, Gordon relays to the head the interns comments on the 'stark' school decor, and is able to receive funding from him to effect improvements. Gordon involves the head as a speaker in two sessions of the General Programme, thereby, he claims, highlighting to the interns the head's significance and influence over teaching styles and the deployment of resources. Gordon refers problems to the head, seeking and then implementing the advice he receives. He includes an account of the advantages to be derived from Internship in the high-profile school development plan, and, later in the year, he discusses with the head the appointment of new mentors for the following year, and feels secure that his recommendations will be accepted.

The support which Gordon derives from the head has significance within the occasionally contentious relationship which Gordon has with the group of mentors in the school. Gordon's remarks in the first interview signal his concern that he is dealing with a group of mentors who are largely established in their ways, and who owe no allegiance to him, since Gordon had no say in their appointment to the role.

He is very concerned to 'pull them together' into 'a team' who respond to him positively, and who share their aspirations and practice collectively as a group. Gordon has a clear model of what he sees as 'positive mentors' who 'share ideas', 'discuss Internship', and seek his advice. In this context, Gordon looks to the meetings of Internship professional tutors at OUDES as a source of advice about the conduct of school-based mentor meetings. He learns from such contacts that the rapport between mentors and Internship professional tutors may be different from his own experiences, especially in the convening and operation of these meetings.

Here, Gordon experiences the difference between receiving advice, which adds to his stock of knowledge, and actually being able to implement such advice within the structures and interplay of roles within the school. This problem takes us to the centre of Gordon's concerns: his continuing aspiration to manage and control the school-based aspects of Internship, and to devise strategies and procedures to enable him to do so.

Gordon finds his desire to call a mentor meeting impeded by institutional structures. Other kinds of meetings abound, the lunch break is short, a visiting speaker calls away his mentors, or a protracted parents' evening leaves no time for mentors to meet. Informal contacts with mentors have to suffice, until a document arrives from OUDES seeking suggestions for intern school-based activities in the final weeks of the course. OUDES requires a response from mentors and the Internship professional tutor.

Gordon now supports the new mentor from his own department, who proposes that interns, in all departments, share in one project to provide valuable materials linked to the school's homework policy. The homework policy is a matter of concern to the head at this time. The proposal meets OUDES' requirements, is supported by the head, and appears in the interests of the school, its subject departments and the interns themselves. The Biology mentor, whose earlier rebellion against the timing of the General Programme intruding upon curriculum time had been 'crushed' by Gordon, declines to accept, goes his own way and is isolated. Gordon later checks that all is going well, by using a session of the General Programme to receive 'feedback' on the interns' progress in the 'homework project'.

Gordon's ambition to secure control is demonstrated in other ways. An important source of control over information is the writing of intern job references. By being the sole school referee for all interns, Gordon ensures that he has good reason to have access to a whole range of information which otherwise might be unavailable to him. Gordon's criteria for achieving quality in the implementation of Internship, at a management level in his school, may be indicated by the proliferation, in the account of his activities, of words such as 'efficient', 'effective', 'organised', 'checklist', 'went smoothly', 'worked well'. He is concerned about evaluation, and 'feedback'.

Throughout the year of the interviews, Gordon, successfully for the most part, constructed procedures and evaluative measures to manage and implement the Internship scheme within his school.

The distinctive features of Derek's involvement as Internship professional tutor

The school's pattern of staff development activities across the year lies at the centre of Derek's interpretation of the role of Internship professional tutor. Derek's range of responsibilities as a deputy head comprise initial teacher training, induction of new staff, school-based INSET, appraisal, and wider staff development. The scope of these responsibilities shapes the way that he makes sense of his own involvement within Internship. Here Derek's role is both defined by, and expressed through, the pattern of the year's events. Time, staff development needs, and actions to provide for those needs are fused together. The interns' induction to the school occurs 'midway' through the training cycle; to Derek the spring term means staff appraisal, the probationers' interim report and two assessment points for the interns.

Therefore, in Derek's articulation of his role, Internship is one part in a continuum of training that spans the different 'stages' of one year, or 'staff development cycle'. Interns are a 'part of school life', not a 'bolted on' extra. The effectiveness of the training which Internship offers to the interns is matched by the staff development opportunities the scheme provides for the school staff who become mentors. Internship is also a source of staff recruitment, as Derek admits: 'we've appointed five interns to the staff this year'. The appointed interns, as a result of their training, are seen by Derek as better placed to be successful in their first year in teaching, and so require, from Derek's perspective, a less intensive induction to the school.

Moreover, as ex-interns, such newly qualified staff, in Derek's view, are close to an understanding of the 'stages' of Internship and, therefore, are able to empathise with the needs of interns. Accordingly, Derek believes that a 'carefully considered gamble' is worth taking in using such ex-interns as mentors. As mentors, they may be close to the needs of the interns, but inexperienced in providing the training to meet those needs. Their inexperience in the delivery of training implies to Derek that they require to be trained in the skills of mentoring. Therefore, they are brought into a new cycle of training, devised by Derek and a more experienced mentor, who is described as a 'super mentor'.

The above example seeks to demonstrate a logic in Derek's practice which was revealed in the various stages of his thinking across the year. The logic was not neat in practice, nor was it preconceived on his part, as far as the data show but such a linkage of actual events and considerations does provide one instance of the way he views the different aspects of his wider role, as parts of one continuum of training. Derek's perception of the value of mentor meetings is a good example of his thinking. In the first part of the year, such meetings, in Derek's view and, he asserts, in that of his mentors, were held to be unnecessary, if they could be by-passed by written information, and informal contacts. In the second interview, his opinion was much the same. By the end of the year, the mentor meetings had assumed a new significance and purpose, as vehicles for implementing the new cycle of training referred to earlier.

The General Programme is also seen by Derek as an element of the larger staff training programme of the school.The interns have distinctive training needs which need to be addressed. Therefore, Derek, who 'plans and runs it', is aware of and can articulate the logic implicit within the contributions which he makes to their training within the General Programme, and the contribution which other staff offer. Each session he describes has a training purpose, and he is very much to the fore in leading sessions himself.

The General Programme has a momentum of its own; the first part is planned and carefully structured; the second part involves the interns in being empowered to identify their own needs, and to offer suggestions themselves, whereby those needs may be met. They run the General Programme, at this stage, as part, it would seem, of their own professional development. Moreover, while the programme is there for interns, it is also available to all other student teachers that pass through the school, and is seen as having potential to train new staff who want to have access to the kinds of expertise which the programme imparts.

An important strand in Derek's view of his role is the confidence he has in his own experience within the school, and in the distinctive and established parameters of his role as 'personnel deputy'. He is confident in the support he can expect from other roles, whether heads of department with whom he negotiates the selection of new mentors; or the wider staff, whose criticisms of intern 'untidiness' or 'cliquey' isolation are seen, by Derek, as reflections of their own teacher habits.

He is confident in his dealings with mentors, whom he sees as a 'stable group', 'experienced', and 'easy to run'. He is happy to delegate to them the responsibility for arranging intern placements in tutor groups, seeing in this no diminution of his own authority. This change, he believes, may offer them a staff development opportunity, and if he is called in, as 'backstop', to clear up 'a mess' caused by lack of co-ordination between interns, tutors and mentors, then such an occurrence will benefit the mentors, and act as a learning experience.

Derek is also assured in his understanding of Internship, and expresses a clear view of the partnership between school and OUDES. The partnership is 'tangible in name and in reality'. His work with the General Tutor is, he suggests, evidence of the reality of partnership. Internship offers the school an integrated and effective form of initial teacher training; it is 'a well worked out scheme'. The school derives benefits from its involvement through the recruitment of well trained teachers, and the provision of staff development opportunities for teachers who become mentors. By taking on large numbers of interns, the school receives funding which enables Derek to sponsor further useful staff development, in the form of the role of a 'super mentor' which has been mentioned earlier. Materials and research into school policies are derived, as a 'pay back', from the intern dissertations, and special end of year projects.

The institutional context within which Derek operates contains no serious challenges to his role as Internship professional tutor. He manages the time table so that his 'super mentor' has the space to carry out the training which he envisages taking place the following year. His wider role provides him with access to the school's INSET policies and appraisal system through which mentors are mostly empowered to assume their responsibilities. His monitoring of interns' involvement across school groups does not present a problem; Derek focuses upon those areas of the school where he is able to intervene, if necessary, and leaves any problems in other areas to be resolved as and when they arise. Overall, Derek appears in control of the events around him. He does not seem to be challenged by other roles or hierarchies, and the dominant strand within his implementation of the Internship professional tutor role is the power his range of responsibilities gives him, when combined with the strength of his extensive experience.

The distinctive features of Mary's involvement as Internship professional tutor

A dominant factor in Mary's performance of the Internship professional tutor role is the institutional complexity that surrounds her. Mary is a deputy head in an upper school (i.e. 13 – 18 age group). In order for the interns to have access to lower school teaching, negotiations have to be undertaken with neighbouring middle schools. These schools have no formal links with Internship, know nothing about the operation of the course, and derive no benefits from any funding in support of the scheme. Organisational links between the upper school and the feeder middle schools are loose and indistinct. At the beginning of the year a new middle school opens nearby, and there is a measure of competition between Mary's school and an adjacent upper school for the establishing of links, and for the placement of interns.

In this context, Mary attempts, at the beginning of the year, to negotiate the interns' teaching time tables, and their placements within the middle schools, without being sure whose responsibility it is to make the necessary connections. Should she assume overall responsibility, or should the task be delegated to the mentors who work in the various middle schools, or should tutors from OUDES handle the negotiations? The head is keen for her to negotiate with the new middle school, in order to establish early links with that school, but she is sensitive to the fact that the new head of the middle school is unwell, and that the staff there are the result of a recent amalgamation of schools, and unlikely to be in a receptive frame of mind.

When her negotiations begin, the middle schools want to receive interns in subject areas that are beneficial to their needs. Their priorities are different from Mary's. While the negotiations are pending, the nearby upper school 'poaches' some intern placements from one of the middle schools in order to resolve their own timetabling problems.

A further complication to the institutional context is the need for many of the interns to travel to a nearby 'sixth form centre' in order to have access to sixth form teaching. With interns, therefore, being off-site on many occasions, either at a middle school or at the sixth form, the opportunities for Mary to negotiate effective placements of interns within tutor groups are severely hampered.

Unsurprisingly, at the end of her various negotiations, with different institutions and different roles, her dominant thought is: 'Does everyone know what they're doing?'

Moreover, the distinctive ethos of her own school presents potentially challenging situations to the group of interns. The school has a strong Christian tradition, which influences the way certain departments are able to approach particular aspects of the curriculum. There is a significant proportion of pupils for whom English is a second language, and whose cultural diversity is substantially different from that which may be found in the majority of schools receiving interns. The school also has particularly flexible attitudes towards discipline, and a strong sense of social responsibility for the pupils in its charge. Therefore, a significant item on Mary's agenda for interns is their induction into the distinctive ways and practices of the school.

Mary's primary concern is with the practical implementation of the course. Her role is not made easier by the nature and extent of her own responsibilities. This is her second year in the post of Internship professional tutor, and her seniority as a deputy head, while offering her the status to enter into the negotiations described above, also imposes upon her a range of other responsibilities in the school, including the very recent responsibility for the school's sixth form. Having only had one full year as Internship professional tutor, she feels inexperienced in performing the role, and attends the

Internship professional tutor meetings at OUDES to gain guidance and clarification concerning her responsibilities.

There is a sense of her own isolation, in Mary's accounts, as she attempts to operate Internship in a coherent and effective manner. She has to plan and oversee the implementation of the General Programme, with very little active support from the new General Tutor. The programme follows as closely as possible the recommendations made in the Internship handbook, but on several occasions she is unable to attend the sessions, because she has to cover the class of the teacher who is addressing the interns.

The interns themselves are scattered across sites and buildings; the science interns remain in their laboratories, and, since OUDES is not very distant from the school, many interns go there straight after school to gather materials for their teaching. Her extensive responsibilities make it difficult for her to talk to the interns as often as she would like, and problems gradually surface through the year, both with the interns and an absentee mentor.

Her own sense of inexperience is reinforced by the fact that three of her mentors are new to the role. Moreover, the complexities of the school's routines make mentor meetings difficult to arrange very often. After initial one to one consultations with the new mentors, 'to allay their fears', Mary relies largely on informal contacts, but 'mostly leaves it to them'. There are many Internship practices and procedures about which she herself is unsure. She is uncertain about what is expected of interns' involvement in tutor groups; she is unclear about whether interns may leave the school if they have no teaching commitments; and she finds the division of the Internship year into Phase One and Phase Two, confusing and hazy.

In conclusion, Mary's institutional context is complex and problematic. The initial advantages, which Mary cites, of the school being small and welcoming may be significantly offset by the dispersal of the interns across other institutions. To add to this complexity, her own role is multi-dimensional, demanding, and time consuming. The other roles within the Internship network around her, who might be able to reinforce her and offer support, are either equally inexperienced or unsupportive. Mary left the school to take up a new appointment at the end of the second term during the year of the study.

The distinctive features of Jane's involvement as Internship professional tutor

Jane replaces Mary at the beginning of the summer term. She is presented with the same institutional context as Mary, but she does not have to face the same tasks, connected with the Internship professional tutor role, as her predecessor. The General Programme has been largely completed by Mary, and the interns' timetables, a source of great concern to Mary, are in place.

The practical tasks facing Jane include completing arrangements for the final General Programme sessions, providing encouragement and support for the interns' school-based, end of year projects, offering guidance in the preparation of the interns' dissertations, and managing the final evaluation of the year's school-based programme.

The transitional period between one Internship professional tutor and the next would prove crucial in establishing Jane in her new role, and in providing her with the opportunities to map out her own agenda of concerns about the implementation of the role, and the methods she would employ to secure her objectives.

Central to Jane's involvement is the personal and professional background which she brings to the role. Her own history provides her with a strong platform on which to build her own distinctive view of her new role, and the means by which to implement, effectively, the school-based aspects of the scheme. Firstly, she is directly interested in teacher training, which provides her with the motivation to apply for the job.

Secondly, she has previous experience as a mentor, so feels she 'knows what to do', and is confident of areas of knowledge connected to Internship: 'Phase One, Phase Two, I know what they're about'. Above all, she is keen 'to get involved straight away'.

Her experience as mentor enables her, albeit from a different perspective, to appreciate what should be involved in an Internship professional tutor's meetings with a group of mentors. The mentors, she believes, need to be aware of what is going on around them in the scheme: they should receive information about the contents of the General Programme. There should be 'a sharing of ideas', and mentors need to have certain information concerning their responsibilities or be provided with certain feedback, at particular times during the Internship year. The meetings, she feels, ought to be a regular part of the school calendar, to avoid clashes with teachers' other meeting commitments, and should be timed to coincide with key aspects of the scheme.

Her experience as mentor makes her appreciate the special relationship which exists between interns and their mentor, and, when combined with her new perspective as Internship professional tutor she also appreciates the sensitivity which is required by the Internship professional tutor in giving freedom to experienced mentors in the performance of their role, and offering support to less practised mentors. As part of her new role, she wishes to 'get to know the interns better', by observing their teaching, but she is equally alert to the view that she must avoid 'stepping on mentors' toes'.

Her experience as Head of Year, a responsibility she still retains, also influences the implementation of her new role. In terms of her own status within the school, her position as Head of Year gives her easy access to senior staff, including the head. As a result of her own commitment to the school's pastoral system, she feels the need to stress the value of interns being attached to tutor groups as an important part of their preparation for their first teaching post. She wants the attachments to be 'tighter' and more co-ordinated, and to be 'checked early on' to determine the effectiveness of the attachments. She wants the interns and form tutors to have clear guidelines to establish practicable expectations, on both sides, of what would be involved in the attachments.

Moreover, she transposes her own pastoral concerns for pupils to her involvement in the interns' general well-being: she senses that the interns need 'more looking after' and that they should be 'cushioned'. She makes a priority of being available to interns on a regular yet informal basis.

In terms of her awareness of Internship, and her own experience of it in practice, she strives to use the range of options and skills available within the structure of the scheme, and, most particularly, the strength that resides in the network of Internship roles when they effectively connect together. Jane builds on her understanding of her predecessor's concerns, and uses the Internship network to resolve a number of difficulties which face her in her first term in the role of Internship professional tutor.

Initially, she is presented with the results of a serious breakdown in the network of roles. Prior to her appointment, a pair of interns were failing to receive the support they should expect from their mentor.

According to Jane, the interns did not want to show disloyalty to their mentor by raising the issue with the Curriculum Tutor; they did not report the matter to other staff in OUDES 'because they felt the school was doing them a favour' by assisting in their training, and they 'did not want to cause trouble'. They did not confide in the school's General Tutor because he 'was rather detached'; nor did they take the matter to Jane's predecessor because 'she was too busy . . . and unapproachable'. A conspiracy of silence ensues, which is only broken and resolved when Jane takes over as Internship professional tutor. Jane immediately focuses the attention of all the Internship roles upon the problem, and brings in the head as well.

A second example demonstrates how Jane uses the power of the network of roles to resolve the very difficult issue of middle schools and their involvement in the scheme. The uncertainties of the links between Jane's school and the new middle school have in part been resolved over the year, in that a liaison group has been established between the two schools to tackle problems of common concern. However, the issue of the middle school's connections with Internship remain unclear, as does the apportionment of responsibilities, across the Internship network of roles, for ensuring such connections are implemented and effective.

Jane is aware of the need to 'co-ordinate' the involvement of the new middle school, and accepts an offer to give a talk on Internship to the liaison group. Using her connections as a science teacher, she negotiates for the science interns to be placed there the following year. She harnesses the contributions of other Internship roles by suggesting that all overarching negotiations on intern placements should be channelled through her.

The mentors would be responsible for the individual timetables of the interns. She urges the General Tutor to visit the middle school to establish an OUDES 'presence' there, and passes on her views to OUDES that Curriculum Tutors might visit interns teaching in middle schools. She also stresses the need for OUDES to co-ordinate a wider policy in connection with all upper schools in the area, and their relationship with middle schools, within the context of Internship.

She conducts a detailed evaluation of the year's school-based programme both to identify interns' concerns, and to support her own planning of the General Programme in the following year. She takes charge of the final General Programme activities, chairs the meetings herself, and plans more active participation in the programme by the interns.

Moreover, Jane is prepared to use elements within the institutional context around her to effect changes and improvements. She contacts the deputy responsible for devising the timetable, and places a bid for mentors to have free time to liaise and plan with interns; she asks for lower school classes, where possible, to be available on 'J' week days; and she asks that mentor meetings be set within the school's calendar of regular meetings.

At the centre of Jane's implementation of the Internship professional tutor role is the strength of her own personal commitment to the responsibilities involved; the harnessing of elements of her own professional background to an interpretation of the requirements of the role; an endeavour to learn quickly from those experienced in the role, and her full use of the power of the combined range of Internship roles to resolve potentially contentious aspects of the institutional context which surround her.

The distinctive features of Peter's involvement as Internship professional tutor

The institutional complications which arise from the size and split-site nature of Peter's school dominate his view of the role he performs within Internship. At many times in the year, these institutional factors impinge upon his co-ordinating functions as Internship professional tutor. The timetable is complex and not always accurate in the information it provides for Peter and his mentors in their attempts to design co-ordinated programmes for interns. Occasionally, at the beginning of the year, during 'J' weeks, mentors design timetables for their interns, which conflict with the timetable which the Internship professional tutor is using in his attempts to arrange tutor placements for the interns. Accordingly, interns are sometimes in the wrong place at the wrong time, depending on the version of the timetable which they attempt to follow.

The complexities of the school cause difficulties for Peter in liaising with mentors. He favours 'informal contacts' with mentors rather than more formal mentor meetings, although some such meetings are timetabled into the school's calendar. Owing to the pattern of teaching which he and the mentors have to follow, informal meetings are difficult to contrive, especially when two mentors remain permanently on a site far removed from Peter's own teaching base. He feels that such constraints impede his efforts to support new mentors, and, as a result, he is 'not doing as good a job' as he would like.

The split-site nature of the school means that the interns are thinly dispersed across the different sites. By being in smaller groups, Peter feels that they are more likely to be integrated within the day to day life of the school, and that staff are more disposed to treat interns as normal members of staff.

However, he hardly ever encounters Curriculum Tutors when they come into school, unless he happens to be in the right place at the right time, so he has little opportunity, especially later in the year, to check on problems which interns may be facing.

Furthermore, a significant concern for Peter, as the year goes by, is the involvement of the wider school staff within the implementation of Internship. While he is anxious that all parts of the school should be involved in the scheme, he is aware that very few staff appreciate the full implications of Internship, and he is 'frustrated' in his attempts to find a way of informing the general staff, and ensuring that his concerns are shared.

Again institutional factors intervene. Full staff meetings are rare, and when they do occur they happen simultaneously on all three sites. An input from the Internship professional tutor is therefore difficult to arrange in a way that will have maximum effect on the whole staff. The school's agenda for INSET days is under pressure from the increasing innovation and demands of the National Curriculum. In Peter's view, there is no room for Internship concerns in that programme.

Moreover, his mentors, who are largely inexperienced in the role, are of lower status than many members of their departments, and, therefore, are in a difficult position to offer advice to those who might benefit, according to Peter, from training in the principles and practices of Internship. Peter believes that if Internship is implemented properly within departments, it offers greater benefits to the quality of teaching, rather than having an adverse effect upon pupil learning. He is at a loss to see a way of promoting the 'trickle effect' of Internship principles within the school.

The obstacles posed by institutional factors also clash with Peter's priorities which derive from his own professional background. He has been a Head of Year, and greatly values the contribution which attachment to the school's pastoral system can provide for interns. However, the tutorial system is under pressure in the school, and is entering a phase of change and development. Many of the staff are 'uncomfortable' in their role as tutors, and, therefore, are unwilling to welcome interns into PSE lessons where their own confidence as teachers is in question. Peter has difficulty, considering the size of the school, in finding enough tutors who are happy to involve interns in their pastoral work.

As the system is to be changed the following year, he feels, at the end of the year, that he has not been assiduous in asking for feedback from form tutors, or in checking on the progress of the interns' involvement, other than in an open discussion during the General Programme, where many of his concerns find echoes in the interns' own experiences.

His enactment of his professional responsibilities is further complicated during the year by his performing the dual role of mentor and Internship professional tutor. As a mentor he appreciates the complexities of designing timetables for interns, and as Internship professional tutor he senses the impracticality of attempting to affect changes in those timetables, when they are so problematic to co-ordinate in the first place.

As a mentor he feels that he can appreciate more directly the 'costs and benefits' accruing from involvement in the scheme, in that he experiences at first hand the problems, expense of 'energy and time,' and 'the draining effect' which derive from having to resolve the problems facing an intern who is under pressure. In this instance, he feels the need of a 'sounding board,' or a support, which, in normal circumstances, would have been himself, in his other role as Internship professional tutor. For Peter, at this time, a role is missing in the Internship network.

At the end of the year, Peter encounters two distinct problems which stem from the internal politics of the school and his own restricted status within the school's management hierarchy. Peter, as Internship professional tutor, finds himself having to adopt the role of advocate for the scheme and the school's continuing involvement in it, in the face of the senior management's concerns over the 'costs and benefits'. Peter is aware that the funding coming into the school, in support of mentors and his own role, is not being used entirely for those purposes, but he has to tread warily, as senior management ponder the checks and balances of the school's involvement in the scheme.

A second issue derives from the strongly independent and powerful faculty system which operates in the school. Peter, from his position outside this hierarchy, has to negotiate with faculty heads to discover, firstly, whether a faculty wishes to be involved in the scheme the following year, and, secondly, the identity of the faculty-nominated mentor.

Each faculty may unilaterally withdraw from the scheme without consulting Peter; and each faculty is entitled to develop its own distinct policy for the rotation of its mentors. Peter is pleased that faculties are interested in Internship, and that they consider the scheme when making their policies, but he is concerned that, in these processes, he is often not consulted before important decisions which affect his role are made.

Finally, he is heartened by the positive atmosphere that is generated by the group of interns within the General Programme. The General Programme, he asserts, is a significant feature of his Internship activities, and he is concerned to promote a varied programme, blending a mixture of styles of delivery, and encouraging the active involvement of interns in their own learning.

The distinctive features of David's involvement as Internship professional tutor

David has been involved in his school, in one capacity or another, for twenty years, and this extensive experience provides a solid basis for the kind of rapport with the staff which he sees as essential in the smooth enactment of his Internship role. His status as a member of the senior management team gives him access to the hierarchy of roles within the school, whose influence enables him both to have 'a free hand in running the scheme within the school' and, on occasions, to 'cut corners' where the tight procedures of a complex school are concerned.

David has had considerable experience in the implementation of Internship across the years. He was a member of the Internship Development Group which helped to plan the scheme, and since that time has been chairman of the Internship professional tutors' group. This experience has given him confidence in assuming more of a role as a 'teacher-educator,' within the context of the General Programme; rather than seeing himself, as he had at the outset of the scheme, as 'just a teacher of pupils'. His own experiences enable him, he feels, to have more confidence in 'shaping and packaging his knowledge' as Internship professional tutor, so that it makes more sense to interns, and is helpful in advancing their own learning.

Here David differentiates between his aspirations to contribute to the interns' learning, as 'whole teachers, not just subject specialists', at a more formal and structured level within the General Programme; and his objective, at a more informal level, both within the General Programme and within the wider context of the school, to 'acclimatise' the interns to the culture and 'ethos' of the staffroom.

David sees the planning and implementation of the General Programme, which he shares with the General Tutor, as a key part of his overall involvement. His priorities here affect what he characterises as the quality of the programme. He monitors the presentation of issues, and the reaction of interns to them, as the year goes by. He feels that the timing of the various inputs should attempt to 'match the interns' understanding and experience' at that stage of their year.

David describes his personal approach to the role of Internship professional tutor as a balance between what he sees as the proactive and reactive aspects of his interpretation of the role. The proactive nature of his responsibilities involves the 'storing of experience' from one year to the next, to enable his planning, for example, of the interns' induction to the school or their involvement in the General Programme to take account of the lessons learned in previous programmes, and to predict the amount of information which he feels interns need to have at that stage in their involvement in the school.

Similarly he adjusts, from year to year, the information and procedures he sets in place for the benefit of staff, and to forestall any problems which his past experience suggests might arise.

A different aspect of his proactive role, as he sees it, depends upon the speed of communications by which potential difficulties are fed to him, so that he can respond before a serious problem arises. He relies upon the mentors to inform him of difficulties at an early stage; or he 'tunes in' to the staff 'grapevine' to detect potentially contentious issues.

His reactive role emerges when problems arise which are unexpected, and which usually require a rapid response on his part. Members of staff may object to aspects of the interns' behaviour or appearance. Heads of department may wish to impose their view of what interns should be doing upon less experienced mentors. Such problems, according to David's experience, may occur at any time. On such occasions, David has to 'prioritise the nature of the problem', and the level of his own response. The concerns of a deputy head over some aspect of Internship; a mentor's problems with an intern; an intern's cry for assistance; all have to be balanced, in David's view, with the limited time at his disposal and the complexities of a split site school. When David's other overlapping responsibilities for students from other teacher training institutions and his responsibility for newly qualified staff are added in, the reactive role, as he sees it, becomes even more pressured.

The institutional factors referred to above play their part in complicating the role which David has to perform. Communication problems arise across the school's three sites, each a mile apart from the other. One solution which he offers is to use himself as 'a backstop' in 'keeping a watching brief' over interns whose mentors are involved in cross-site travel. A second development which he promotes, in order to overcome the problems caused by the split sites, is the concept of 'joint mentors'. This idea involves the principal mentor, on one site, being supported in his supervision of interns by a second mentor on a different site which the interns visit during their teaching timetable. Otherwise, David remarks that it is easy to 'lose contact' with an intern or a mentor within such a context.

Moreover, as most interns, like members of staff, tend to teach only on one site, it is easy for interns to lose sight of the wider school picture. David's attempts to resolve this sense of isolation by rotating the General Programme meetings across the sites go some way to easing this difficulty. However, he finds that this solution presents more problems, in that interns have transport difficulties in travelling across sites to reach the location of the General Programme, and often, by arriving late, the interns cut short the available time for the programme itself. Of equal concern to David is the impact of the interns' cross-site teaching commitments upon the continuity of their involvement within tutor groups. He values the contribution which the interns' involvement in the school's tutorial system offers them, and is uneasy that their cross-site teaching sometimes offers interns the excuse to be less committed to the tutorial work, which some of them see as less important than their commitment to their subject departments.

Experience has taught David, so he claims, to have a sense of realism in the way he performs his role. Firstly, he has scaled down, over the years, the 'information pack' which interns receive at their induction to the school. He believes that the interns can only take in so much information, and that they tend to ask questions directly, concerning the things they need to know, rather than consulting staff hand books and policy documents.

Secondly, he wants to observe the interns teach, to obtain a more rounded view of their contribution to the school. However, he senses that it is impracticable for him to arrange to see thirteen interns 'in a meaningful way', and he, therefore, leaves the interns the option of asking him into a lesson, if they feel it will be helpful to them. Thirdly, he attempts to monitor the involvement of interns across the range of classes which they teach, to avoid any possible 'overloading' of pupils within the same combination of teaching groups. Again the complexities of the school timetable make any substantial intervention on his part in changing those timetables, unrealistic.

Another important element in David's account of his performance of his role within Internship concerns his collaboration with, and support of, the group of mentors in the school. He combines regular informal contacts with a pattern of more structured meetings during the course of the year. The meetings, in his view, enable the mentors to exchange ideas, review the progress of their respective interns, react to initiatives from OUDES, and to plan ahead. He values the feeling of the mentors that they are part of a 'team,' which enables them to be more supportive of his efforts to make the scheme within the school coherent and co-ordinated.

Evaluating the scheme's implementation within the school, and, in particular, his contribution to it as Internship professional tutor, is an important process for David. The form tutors provide written and informal feedback to David; and the mentors, through the regular meetings, also contribute their views on the success or otherwise of the year's programme. The interns, too, provide a detailed written evaluation as part of their final General Programme session. The whole process, according to David, helps him to move forward in the attempt to modify, and often 'look afresh' at the planning of the school-based course.

CONCLUSIONS

Common factors across different Internship professional tutors

This section presents an overview across the Internship professional tutors, distinguishing those factors within their various contexts which they have in common and those factors which differentiate them. The overall discussion of these distinguishing factors leads to the drawing of conclusions which are relevant to the first research question.

All the Internship professional tutors interviewed attempted to fulfil specific requirements of the post, as envisaged within the guidelines set down for the enactment of the Internship scheme within schools. They all set up an induction programme for their group of interns; they all planned and put into operation a school-based General Programme; they all involved their interns within the tutorial system operating within the school; they all assumed an overview of the operation of the mentors within the school, and interacted with people in a variety of roles within the staff, and with those tutors representing OUDES. These are all 'typical' actions which would be expected of a 'typical' Internship professional tutor working within the framework of the Internship scheme.

Across all the schools, institutional features such as the school timetable, pupil grouping policies adopted by subject departments, the pattern of school meetings, departmental strategies and hierarchies, the teaching commitments of staff, and the nature of the tutorial system in operation within the school present Internship professional tutors with administrative problems as each of them strives to integrate the interns into his or her school in ways that are beneficial for both them and the staff. The Internship professional tutor is also involved in balancing the responsibility which he or she has to the needs of the school as an educational establishment for the instruction of pupils, with the smooth and effective operation of the scheme whose aims focus upon the training of beginning teachers.

In pursuing these ends, the Internship professional tutors involved in this study encounter problems which are not solely administrative, but involve each of them in anticipating, reacting to, and resolving difficulties of communication between different individuals and groups. They also seek to deal diplomatically with any conflicts which arise as a result of a lack of awareness, on the part of the school staff, of the needs and expectations of interns; or, on the part of the interns, of a lack of awareness of the culture or ethos of the school, or, more specifically, of the school's accepted practices, procedures and methods of communication.

Internship professional tutors, in whatever school context they are placed, rely for much of their effectiveness upon successful interaction between their own role as Internship professional tutor and people in a wide variety of other roles. In such situations, each Internship professional tutor's personal approach, responsiveness, tact and speed of reaction appear to be significant characteristics which determine the successful management of such interactions.

Factors which differentiate Internship professional tutors

The understanding, within any one school, of what constitutes the Internship professional tutor's role may determine the status awarded to the post, the kind of person who is given the role, the range of responsibilities that accompany the position, and the kind of experience that may be seen as necessary for the job's fulfilment. Moreover, the distinctive composition of the role within any one school may affect the amount of time that its incumbent may have available to devote to the specific tasks, and the priorities that the particular Internship professional tutor establishes for implementing the role.

There are some factors which, among the five schools represented, appear as unique to a particular school. Derek's experience as Internship professional tutor has largely been shaped by the distinctive nature of his wider role as personnel deputy within the school. Jane's and Mary's concerns as Internship professional tutors reflect their institutional context which combines the features of an upper school, which has a distinctive Christian ethos, with links to outside organisations in the form of middle schools and a sixth form centre.

Even when significant similarities appear, the combination of factors within an individual Internship professional tutor's overall context make straightforward comparisons difficult to achieve. All Internship professional tutors are affected by the design and complexity of their respective school timetables, and the fact that these timetables are designed for a purpose different from that of being convenient for the enaction of a school-based teacher training programme. However, each Internship professional tutor devises strategies, according to his or her individual context and priorities, to overcome these difficulties, or, at least to marginalise the problems posed by the timetable.

Conclusions drawn from the data which address the second research question

The second research question concerns those criteria of 'good practice' which are not captured within the original guidelines for the role but which are reflected in the Internship professional tutors' notions of 'quality'.

There is a concern for quality within the practice of each individual Internship professional tutor, but that concern expresses itself in different ways according to the priorities which the Internship professional tutor brings to the role, and the possibilities arising from his or her personal commitment to the role, professional background and institutional factors. In this respect, the two research questions, which form the focal point of this final stage of the research programme, are interlinked; the range of factors which influence and shape each Internship professional tutor's practice affect that individual's perception of quality in terms of what is practicable and attainable or what is desirable and yet a distant goal.

In order to understand what each individual Internship professional tutor sees as quality, one has to grasp the nature of that person's day to day activity, within his or her professional context.

Individual Internship professional tutors' concerns with the notion of quality

Gordon

For Gordon, the concerns with quality which underpin his enactment of the role relate to ensuring that the component parts of his responsibilities are carried out efficiently and pragmatically. He feels secure in staying close to the guidelines and to practice recommended by other Internship professional tutors. The interns' induction to the school is carefully planned; their placements within tutor groups are thoughtfully orchestrated; and administrative tasks are meticulously implemented. Moreover, he is concerned with his role in relation to the school's mentors, and his efforts 'to pull them together' into a team. This is a central issue as far as his view of the quality of his performance is concerned.

Derek

Derek's criteria for judging the effectiveness of the Internship scheme within the school and his part in its implementation revolve around the ways in which the components of the scheme fit into the pattern of the school's wider staff development policies, and the particular dimensions of his own role as 'personnel deputy'. In particular, Derek sees ways of using the Internship partnership to strengthen his own priority to provide more intensive training for mentors.

Mary

Mary's notion of quality concerns her ability to make Internship operate within a difficult set of institutional factors. She wants to ensure that each part of the interns' programme is in place and is functioning. She strives to cope, to put all the pieces of the year's programme together so that, having done that, she can accommodate all the other responsibilities which she has to fulfil.

Jane

Jane, within the same context as Mary, but taking over from her later in the year, has different priorities and approaches to performing the Internship professional tutor role. For her the quality of the General Programme depends upon the active involvement of the interns within it. She draws upon her criteria for success as a former mentor and Head of Year to prioritise a close working relationship with mentors and interns. Her direct interest in teacher training, combined with the impetus offered by her acquiring a job as Internship professional tutor, which she actually wanted and which was not 'bolted on' to other responsibilities, drive her on to initiate changes in the way that Internship operates within the school, and in the way that she taps into the strengths of the Internship partnership.

Peter

Peter's notion of quality concerns the effective operation of the scheme within a complex institution. His priorities revolve around lines of communication between himself, mentors and other staff within a split-site school. His role as mentor makes him conscious of the need to make other staff, who are outside the Internship network of roles, aware of the practices which Internship requires of them. In terms of the General Programme, Peter seeks to ensure that the methods used in its delivery are varied, and involve the interns in active participation. Overall, the quality of Peter's work as Internship professional tutor is affected by the strong independence of the school's subject departments, and his senior management's application of 'cost effective' criteria to the operation of Internship within the school.

David

David's concerns with quality centre around the development of close links between the various roles within Internship, and an increasing focus upon the Internship professional tutor as a 'teacher educator', both within and beyond the delivery of the General Programme. His priority lies in matching the ways the interns learn about school with the timing of inputs within the General Programme, which aim to support that learning process.

The effectiveness of his own role is dependent upon the balance between reactive and proactive functions; between his learning from experience to forestall problems, and his making the right decisions in the face of unexpected events.

Conclusions relating to Internship professional tutors' concerns with quality which extend beyond the guidelines

The guidelines originally stressed the importance of six key processes within an Internship professional tutor's management of the scheme:

- induction,
- co-ordination,
- integration,
- support,
- monitoring,
- evaluation.

The work of the six Internship professional tutors examined within the final stage of the research programme demonstrates that there is still a preoccupation with these processes. Effective planning, administrative efficiency and overall control are elements which run through each Internship professional tutor's practice, no matter what the differences may be between each one in terms of experience in the role, status within the school, or personal commitment to the role.

More experienced Internship professional tutors, while still appraising their practice by its administrative effectiveness, have built up their confidence over the years, and feel more assured that they can achieve control over the running of the scheme in their respective schools. In certain areas, referred to in the guidelines, such as monitoring the impact of interns upon pupils' learning, they may acquire a sense of realism, that relatively little can be done by them to monitor this aspect successfully, in a proactive way. Increasingly, such Internship professional tutors become more preoccupied with the evolution of the scheme within their own schools, giving more attention to such notions as how interns learn during the General Programme (David), or how staff participation in Internship may advance staff development opportunities within the school (Derek).

In other respects, issues which may have been only lightly referred to, or indeed overlooked, in the guidelines, assume increasing importance to Internship professional tutors within the study.

Firstly, individual Internship professional tutors ascribe different reasons for wishing to promote effective school-based mentor meetings, but all see these sessions as valuable contributions to the effective management of Internship within their respective institutions, in a way which was not apparent in the guidelines.

Secondly, the guidelines, while mentioning the Internship professional tutor's role in addressing interns' problems, give no further pointers to the specific nature of this element of the role which is extended and developed, in the practice of some of the Internship professional tutors, to include mediating between the interns and the wider staff, when the latter encounter the habits of interns which are different from accepted staffroom practices. Here the Internship professional tutor may function as counsellor, mediator or advocate, thereby being instrumental in shaping the interns' understanding of teachers' professional codes and attitudes.

Thirdly, in their practice, four of the Internship professional tutors use interns' involvement in tutorial work as a means of spreading Internship to a wider range of staff than those in the few curriculum areas which are represented in the scheme. Furthermore, most of the Internship professional tutors give a higher priority to the tutor role aspect of the interns' work than was originally envisaged within the guidelines.

Finally, a significant element in four Internship professional tutors' perception of how the quality of the scheme in their respective schools may be enhanced concerns the need for the wider staff to be made aware of the ideas and practices of Internship. This was not an aspect of the course which featured in the guidelines.

In conclusion, it may be seen that a vital aspect of the Internship professional tutor's work involves developing effective relationships with interns, mentors, other Internship roles, and with the school staff as a whole. If there is a breakdown in any of these relationships, the overall effectiveness of the scheme suffers as a consequence.

At the centre of many Internship professional tutors' practice is a concern for the process of interns' learning which their work helps to promote, and here their criteria of quality extend beyond such processes as 'induction, integration and evaluation', referred to in the guidelines. Of primary concern to many Internship professional tutors is the learning which the interns acquire through their induction to the school which in turn feeds into and is supported by the General Programme in the way that it is structured, timed and delivered, to coincide with the curve of learning of any one group of interns. In this way interns acquire learning of a less formal kind which involves their being guided to an appreciation of professional values and staff culture.

Internship professional tutors, in many cases, are concerned to foster learning within three other groups. Firstly, all the Internship professional tutors, in various ways, strive to develop mentors' awareness and understanding of the scheme, notably through the school-based meetings which each Internship professional tutor promotes. Secondly, Internship professional tutors see themselves as instrumental in developing the awareness of the wider school staff towards Internship; whether this is achieved by means of spreading contacts between interns and staff as widely across the school as possible, largely through the interns' involvement in the school's tutorial system; or by arranging more formal INSET presentations. Such awareness might also be developed by the Internship professional tutor mediating with staff over problems and concerns which arise as a result of the interns' impact upon the staff. Thirdly, Internship professional tutors, through their regular termly meetings at OUDES, are concerned to promote their own learning by means of contacts with other Internship professional tutors, and so share ideas, concerns and notions of good practice.

WIDER IMPLICATIONS OF THE STUDY'S FINDINGS FOR POLICY AND PRACTICE WITHIN SCHOOL-BASED INITIAL TEACHER EDUCATION

Firstly, the study demonstrates both the need for, and the complexity of, a co-ordinating role such as that of the Internship professional tutor. Individual subject mentors play a major role in their own distinctive contributions to initial teacher education, but it does seem necessary for these contributions to be complemented by another role, accepting wider whole-school responsibilities within such schemes. The experiences of the Internship professional tutors clearly show the importance of structuring school-based teacher education into the life and work of the school. Those Internship professional tutors who consider themselves successful in their role are those who most adeptly integrate the operation of the teacher training programme into the close grained texture of their respective schools.

Secondly, the research shows that both the situations and the concerns of the selection of Internship professional tutors are very diverse, even within one small county and one small scheme. The original guidelines for the role were very clear and detailed, and it would be relatively easy for OUDES to have unrealistic over-rigid expectations of how that role would be enacted. Yet the study highlights both subtle variations and significant shifts of emphasis in different professional tutors' operation of their role. Moreover, these modulations, when examined closely, appear to be amply justified given the context of each school, and of each professional tutor. In these circumstances, it is apparent that considerable efforts are necessary at the whole-scheme level to achieve adequate quality control and assurance.

REFERENCES

Ball, S.J. (1987) *The Micro-Politics of the School. Towards a Theory of School Organization*, Methuen, London and New York.

James, Lord (1972) *Teacher Education and Training: A Report by a Committee of Enquiry appointed by the Secretary of State for Education and Science, under the Chairmanship of Lord James of Rusholme*, Her Majesty's Stationery Office, London.

Pell, D.J. (1994) *The Role of the Professional Tutor within the Oxford University Department of Educational Studies' Internship Scheme for Post Graduate Certificate of Education Students*, D.Phil. thesis, Oxford.

Silverman, D. (1970) *The Theory of Organisations: A Sociological Framework*, Heinemann, London.

10

THE IMPACT OF STUDENT TEACHERS ON THE CLASSROOM EXPERIENCES OF PUPILS

Stephen Carney and Hazel Hagger

The focus of this chapter is one of the five studies undertaken as Oxford University's contribution to a national research project on mentoring in schools.[1]

By the summer of 1993 when the project got under way, the Internship partnership between schools and the university had been in place for six years. It made sense, therefore, from the outset to call on the partner schools' experience of school-based initial teacher education. To this end, teachers were invited to discuss with the researchers issues of interest and concern in relation to Internship that might be investigated. In this way, schools were able both to articulate their particular concerns and to play a major role in the subsequent design of the studies. Five studies were conducted on the basis of these concerns, and a summary report of all of them is available in Carney and Hagger (1996). This chapter focuses on just one of these studies.

One school, a relatively small 11–18 mixed comprehensive, was interested in the implications for the school of hosting an annual cohort of 8–10 interns over a number of years. In particular the school sought to understand the ways in which mentors and other staff worked with interns to promote pupil learning, how mentors monitored the learning of the pupils working with interns, and whether or not pupils themselves were differentiating between

[1] The authors would like to thank the Esmée Fairbairn Charitable Trust for its generosity, support and enthusiasm. The project, a collaborative one conducted from 1993 to 1995, involved six universities: Keele, Leicester, Manchester Metropolitan, Oxford, Sussex and Swansea. The joint final report, *Mentors in Schools: Developing the Profession of Teaching* (1996), is edited by Donald McIntyre and Hazel Hagger, and published by David Fulton, London.

their normal class teacher and the interns in relation to their own perceived learning outcomes.

The research was based in two of the larger subject departments, referred to as 'A' and 'B' in the discussion that follows. Data were collected through semi-structured interviews, complemented by observation in lessons and within the host departments, and in two phases, in recognition of the different ways in which interns worked with mentors, subject teachers and classes at different stages of the Internship year. Thus, the first wave of interviews and observation took place in March, and the second in May.

In each of the two departments one intern was observed teaching two classes, one from Year 7 and the other from Year 9. From each of the four observed classes, the intern and mentor were asked to select for interview four pupils. Thus, a total of sixteen pupils (eight boys and eight girls) were interviewed in mixed-sex pairs. Pupils were selected on the basis of their perceived preparedness to discuss their classes openly and honestly.

Mentors were asked to describe their plans for interns' classroom teaching and to describe the ways in which they and their departmental colleagues were working with the interns at that particular point in the Internship year. Prior to each observed lesson, interns were interviewed and asked to explain the aims of the lesson and the nature of any planned activities or strategies. They were also asked to talk about the ways in which they were working with their mentor and other department staff at that time and to describe the pupils selected for interview. Following these lessons, interns were interviewed to discuss the lesson, how it related to their plans, how they had been working with the class and more generally the arrangements in the school department that had helped their work with pupils as well as with their own learning as interns.

Pupils were interviewed briefly immediately after each observed lesson and asked about their views of the subject, the nature of their work with the intern, any perceived differences between lessons with the intern and those with their usual teacher, and the impact, if any, on their learning of having interns teach them. All interviews were audio-taped and transcribed verbatim.

While recognising the limitations of this small scale study in one school, we would claim that two interesting and potentially significant themes emerged from analysis of the data. First, it was apparent that both pupils and mentors saw the involvement of interns in their classes in an extremely positive light. Secondly, it appeared that the extent of the benefits of working with interns – especially for pupils – was greatly influenced by the quality of the supporting arrangements for interns established by host departments. These two conclusions are now discussed in more detail.

REACTIONS TO WORKING WITH INTERNS

In both subjects, the pupils interviewed tended to describe the lessons taught by the intern as 'more fun' or 'less serious' than those taught by their usual teachers. Typical of their comments are the following:

> It's nice with her, she's thoughtful when she's teaching us. She sort of makes it fun. She likes talking to us rather than just teaching and that's it.

and

> (the intern) puts an enjoyable side to it as well as a learning side.

A number of explanations were offered for these views. Eight of the pupils in subject 'B' and five in subject 'A' suggested that the interns, as younger teachers, were able to relate more closely to them:

> I think they both try and make lessons fun, but I think because [intern], I think she's younger than [teacher], it makes it a bit better.

> Well, I think I probably feel more comfortable talking to [intern] than [teacher], probably because she's younger. We don't always stick to the lesson, we talk about other things.

In terms of classroom interactions, many subject 'A' pupils across both Years felt that the intern offered more individual attention, considered pupils' views more and tried to develop better relationships:

> [the teacher] is usually sitting at the desk marking things and you don't want to interrupt, but [the intern] is usually walking around, speaking to people, making sure they're doing all right.

> She's more of a friend than a teacher really.

> we'll talk about it as a group with [intern] but we just write it down with [teacher].

> She [intern] tries to get on with us and she makes friends with us, but she also helps a lot, so it makes it easier, if you want to go for help, it makes it easier because, you know, if you get on with her it makes it easier and you feel better going there.

Pupils in subject 'B', whilst less forthcoming, expressed similar sentiments:

> Sometimes, you know, you might want to go a step further because the reaction might be a bit more . . . something that [teacher] says there's no time for it but [intern] would probably show it to us.

> If we sort of put our hands up for one question, [teacher] will probably get the answer, and you know, [intern] listens to all our opinions.

Many pupils suggested that this had implications for their work. Four of the subject 'A' respondents felt that in the intern's class they were inclined to contribute more. Two more felt that they 'work better' and another offered 'I ask for more help'. Others suggested 'I've got more personality in my work' and 'I'm more confident and put my hand up and things'. In terms of the interns' ability to explain classroom tasks, subject 'B' pupils across both Years felt that interns used the board and OHP more, provided more worksheets, set up more experiments and were inclined to 'show more'. In some cases subject 'B' pupils in Year 7 felt that the intern's worksheets were more demanding.

With regard to the question of perceived differences between the intern and their usual teacher, pupils' responses were generally consistent in both phases of data collection. Approximately half of the respondents across subjects suggested that they were unable to clearly 'rank' one teacher above the other. Comments like 'both are thoughtful', 'both are interesting', 'both made lessons fun' were typical. Interestingly, no pupil in either subject felt that the interns were harming their learning. Indeed, half of subject 'A' respondents felt that their learning was greater with the intern while the others were unable to discern a difference. From subject 'B', three respondents suggested that the interns made 'a difference' to their learning with a further two suggesting that their learning was greater with the interns while the remaining three suggested that it was about the same. Typical comments from these pupils included:

> I think they're both good, and they're both very good teachers when it comes down to it, and they're both sticking to what we're supposed to be learning and they seem to get the message across.

> I don't know, it's a bit more lively, all the group work. She [intern] gives us more inspiration, sort of thing. She makes us think, gives us ideas and makes us think about those ideas.

> I think I probably understand it more with [intern], so if I understand it I learn it.

> They [interns] don't give loads of facts, they talk to you in a way so you'd understand.

Two Year 9 pupils in subject 'B' suggested that the superior subject knowledge of the normal class teacher and her greater experience meant that their preparation for examinations would be better than it would be with the intern. Another noted that there were particular benefits in 'joint' lessons (those taught by the two interns together with the mentor in a supporting role).

> even if [intern no. 1] is talking to us, if he's missed something then [intern no. 2] will always kind of like chip in. They do that quite often, which helps. Because with three teachers you get more.

Mentors echoed the enthusiasm of their pupils for working with interns and suggested that their impact could be felt in many different ways. They argued, for example, that as a consequence of having more 'hands' in the classroom they were able to offer greater attention and resources to individual pupils. Further, they claimed that working closely with another adult in lessons led to their developing new insights into the nature and needs of individual pupils. The two mentors were in no doubt that these perceived benefits of working with interns impacted positively on student learning:

> Person power. There's the planning, there's the ideas, there's the effect on individual kids.

> where the communication is good and you share in the same objectives, then they're [pupils] getting twice as much attention.

> It's also meant that we've been able to . . . follow up work and return it to them [pupils] very quickly because there's two of us on the job.

> While I've been here I would say that I don't think there's any examples of kids losing out.

Indeed the mentors were fulsome in their praise of the interns for the insights they offered on individual pupils:

> Because for those pupils, it's really – it's not so much whether the perceptions are accurate or not, although I think they are – but it is the fact that those individuals are being much talked about by their teachers. I mean, if it was just me, I wouldn't be talking about the individuals in my classes with anybody else to this extent, because they've all got their own. And so, we're having very full discussions of certain individuals and thinking about what they need. It's helping me. I think we're bouncing ideas off each other and that sort of thing, and it's actually meaning that that child, though they don't know it, is receiving quite a lot of focus.

In addition to these perceived benefits for the learning of their pupils, both mentors were clear in their view that involvement in Internship was having an important influence on their own teaching and thinking.

> because we have to be explicit about what we're doing, therefore we have to articulate our aims . . . And when you're working with an intern you can't . . . just wander into the classroom and make the lesson up . . . you have to talk to them about what you're going to do and I think that's good for you as well.

> if you have an intern with imagination . . . then she does bring new ideas in. There have been a few things that she's done and I've thought 'Oh, that's a good idea, I'll try that'.

> The other thing that the interns do is that it doesn't half keep us on our toes. It's sharpened me up no end because I can't criticise other people without considering what I'm doing, and it's been a tremendous bit of extended education for me. And that really, for me, on a personal level, that is very significant, very important. I've just learnt so much this year. So I hope in the future the kids will benefit, you know, from my improved approach.

Mentors also felt that the processes and procedures for managing interns' learning across the department were influencing, in positive ways, the professional relationships amongst colleagues and stopping the department from becoming 'too insular' or 'kind of dreary'. Increased communication within the departments and the school as a whole was seen as a positive outcome of involvement in Internship:

> I like the other interns as well being in the staff room. It just means that the school can't get away with just working its own little code . . . it has to be open . . . And it means that I talk to my colleagues. For instance [colleague] is devising a unit of . . . work to do with [intern]. It means she and I are talking about [this] work, so it means that we're collaborating more than we would otherwise do. So I think it improves communication, not just intern and permanent teacher but between the teachers.

DEPARTMENTAL ARRANGEMENTS FOR INTERNS

It seemed clear from the data that the support offered to promote the interns' development differed substantially between the two departments. We would go further and suggest that the level of this support was an important factor in the learning possibilities for those pupils working with interns.

During the interviews each mentor was asked to describe the timetable for their intern and the factors of which they took account in drawing it up. They were asked for details of the ways in which they had been working with their intern at that time, the ways that the intern had been working with departmental colleagues, and the focus of the work in the classroom. Each mentor was also asked to discuss the intern's progress and learning and how, if at all, that progress was being monitored within the department. The mentors' responses to this area of questioning, supported by data from the interns' accounts and our own observations, point to at least two factors which might affect the impact of interns on pupil learning.

First, in devising interns' timetables, mentors attempted both to expose interns to a balance of classes across the age and ability range and to be sensitive to the learning needs of pupils. Mentors were especially concerned about the impact that learner teachers might have on examination classes and, in line with (unwritten) school policy, they attempted to avoid involving the interns with classes in Years 11 or 13. As the mentor in department 'A' explained:

> and I have to make sure that each of them has a lower school class of mine because it's not policy to leave them to it with a GCSE group, because the older kids are less accepting of that situation and also there's too much responsibility, they have to do the work . . . So once I've put that in, I then try and give them a 7th Year and 8th Year and a 9th Year if I can, because those will be

the groups that they can eventually take all the time. And then I give them a Year 10 GCSE . . . to team teach with a colleague.

Secondly, it was clear that the nature of mentors' work with their respective interns changed as the course progressed. Mentors characterised the Joint week period – from October to January – as one of close contact with the intern where lesson planning, observation and thorough de-briefing of class-room strategies and decisions occurred regularly; and they cited the timetabled 'mentor period' as essential for this purpose. They characterised the School week period – from February to June – as a time during which the interns would become increasingly independent of themselves and of the other teachers, and would exhibit more ambition in their planning and teaching.

By the time of the first phase of data collection (March) one intern was 'solo teaching' classes from Years 7, 8 and 9 and teaching collaboratively with the mentor in Year 10. By the time of the second phase of data collection (May), this intern had moved on from supporting her mentor in Year 10 work to personally evaluating what the pupils had achieved, suggesting activities to the mentor, planning new work and delivering lessons. Similarly, this mentor was no longer examining her intern's lesson plans, saying instead, that 'we're confident that she can structure lessons properly'. By this time the working relationship was described by the mentor as one of 'engaging each other'. Relationships between interns and mentors were also marked by a higher degree of informality although mentors claimed that they continued to be alert to the impact of the interns on their pupils. The mentor of depart-ment 'A' claimed that at this stage in the development of the intern's learn-ing, mentor and intern could collaborate as partners to promote student learning:

> We know what we're doing and [intern] is suggesting activities to me and I'm suggesting them to her . . . She's taken some lessons [with Year 9] without me. She's set timed essays for them and marked them, so she's assessing, marking work. At an earlier stage I would have said, 'Right, I would like them to gain an understanding of this character next week in this lesson, and would you like to plan an activity that would do that?' And we would then both deliver it, but [intern] would lead off and present it to the group and I would be there assist-ing in the class. So it would be more formal. But now it's working much more informally that we're both interested in what's going on and we're discussing the kids together and what we think their understanding is, jointly devising activities.

As the interns became more independent, mentors and other teachers limited their observation of lessons but continued to maintain a presence and to keep in touch with the progression of the class:

> I've been in. Not for formal observation, but I usually drop in. You know, it signals to the class that the pair of us are still responsible together for the learn-

ing, so I come in and make a point of showing that I know what they're doing and even kind of asking her a bit sometimes.

Similarly, as the S weeks progressed, timetabled mentor sessions were becoming much more 'open-ended' and dominated by interns' needs and concerns. By the time of the second round of interviews mentors said that interns were 'fine-tuning' their material and the structure of their lessons and focusing on things like differentiation and preparing for the reality of teaching life on a full timetable. One mentor added that by now her intern was working more broadly within the framework of the school in order to support the learning of pupils:

> You know that she's concerned about so and so, that she thinks a certain person's anxious or unhappy about a piece of work or something. And where she suspects there might be an emotional problem or something going on with a pupil, she's going straight to their tutor now to talk to them, or she knows, you know she knows around the staff room who knows that child, who she should talk to. So she is also going to get information on kids, just as I would do if I was wondering what was going on – I would go to a pupil's tutor. So if [intern] mentions it to me, and I say 'Oh you could see her tutor', [intern] says 'I've done that'. So she's following things up with individual pupils, she's using the same systems that we would use.

Cutting across these two common features, however, were striking differences between the ways in which the interns worked and were supported in the two departments studied. In department 'A' the mentor, whilst not involving herself in other teachers' classes, would nevertheless discuss the intern's work in all classes with other staff. As a consequence, teachers working with the intern had a clear idea of her overall progress, and understood how they could support her in developing her classroom practice. This close interaction between the mentor and her departmental colleagues was in part due to the mentor's position as head of department. It was also due to the recently appointed second in charge of the department who appeared to work very closely with the head of department in relation to Internship and was herself eager to work with the intern as a class teacher.

In contrast, the mentor of department 'B', although an experienced teacher, was 'the newest appointment in the department' and in her first year as a mentor in Internship. Although the department contained two former mentors and others with experience of Internship, the mentor, in coming to grips with the role, did not feel in a position to call upon other staff for detailed guidance or advice:

> I think you have to train your associates [departmental colleagues] right from the start . . . I didn't do it this year because as a new mentor, working with teachers with more experience than me, I don't think I was in a position to say 'hey, this is how we ought to do it'. . . [or] . . . 'look, this is what I would like you to consider today when you're observing [intern]'.

> I don't want to overload people with long discussions with me trying to pin people down when they don't have time. That's not going to be popular.

It was clear that both mentors were best able to evaluate interns' work with pupils in relation to their own classes. Here, they felt justified in continuing to observe (in many different ways) and participate in lessons throughout the intern's school experience. Indeed, mentors allocated interns to one of their own classes expressly for this purpose:

> Then when I do the S weeks, I first of all have to make sure they're all teaching at least one group with me – because I have to do observations, you know – that they will then take over from me.

Whilst both mentors were able to maintain a close involvement with these, their own, classes, they monitored their interns' work with colleagues' classes in two distinct ways. First they used the timetabled mentor session to question interns:

> in the mentor session every week I'm always saying you know, 'Are there any concerns? Is there anything we need to talk about? Are all your classes going OK?' . . . and [intern] might have said 'Well, there's a problem there, but I'm seeing [teacher] about that'. And I'd say, 'OK', and then follow that up with [intern] or [teacher].

Secondly, they engaged in discussion with relevant colleagues. As we have suggested, the data indicate that the extent of this discussion varied between the two departments studied. In department 'A' open, detailed and regular discussion between the mentor and intern as well as between these two and other colleagues characterised the process of monitoring interns' developing classroom skills:

> we are talking about the interns a lot . . . and sharing regular bulletins on how they were getting on. I was just talking to [second in department] about [intern no. 1] and talking to [third colleague] about [intern no. 2].

The second intern in department 'A', whilst not involved in the study, was the focus of particular attention by teachers across the department:

> there were problems with [intern no. 2], for instance. I was concerned so I asked [subject colleague] how things were in her lessons. She gave me her concerns, so I then went round all the people he had contact with to get the full picture and then we had a long meeting when we went through all the concerns.

Similarly, her greater experience of guiding student teachers' learning enabled this mentor to be much more specific in verifying her claims about interns' learning within the context of its impact on pupils:

> It's hard to monitor pupils' learning when they're all doing slightly different things. You know it's very easy when you set one piece that's for a short period of time, but if it's a project where they have to plan and they have to complete

a number of different pieces of work and they have to, say, organise themselves in pairs or in groups to do that, delegate tasks and then come out with a group product, which she [the intern] can, then she can assess the input of individuals into that. She did all that extremely quickly . . . So that she's learning and responding very quickly and making very accurate judgements about pupils, devising very appropriate learning materials for them. They're responding very well to what she does now.

In contrast, it seemed that the level of discussion amongst colleagues about the progress of the intern and her impact, if any, on the classroom experiences of the pupils which was so evident in department 'A', was far less apparent in department 'B'. Here, the mentor said that she had no knowledge of how either of the two interns in the department were working with other staff and any feedback from colleagues tended to concentrate on the interns' 'problem areas'. The mentor herself recognised these arrangements as unsatisfactory:

No, this is a hole. This is, I mean I think the discussion I had with you last time, this highlighted the fact that there's definitely a hole in what I'm doing, and I started talking about – well we had a mentor session with the two interns to decide how we could communicate better with other teachers.

The intern's account tended to support the mentor's description of these working arrangements within department 'B': she asserted that it was the mentor who worked most closely with her in relation to lessons and that she was the only teacher in the department to provide substantial critiques of lessons. For the most part she saw herself being left 'just to get on with it'.

Moreover, the mentor in department 'B' was less confident about detailing the learning and development that was taking place in her interns, particularly with regard to classroom teaching skills:

I mean, I just don't know how you measure something like that . . . we talk a lot. You know, any time of the day, if I'm floating around, then either of them [the interns] can come and have a chat.

Unlike the intern in department 'A', the intern in department 'B' experienced difficulties in detailing the progress of pupils in her classes:

but I don't know whether they've been on task before I've got to the groups. I don't know. I don't know how to deal with that at all, I must admit . . . it's just impossible, isn't it?

Intern 'A', however, was constantly evaluating the progress of pupils and relaying this to the mentor and other class teachers within the department:

but I think [subject teacher] will need to know when she takes over again. So I've actually written something down for her. I keep [Mentor] informed as I go along and will just make sure, I think, that we finish this particular unit we're working on for me to hand back over to her, and she'll start again with them.

Strategies to focus on particular skills were a central theme of that intern's lessons and the usual class teachers often supported this by working with individual pupils on a withdrawal basis. As a consequence the intern saw her role much more in terms of its impact on student learning. In department 'B' this emphasis was less apparent although it would be inappropriate to draw conclusions from a relatively small sample of interviews and interactions. It is clear, however, that intern 'B' engaged in discussions with other teachers to far less a degree. Moreover, this intern found it difficult to talk about her teaching in terms of student learning outcomes.

It was clear from the interviews with mentors and interns, and from our own observations within the two departments, that pupils' learning need not be adversely affected by engagement with student teachers. In department 'A', the mentor appeared to be more aware of the impact of interns on pupils' learning and was able to offer strategies to monitor that learning. This included the development of Internship as a departmental commitment so that pupils' progress was monitored both in her classes and in those of her colleagues. This approach was in contrast to arrangements in department 'B'. Here, an inexperienced mentor was unsure of the influence that the intern might have been having on the learning of pupils and was unable to gain the support of her colleagues either to improve her own practice or to enhance the arrangements in their classes.

IMPLICATIONS AND RECOMMENDATIONS

Schools engaging in initial teacher education are quite properly concerned that their pupils as well as the student teachers benefit from it. The results from this small study initiated by a school with such concerns offer some reassurance: far from providing evidence that working with interns was having a deleterious effect on pupils' learning, the data suggests that the pupils themselves and their teachers believed that they benefited from the engagement of the subject departments in Internship. It was also clear that the extent to which pupils benefited was dependent on the appropriateness of the provision for the interns' learning. In the case of one of the two departments discussed in this chapter, in which a teacher new to mentoring was working with minimal support from departmental colleagues, the pupils nonetheless tended to claim that they were benefiting from the presence of interns, and certainly none thought that their learning was suffering. In the other department, however, where the mentor had secured the collaboration of colleagues and had established agreed ways of working designed to ensure the progressive development of the interns' learning, the pupils (and mentor) were unanimous about the benefits to the pupils.

Following discussions of the findings with selected members of the school staff – the two mentors involved in the study, the professional tutor, the deputy headteacher with responsibility for staff development and the head-teacher – it was agreed that the research team would draw up for the school's consideration a list of recommendations with regard to its engagement in Internship. The suggestions made came under four broad headings – collective departmental responsibility; mentor development; selection of departments; and the role of the professional tutor.

Collective departmental responsibility

It was felt that a greater emphasis on the collective responsibility of the department or faculty hosting interns would lead to shared understandings of the skills and strategies involved in being school-based teacher educators. It was suggested that the head of department had a critical role to play in ensuring that the whole department took seriously its responsibilities in relation to initial teacher education, and that s/he could support the mentor by, for example: ensuring Internship was a regular item on the agenda of departmental meetings; working positively with the interns wherever possible ; and making it clear to colleagues that the mentor had a managerial role in relation to the interns' learning within the department.

Mentor development

It was suggested that the professional tutor encourage the sharing of mentoring expertise across different subject departments by, for example, concentrating on mentoring skills and strategies rather than on individual interns at the regular meetings of the school team of mentors; setting aside some Inset time to focus on mentoring; and making more use of the expertise available at the university to support mentors, especially those new to the role.

Selection of departments

It was proposed that in deciding each year which subject departments should host interns, the school should strive to achieve a balance between introducing new departments to Internship and consolidating and building on the expertise in those departments with experience of working with interns. It was felt that the school needed to consider the potential benefits of extending Internship to other areas whilst at the same time ensuring that the expertise already gained was able to be exploited in order to maximise the benefits to teachers and pupils alike.

The role of the professional tutor

The professional tutor was encouraged to take leadership of the school ITE team rather than adopt a more passive role as Internship administrator.

The proposals were put to the Headteacher and the deputy head at a lengthy meeting in the school. Their response to the research report and to the subsequent proposals was positive. Primarily, the finding that pupils found working with interns a positive and rewarding experience was felt to be of great interest to school governors in particular who, from time to time, had voiced concerns about the extent of pupils' involvement with interns. Further, there was strong acknowledgement that both pupils and mentors were perceiving positive benefits from Internship. However, acknowledging that the extent of these benefits was closely related to the support provided by host departments, the Headteacher expressed concern at the apparent drift in commitment displayed by department 'B', suggesting that interns 'cannot just be left to get on with it'. As a consequence, the Deputy Head was to consider both how Internship was monitored across the school and how experienced mentors could be involved in the continuing development of less experienced colleagues.

REFERENCES

Carney, S. and Hagger, H. (1996) Working with beginning teachers: the impact on schools, in McIntyre, D. and Hagger, H. (eds.) *Mentors in Schools: Developing the Profession of Teaching*, David Fulton, London.

The Oxford Internship Scheme: Glossary of Terms

Intern: Student-teacher. The term 'intern' is borrowed from the final on-the-job phase of medical training, and is intended to emphasise the student-teacher's status as a learner, but also as like a junior member of staff

Mentor: Subject teacher who takes primary responsibility for the professional education in classroom teaching of (usually) two interns

Professional Tutor: Senior teacher who co-ordinates a school's part in the Internship Scheme, usually with at least eight interns, and leads a General Programme (later called a Professional Development Programme) of school-based seminars on whole-school and cross-curricular issues for the interns

General Tutor: University lecturer who liaises with a school, and especially with its professional tutor, and shares responsibility for the school's General Programme

Curriculum Tutor: University Lecturer with a subject specialism who jointly with the mentors in the same subject area plans the Curriculum Programme for interns' learning about classroom teaching of the subject, implements the university-based part of the programme and visits interns and their mentors to contribute (once every few weeks) to the school-based part of the programme

Joint or 'J' weeks: First part of the course, from October to late January, during which interns spend two days each week in schools and three days in the University. (In the early years, there was also a brief second J-weeks period at the end of the school year.)

School or 'S' weeks: Part of the course from late January until June during which interns are based full-time in the same schools as they were in during 'J' weeks

Profiling Points: Three occasions during the year when interns discuss how far they have progressed in developing specified necessary classroom teaching abilities and qualities individually with their mentors and curriculum tutors, and broader professional abilities and qualities with their professional and general tutors

Phase 1: First part of course, usually lasting to about Easter, during which interns focus on developing abilities and qualities necessary for competent classroom teaching; Phase 1 ends when an intern is judged to consistently manifest these abilities and qualities to a sufficient degree to justify Qualified Teacher Status

Phase 2: Remainder of course, during which interns focus more on developing abilities and qualities necessary to be a self-evaluating and self-developing teacher.

INDEX